We Must Make
Haste–Slowly

For Leona, who loved Chile
because the streets were crowded and safe at any hour

Contents

Introduction

"Ours will be a revolution, *a la chilena,* with red wine and empanadas," declared Salvador Allende, Chile's President-elect, shortly after his victory in September 1970. Revolution *a la chilena* meant a revolution within the existing judicial and legal structures, a revolution that would use the political arena as the debating ground and the ballot box as the final arbiter of social policy. Such a prospect was difficult for most international observers to comprehend. Revolution usually brings to mind armed guerrillas storming the centers of power—Fidel and his bearded legions marching into Havana on New Year's Day of 1959; Mao and his millions coming out of their caves and sweeping across China in 1947; the hungry soldiers of Tzarist Russia dropping their arms and turning wearily homeward that winter of 1917. The possibility of radical change through free elections, after campaigns in which basic ideas are explored and debated, or the possibility that radical change can come about gradually, evolving with increasing participation of the people, are concepts alien to the general notion of revolution.

North Americans reacted typically to Allende's victory. Both conservatives and radicals in the United States viewed the situation blackly. The Left was skeptical and wary. Politicians, they believed, were notorious for leading the people down the primrose path to disaster, so why would Chile prove different? The enormous economic problems in Chile plus the strength of its army would, they predicted, prove impossible to overcome without some sort of massive upheaval. The conservatives in the United States had another attitude, but it was equally cynical and crude. To them the victory sounded the death knell of democracy in Chile. Although the Socialists had won in a free and democratic election, they said, it was common knowledge that, once in office, socialists and communists never permitted their power to be threatened. The Chilean people had chosen, through desperation and shortsightedness, not merely another political tendency, but eternal slavery.

I went to Chile in December 1970, a month after the newly elected Socialist Government took office, to explore the revolutionary process in Chile and to try to understand and describe that process to North Americans. I went armed with what I thought was the necessary basic data. I knew that Chile was a long, narrow country on the west coast of South America with a population of nine million; that it had a long tradition of democracy; that its primary export was copper; that it had a beautiful climate comparable to southern California with the potential for being a world producer of fruits and vegetables. I knew that the liberal Christian Democrat Government had taken office in the mid-1960s and had begun an agrarian reform program supported lavishly by the Alliance for Progress and U.S. politicians.

Yet in a profound sense I lacked any knowledge of Chile. My prejudices and preconceptions were purely North

American. I assumed, for instance, that traffic there would travel in an orderly manner, staying on one side of the center white line, and that a bus would come to a complete halt before letting people get off. I assumed that politicians either regularly lied to the people or told them just enough to satisfy them, that press conferences were usually planned in advance and were always bland and unproductive. I assumed that what the newspapers printed did not reflect or substantially affect Government policy. In all of these assumptions, and in many more, I was wrong.

I discovered a country where the people have an almost fanatical love of liberty and democracy, a country where politics and legalism constitute a way of life. Politics pervades every facet of Chilean society. Politicians are superbly trained in the art of compromise and negotiation. Thousands of neighborhood organizations which on first view seem apolitical are really tied strongly into one of the national political parties. The Centers of Mothers, where women learn sewing and other family skills, the sports clubs, the neighborhood centers—all are tied to political parties. Most of the newspapers are political party news organs, reflecting their respective party ideologies.

Always present with this politicization is a belief in law. The two are related. If one believes that law is truly an important concept, and that to make a revolution one has merely to change the laws that need changing and enforce the existing laws that support the goals of the revolution, then the composition of those laws becomes important. I remember the case of a small slum area in southern Chile where Peace Corps volunteers were trying to establish a self-help community corporation. The residents spent interminable hours during the first three months discussing the proposed constitution, painstakingly going over it line by line to examine fine legal as well as philosophical points. The example is by no means atypical.

But I discovered also that political ideology in Chile

begins where North American politics ends. Labels that may be appropriate in a North American context lose their validity in Chile. In Chile the political spectrum begins with what we would call liberalism. An arch-conservative in Chile has a political ideology and program similar to that of Teddy Kennedy. He believes in capitalism, foreign investment, and private control of a major portion of the economy, but also in strong social legislation, strong central government, and deficit spending. In Chile conservative governments have begun price controls and a timid agrarian reform program.

From this point the political spectrum moves only left. The Christian Democrats in Chile are perhaps equivalent to the Socialist party of the United States in the 1930s when Norman Thomas was the party's presidential candidate. They favor a strong central government and Keynesian economics and are concerned primarily with helping the people on the lowest rungs of the social ladder. Trade unions, rural unions, and local organizations are their bases of power, and public housing, price control, and redistribution of income are their goals.

As for the multiparty coalition that forms the present Government in Chile (there were six parties in the coalition when the Government took office; by the spring of 1972 eight parties were involved), there is nothing comparable in the United States to serve as a frame of reference. The Radical party in the coalition is undoubtedly the most conservative, the Communist party is more conservative than the Socialist party, and so on. On the one hand, the differences are at times trivial and slightly bewildering when all parties espouse essentially the same program; all are self-proclaimed Marxists, and all are working together. However, there can be just as much diversity among Marxists in Chile as there is among capitalists in the United States.

In a final blow to North American preconceptions, there is in Chile a strong movement called the Far Left—

composed of those who will not participate in governmental politics; who believe that workers, peasants, and students should be in the vanguard of any policy making and power brokering; and who are arming the people for the day of reckoning when the army will intervene to stop the revolution.

Although each political party has its own ideological interpretation of what is happening in Chile and of what is necessary to effect change, the overall political system in that country has been flexible enough to respond to the increasing demands of the lower and middle classes and to give continuity and direction to Chilean politics over the past two decades. As the electorate has broadened and increasingly larger groups of people have been organized into local and regional groups linked to and tied into national political parties, the entire country has responded by moving slowly leftward. For instance, it was a conservative Government led by a businessman that pushed through a constitutional amendment to permit the formulation of an agrarian reform program. Of course, that Government only enacted the legislation; it never used it. The next Government, that of the Christian Democrats, in fact began radically restructuring rural Chile, organizing hundreds of thousands of peasants into rural unions and rural cooperatives. The current Government has gone one step further, establishing an agricultural bureaucracy staffed and controlled by the peasants themselves and changing the basis of the agrarian reform program to one that not only distributes land to those who presently work the patrons' farms but also integrates subsistence farmers and migrant workers into this reform. Yet there is still, as always, pressure from the Left. At present the guerrilla groups in the rural areas are forming people's militias and fomenting takeovers of farms. The delicate tension between the Government and the people is in constant flux, but it is the tension inherent in a true democracy. There are endless examples of this continuity and dialectical process of revolution in Chile. To oversimplify, the conservative Government enacts reform legislation, the liberal Government begins to exercise such legislation, and the socialist Government utilizes it to change existing social patterns. For example, the conservative Government of Jorge Alessandri between 1958 and 1964 created DIRINCO—an organization that was supposed to control prices and check quality. It was a paper tiger. Then Eduardo Frei, the Christian Democrat President from 1964 to 1970, developed the organization, establishing an institutional integrity and using the sanctions written into the law to control certain prices. Finally, the current socialist Government put at the head of this organization a man who worked on the central committee in Cuba for several years, a man who believes that true controls can only be imposed when neighborhood groups are formed to check on their own stores and examine the kitchens of their own shops and restaurants.

The dialectic in Chile continues to develop. Yet, as with all such processes, there is always an alternative, a possibility of reverting to some former level of economic or political development, a tendency to react to mass demands with force and repression. Chile has had its share of such experiments, but they have been mild—much, much more mild than in other Latin American countries. In fact, the extent of political repression in Chile even at its peak in the last years of Frei's administration probably did not equal the political repression in the United States during the same period (the conspiracy indictments in Chicago, for example).

The liberal thrust in Chile has had to face economic realities. With debts increasing, industry stagnant, and export industries controlled by foreign corporations, there has been increasing pressure on the Government to impose austerity programs, freeze wages, and break the back of popular struggle. It is the tension radiating from an underdeveloped economy and an overdeveloped or rapidly maturing political sector that defines much of recent Chilean history.

I went to Chile skeptical and cynical. I left, shortly before the municipal elections in the spring (our spring, their fall) of 1971, convinced and respectful—in part because of the accomplishments of the new Government even during its short tenure in office, but more because of the dialectical process of Chilean history, the process of the revolution. I discovered a country where the role of the people has become increasingly paramount, where in past decades increasingly larger groups of people—peasants, workers, women, students, slum dwellers, the unemployed —have organized themselves and pushed against the centers of power. And those centers of power have been flexible enough, for the most part, to flow with the growing social demands and changes in national power blocs. The flexibility of the Chilean political system has permitted this Government (although at times just barely) to give the people space and time to organize and explore new avenues for development. It is this process, in my opinion, that makes Chile unique, and it is this process that the current Government believes will continue until true socialism is finally achieved.

The process is all-important. No one in Chile pretends to be constructing socialism. Rather, even this Government composed of socialists, Communists, and Marxists of all political persuasions sees this as a period of transition toward socialism. Allende himself describes his Government as "a riverbed to channel the aspirations and energies of the people." There is general agreement in Chile that the revolution took a great step forward in the election of 1970. Yet Chileans also generally believe that the roots of the revolution go back many years and hope that the revolution will eventually overtake even the new Government, forcing ever more radical leaders to come to the fore and lead newly organized and conscious political masses. In Chile the expropriation of factories and the restructuring of the economy, although tremendously important goals, are also the most easily achievable. Decentralizing power, giving the masses a sense of power over their own lives and institutions, and changing the popular concepts of justice, freedom, and work are the more difficult and long-range aspects of the revolution.

In this book I have tried to give a glimpse into Chile during the period from 1965 to 1971. I have concentrated on the period after the socialist Government took office. In examining current Chile I have tried to describe some of the ideas, dreams, and projects of the new Government as well as some of its weaknesses and confusion. The picture is incomplete because the process is incomplete. The theory of social change has sharpened considerably even during Allende's first year in office, and the practice of social change has begun. Chileans are learning as they go. As one political leader put it: "We are building the road to socialism as we walk it."

I have tried to convey a feeling of movement, of motion, sometimes of disarray, yet a movement that is generally in the direction of socialism. But the goals are not yet achieved. In the factories workers may have certain political power, but it is the trade union leadership, not yet the rank and file, who exercise such power. In the rural areas peasants do indeed have enormous power over agricultural prerogatives, but generations of paternalistic practices cannot be overcome in a few months or even in a few years.

This is not an exhaustive study of Chile. The history of Chile and the personality of its present chief executive, Salvador Allende, are very important topics. But such areas have been treated well elsewhere. I suggest to those who are interested in a detailed examination of the history and composition of Chilean political parties that they read Federico Gil's *The Chilean Political System*. Those who want an excellent examination of Chilean economics, especially the relationship to the United States and U.S. penetration internally, should read *New Chile*, a study by the North American Congress on Latin America (NACLA). And of course there is the incomparable self-portrait of Allende that emerges from Regis Debray's interview, *Conversations with Allende*. Finally, for those interested in the process of revolution—read on.

1

A Brief History of Government in Chile

Chile is ordained by its natural situation, by the simple customs of its virtuous inhabitants, to enjoy the prosperity proportioned by the just and sweet laws of a republic. If any republic is to last a long time in America, I think it will be that of Chile . . . Chile can be free.

—Simon Bolivar

In 1535 Diego de Almargo, Francisco Pizarro's original partner in the conquest of Peru, struck out to continue the conquest of South America by the Spanish conquerors. Requisitioning hundreds of Spain's finest men and livery, he rode southward from Lima in search of reported treasure troves of silver, gold, and other precious metals. Instead he encountered the Araucanians, a fierce, proud race of Indians who understood intuitively what their brethren in North America were soon to learn—that the white men were harbingers of disaster and extinction—and who reacted accordingly. Repelled by the Araucanians' fierce at-

13

tacks, and discovering to his bitter disappointment no metals of any worth, Almargo went back to Lima, never to return to Chile.

But although the explorers were disappointed in their search for metals, they did encounter one of the most fertile and beautiful lands in the entire world. Tales of the natural bounty of Chile, its huge forests and fertile valleys, its magnificent flora and natural fruits, sparked the interest of another great Spanish adventurer, Pedro de Valdivia. Renouncing huge estates in Peru that he had been given by the king of Spain and a fortune estimated at over $300,000, Valdivia chose in 1540 to go to Chile. It was a decision that caused even his closest friends to question his sanity. For, as one author described it:

> Chile now lacked even the glamour of the unknown. She had been stripped of all the exciting possibilities which had attracted a man with the temperament of Almargo. It was with a good knowledge of both her lack of mineral wealth, and of the excellent fighting qualities of her inhabitants, that Valdivia chose her. His purpose was to found and build, not to despoil.[1]

This partially explains Chile's early history. Unlike the area around Lima, or the viceroyalty of Mexico, it had no instant treasures to be gained by deceiving or looting local Indian vaults. Unlike Argentina or Brazil, it had no great ports from which to embark toward Europe or Africa. Wealth would come only through bitter struggle, both with the land and with the people who inhabited that land.

Simon Bolivar once called Chile the "uttermost part of the earth." This very remoteness and isolation has given it a certain uniqueness. Almost 2,700 miles in length, as long as the continental United States, Chile averages only sixty miles in width. It is a great ribbon of earth bordered by the Pacific Ocean on the west and by the Andean mountain chain on the east. To the north is the desert of Peru and to the south the South Pole. Cut off from the rest of the continent by these natural barriers, Chile has a unique and unified history, culture, and language. As William Johnson has noted:

> Where the other Andean nations are divided by the Andes, Chile is in fact unified by them. There is little of the regionalism that produces distrust and misunderstanding between Quito and Guayaquil, La Paz and Santa Cruz, or Lima and the rest of Peru.[2]

To Simon Bolivar this isolation meant that Chile was insulated from the "vices of ancient Europe and Asia." Certainly Chile's isolation caused it to be less subject to the whims of Spain than most of the rest of South America was under the rule of the Spanish monarchy. Chile's principal contact with Spain was by means of the few ships that stopped in its ports for provisions on the way to or from Europe via Cape Horn.

Its geographical isolation and its lack of treasure made Chile an uninteresting colony for Spain. By the late 1700s it was administered by a captain-general—a type of government reserved for the less important parts of the Spanish empire. While most of the other Spanish colonies developed around flourishing port cities where the leisure, merchant classes held sway, in Chile the descendants of the Spaniards worked the land themselves, becoming tough, self-reliant, and increasingly independent. As a result of this independence many of the irritations that caused the rest of Latin America to flare up in rebellion against Spain were only minor irritants in Chile. In fact, Chilean independence from the Spanish crown was not declared until 1818, after the last great decisive battle against Spain had already been waged and won.

The early history of independent Chile was similar to that of other Latin American republics in that its struggle was between those who favored a strong central government and those who favored the congressional, or parliamentary, system in which rural areas would become more important. Yet unlike other countries, Chile eventually managed to resolve this problem, primarily through the strong leadership of Diego Portales, a virtual dictator in Chile in the period from 1830 to 1833. The thirty-seven-year-old aristocrat had had a business career but had not been involved in politics until a few years before. He was never actually President of Chile, but he was the real power in the Chilean Government, able to make and unmake presidents.

The Constitution of 1833, of which Portales was the chief architect, represented a compromise between those who wanted a strong executive and those who argued in favor of a strong Congress. As Donald Dozer describes its provisions:

The president, who was given considerable powers, was to be chosen by indirect elections for a term of five years and could be re-elected for another term of five years. His cabinet members were given the privilege of sitting in Congress, but they could not vote. When Congress was not in session the president, with the consent of his council of state, could declare a state of siege; but when Congress was in session, only it could authorize him to do so. The Congress was a bicameral body, elected by popular vote; when it was not in session a commission composed of members of both houses acted in its place as a continuing committee. The suffrage was limited to male citizens 25 years of age and over who could read and write and who owned a specified amount of property. Under this constitution the government of Chile was completely centralized and the provinces were reduced to departments headed by governors appointed by and responsible to the government in Santiago.[3]

The 1833 document, coupled with the leadership of conscientious political leaders, gave Chile a period of political stability unrivaled by its Latin American neighbors. The

Constitution of 1833, except for certain amendments, remained basically in force until 1925.

During the nineteenth century Chile's political institutions remained stable while its economic situation changed dramatically. New areas of wealth were either discovered or taken over by conquest, yet as soon as they became part of the Chilean polity they were quickly given over to foreign—usually British—control. In 1879 the Chilean army fought its War of the Pacific against the combined forces of Bolivia and Peru. Soundly defeating these countries, the army gained enormous mineral wealth. The southern third of Peru was seized, along with the richest copper deposits (although copper did not become a major source of revenue until after World War I), and Bolivia's access to the ocean was cut off (which to this day is a thorn in the side of Bolivian-Chilean relations). But British interests quickly moved in and gained title to the rich deposits of nitrates and copper in northern Chile.

The Parliamentary Era: 1891–1924

As the nineteenth century drew to a close, the combination of an increasingly powerful trend toward parliamentarianism and the intervention of North America and British business interests caused Chile's political system to disintegrate into civil war. On one side stood José Manuel Balmaceda, the Chief Executive and a supporter of a strong Presidency, and the Chilean army. On the other side were the rural leaders of Chile and those who wanted to continue the unofficial trend toward increasing power on the part of the Congress. These people were supported by the Chilean navy and by British and U.S. investors. Civil war broke out in 1891, lasted eight months, and ushered in a thirty-year period of parliamentarianism, a period of partnership between Congress, foreign business interests, and the large landholders in Chile. Supporters of the parliamentary form of government feared the concentration of power in the hands of Balmaceda partially for philosophical reasons, but mostly because they thought he would use such power to lead a liberal program of national action which would extend educational facilities, further curb the powers of the Church, begin a national program of public works, and broaden suffrage.

Weakening central authority did not in fact presage a period of increased democracy in Chile. Rather, the thirty years of parliamentarian rule are remembered in Chile as years of corruption, of indifference to rising pressures from the working class, and of almost obscene opulence by the ruling classes. Elections were viewed as being, at best, means for redistributing wealth through the buying of votes. As one author wrote:

> The parties did not send the most capable men to Congress but the richest—those able to pay for an election. . . . An election for deputy might cost from 20,000 to 100,000 pesos, and an election for senator from 100,000 to a million. The amount depended on the location of the candidacy, and was in proportion to the resources of the adversary.[4]

The custom of selling votes became so widespread that one popular story tells of villages where the people, when presented with only one list for whom to vote, rose up and stoned the best-known electoral agents because they had denied the people the chance to sell their votes. The masses had become convinced that it was the "duty" of a candidate for Deputy or Senator to bribe his electors.

Meanwhile, throughout these years worker militancy and the twin processes of economic depression and high inflation put pressures on the Congress. Between 1895 and 1912 more than thirty thousand workers, most of them skilled, emigrated to Chile from northern Italy and Spain, contributing to the syndicalist and anarchist orientation and ideology of the labor movement. Labor newspapers sprang up, unions were established, and strikes multiplied. The Government responded with force. In 1905, for example, the workers of Santiago, the capital city of Chile, protested the taxing of beef imported from Argentina and staged a march which quickly became a bloody debacle. Edward Alsworth Ross, writing nearly a decade later in his book *South of Panama,* described the scene:

Even a decade ago, the temper of the people was so ugly that once, when the troops were absent at maneuvers, a fearsome mob of three thousand persons, that seemed to spring from the gutter, like the Paris revolutionaries of the Faubourg Saint Antoine, marched about Santiago destroying property. Nothing but the desperate exertion of the mounted police who, by remaining in the saddle 48 hours, were able to keep the rioters within certain bounds, prevented the burning and sacking of the city. The soldiers were brought back as soon as possible and 400 persons were shot down.

Most of the protests came from the miners. In 1906 150 miners were killed in Antofagasta while protesting company policies and high unemployment. In 1907 the Iquique miners marched in protest against the practices of a company store and against the lack of protective screening in nitrate-dissolving ovens, as well as against inflation; two hundred were killed and three hundred wounded.

Meanwhile the ruling class was living in luxury and leisure. The same year that the miners were protesting inflation and being murdered on the streets of Iquique, Chileans were expending 6.8 million pesos to import champagne, jewels, silk, and perfumes and only 3.8 million pesos to import industrial and agricultural machinery.[5] As one observer has written:

The new ruling alliance became an inert social force, which was reinforced by foreign capital, to wit, nitrate taxes which obviated land taxes, and enabled the growth of a swelling, corrupt bureaucracy, a dominating ethos of conspicuous consumption; the beginnings of endemic Chilean inflation.[6]

The discovery of synthetic nitrates during World War I pulled the prop from the economic system. Unemployment rose to the tens of thousands in the nitrate industry. National depression set in. Strikes multiplied. The Socialist Workers party was established and a Communist newsletter was created. But Congress, long allied with the rural and foreign business groups, found itself unable to respond to this change in national forces. Although social legislation concerning minimum wage and maximum hours, protective health insurance, and workmen's compensation was introduced into Congress, these bills languished in congressional committees for five years, each year being tabled and postponed for floor votes.

Congress held back on every item of social importance. Finally, in the straw that broke the political system, one morning in September 1924 it voted to raise its own salaries while deferring a bill for a military pay increase. The troops marched quietly into the congressional building and filed into the galleries, rustling their sabres in disapproval as they sat and stared at the Congressmen. Although more social legislation was passed by Congress under the stern visages of the military officers in the next few days than in the past five years, it was not enough to save the parliamentary system of government. A conservative military junta took power and in less than five months this junta was overthrown by a group of younger officers, among them Major Carlos Ibanez and Major Marmaduke Grove. They turned with approval to the Lion of Tarapaca, the nickname given to the leader of the Liberal Alliance, Arturo Alessandri, who had been elected in a narrow vote to the Presidency in 1920. The Liberal Alliance was a political coalition representing the middle and lower classes. A powerful orator, a clever politician, and a charismatic personality, Alessandri accepted the draft of the younger military and returned to the Presidency. Within months a new constitution was drawn up to replace the conservative Portales Constitution of 1833.

The new document provided for a strong, independent Chief Executive. He would be elected for a six-year term by a direct vote of the eligible voters and would be ineligible for immediate re-election, although he could be re-elected after a term out of office. To him and not to Congress the members of the cabinet would be responsible. The President's budget could be put into effect without sanction of the Congress. The Constitution separated Church and State, provided for a graduated income tax, and granted suffrage to all literate males over the age of twenty-one. The Constitution was approved by a popular plebiscite and went into force in 1925.

The Return of a Strong Presidency and the Experiment of the Popular Front

The collapse of the parliamentary system ushered in a period not only of strong executive rule but also of interventionism by the army. Ibanez, then Minister of War, eventually forced Alessandri's resignation and himself became President. His regime was efficient but dictatorial. One important side effect of his introduction of social legislation by fiat was the beginning of an association with the Government for many of the previously quite independent and syndicalist unions. The newly established Communist party urged its members not to cooperate with Ibanez, but the twin pressures of poverty and the promise of approval and largess from the Government overrode ideological considerations.

Yet Ibanez could not survive the effects of the world depression, which exploded in Chile in 1929. In fact, Chile may have suffered more from that depression than any country in the world. In the fifteen months following Ibanez's downfall there were three different Presidents. In June 1932 the Chilean air force installed in power a junta led by Colonel Marmaduke Grove. Under the direction of Carlos Davila, who was a partner with Grove and who made himself provisional President, Chile became a "socialist republic" for one hundred days. During those hundred days a flood of social legislation came pouring out of the Chilean White House as decree after decree was put on the books. But the attempt to make Chile into a socialist state (or rather, into a state that resembled the national socialist states of Europe) caused the army to step in once again and overthrow Davila. In that brief struggle a medical student named Salvador Allende was arrested for protesting the overthrow of the socialist republic. Donald Dozer writes:

> The political situation disintegrated into anarchy. In Santiago, 160,000 unemployed Chileans, largely displaced from the nitrate industry, roamed the streets; other industries were paralyzed; and the national treasury was bankrupt, with a foreign debt of three million pesos.

Into this chaos stepped Arturo Alessandri, who returned to the Presidency in 1932. But as one observer writes, this was a changed Alessandri, one who was more cynical of the possibilities of democratic government:

> From the beginning his new administration followed a repressive course, putting the maintenance of public order and constitutional stability above human rights and freely using the militia and the police for this purpose. The early Alessandri, champion of popular rights, went over wholly to repression of popular rights. When he was confronted with a railroad strike early in 1936, he ordered the army to take over the railroads, declared a state of siege, dissolved Congress, closed down the opposition press, and banished popular leaders who criticized

his government. . . . As his candidate for the presidency in the election of 1938 he selected his Minister of Finance, Gustavo Ross, one of the wealthiest men in Chile.[7]

The heavy-handedness of Alessandri's regime, along with the prospect of the wealthy elite coming back into power, caused the leftist parties in Chile (in 1932 the Socialist party had been formed) to gather together under the banner of the Popular Front and, by a narrow margin, wrest victory from Ross. The Popular Front ruled for the next fourteen years and served as a lesson for future coalitions. The primary lesson that the socialist Left learned was not to accept as presidential candidate someone from the least revolutionary of the parties, even though that person might have widespread popular support, lest he tend to become more conservative once in power. The candidate who demonstrated this tendency was Pedro Aguirre Cerda. He was a member of the Radical party, which supplied 55 percent of the Popular Front's strength in Congress and held six of eleven cabinet posts. Throughout the fourteen-year period Radical party Governments, each one more conservative than the last, ruled Chile. They ruled partly because of the divisiveness of the socialist Left in Chile. For example, in 1941, because of the growing influence of the Communists in the Government of Aguirre Cerda, the socialists left the Government. In 1942 the anti-Communist candidate, Juan Anconio Rios, backed by a coalition of conservative parties, was victorious over Ibanez, who was then running as the candidate of the liberals, the conservatives, and the Nazis.

In 1948 Gonzalez Videla became President, this time with the support of the Communist party, but almost immediately after the election he turned on the Communists, purged them from the labor movement, and prohibited their participation in national life. Whether this was done because of pressures from copper companies, as was rumored at the time (the rumor was that Videla, in return for upping the taxes on North American-owned copper companies, would seek out and destroy the Communist leadership in political and labor circles), or because of fear after World War II of Communist penetration into influential positions, is not known. What is known is that the socialist Left in Chile compromised its own positions one by one for an entrance into the Government and each time was burned in the process. As one socialist, writing in 1961, sums up that era:

> The Popular Front was a gigantic political error that saved the Radical party from falling apart, deprived the masses of their revolutionary initiative, and held up the offensive of the workers for a long period. The Popular Front was an act of social legerdemain that transformed the people's aspirations into mere verbalism and never was intended to modify the structure of landed property or to retrieve the ownership of our natural resources. Instead, it increased the already excessive proliferation of bureaucracy by incorporating thousands of petty bourgeoisie elements into the state administration and wasting the energies of the nation in a multitude of new, ineffective, and inoperative organisms. One after another, and with uniformly increasing speed, the Radical governments led to new disappointments and to mounting resentment from the masses against the parties and men responsible for cheating the people out of fulfillment of their true and deep desires.[8]

For the people it was a period of profound disenchantment with the political process. But it was also a learning experience for future politicians. Salvador Allende had served briefly as Minister of Health under Aguirre Cerda and had resigned in protest to Government policies. Eduardo Frei, who later became the presidential candidate of the Christian Democratic party, served as Minister of Public Works under Videla and also resigned in conflict with the repressive policies of that Government.

Voters were disenchanted. In 1952, with the political parties in disarray, with the word "politician" an epithet in many circles, with almost a dozen candidates running for the Presidency, aging Carlos Ibanez ran—and won—on an independent ticket, standing above political parties. His symbol was the broom, indicating his program for sweeping corruption out of the Government.

1952–1964: Experiments in Capitalism

Carlos Ibanez, like many of his predecessors and all of his successors, found economics rather than corruption to be the nemesis of his administration. Elected in an overwhelming condemnation of corrupt politics and politicians in general, Ibanez had to shoulder the burden that the ending of the Korean War was to impose on Chile. In the next two decades economists of every school and every political persuasion would attempt to solve the huge problems of underdevelopment in Chile. Each would go about it with honesty and, for the most part, self-conscious dedication. Each would have limited success, with perhaps the most positive contribution being the negative one of eliminating for the new incumbent one more alternative. Yet each school of economists would have to admit failure, brought about by international and national forces they did not understand. And as each new palliative was tried, the people of Chile awakened further to the need for their own organization and participation in power. An underdeveloped economic system and a highly developed political sector created a tension in Chile which would grow during the 1950s and 1960s until the resulting stresses on the national polity brought the Chilean political system close to destruction.

The Korean War serves as an example of how Chile, like most other Latin American nations, is tied into the economic cycles of the United States, the chief trading partner and chief consumer of Latin American products and raw materials. During wartime the United States economy expands and its imports increase—especially imports of raw materials (such as copper from Chile). The underdeveloped nations that supply these materials get pulled along. After the war, the cooling of the economic center (the United States) sends ripples of depression, inflation, and social instability through the periphery (Chile).

During the Korean War real wages in Chile increased, although for most workers the living wage was still miserably low. The number of unions stayed fairly constant, as did the number of strikes, both legal and illegal. But in 1953, with the end of the war's active phase, Chile's capacity to import dropped by 27 percent. There was an associated 21 percent drop in exports, with no improvement the following year. By the end of 1955 the cost of living was galloping away at the almost unbelievable rate of 84 to 88 percent yearly.[9]

The end of the Korean War was not the only cause of Ibanez's domestic problems, however. It can be argued that recent international wars have merely been aspirins to the Chilean economy, temporarily relieving profound structural weaknesses. In the 1940s and into the 1950s Chile, like most other Latin American nations, experimented with import substitution, then a widely acclaimed panacea for the woes of underdevelopment. The theory behind this process was that a country could gradually produce within its borders goods that had previously been imported, thus saving precious foreign exchange, which could better be used to buy the necessary industrial and agricultural machinery needed to raise productivity. As with many other "solutions" to the problems of underdeveloped countries, this one brought only temporary relief. During the 1940s and 1950s factories were working two and three shifts. By 1960 industrial employment had risen from 287,872 to 406,000. But even by the middle of the 1950s people could see that the process had reached a peak. The number of manufacturing workers stagnated at the level of the 1950s, and only nonproductive sectors such as service and part-time employment rose. Import substitution had succeeded only in developing an inefficient national industry with low-paid workers and an underutilized industrial capacity.[10]

With the serious inflationary crisis, Ibanez turned to international financial organizations for loans and advice. The International Monetary Fund promptly dispatched a group of economists to draw up an economic game plan for the Ibanez government. This group, later dubbed the Klein-Saks Commission, recommended severe changes to stem what it believed to be the problem—a too rapidly rising demand for a limited quantity of goods. Its solution was simple: Freeze wages. Lower wages would increase profits, causing higher investments, which would in turn increase production and lead to a greater supply, eventually bringing the prices into line with demand. To permit this free market fluctuation, of course, price controls on all but essential foodstuffs were eliminated, as were all subsidies. A free exchange rate was also established.

However, although Ibanez, either through inclination or pressure, accepted the IMF loan and its conditions, implementation necessitated strong measures. Freezing wages meant dealing with a trade union federation that was very powerful even though its Communist leadership had been purged by the previous administration. Workers are usually unwilling to reduce their already precarious hold on life, and Chilean workers proved no exception. The number of strikes rose in 1954 and again in 1955. The real living wage dropped by about 25 percent in 1955 (and did not rise to Korean War levels until 1971).[11] A general strike was called for September 1955 to protest Government policies, but it was postponed until January 1956. Ibanez, taking advantage of this delay, moved in rapidly, arrested most union leaders, and placed the nation under a state of siege. The January strike failed, and the back of organized labor was broken. Labor activity in the following years remained minimal. In 1957, despite a continuing drop in real wages, there were only eighty strikes as compared with 305 the previous year.[12]

Inflation was arrested, but only for a short period, and only at terrible social cost. The recession in the United States from 1957 to 1958 decreased the amount of copper being consumed there and raised the price of finished products, causing inflationary pressures to erupt in Chile once more. In the short run, the harmful effects of inflation were mitigated by a tremendous increase in net foreign investment and loans, from $5.5 million in 1956 to $91.1 million the next year, and to $102.1 million in 1958.[13] But the building pressures could not be contained forever. Just before the 1958 political elections inflation broke out, as virulent as ever, and continued to be the major issue in national political contests.

In preparing for the 1958 elections the Left, through a mighty effort, patched over serious internal differences and agreed to unite in a common front. The Communist party, which had been legalized by Ibanez as a farewell gesture, and the Socialist party were the two main pillars of the coalition. The standard-bearer was Salvador Allende, founder of the Socialist party and losing candidate for the Presidency in 1952. The 1958 campaign was hard fought and the Left, to the surprise of everyone and to its own utter delight, came within an eyelash of winning. Allende might have won but for the last-minute candidacy of a defrocked priest. The priest ran in rural Chile and won forty thousand votes that would likely have gone to Allende, throwing the election to Jorge Alessandri, representative of the business community and grandson of Arturo Alessandri (who had been President three times in the 1920s and 1930s).

The 1958 election was a turning point in Chilean

politics. It brought the parties of the Left together in a unity that carried them through the next three elections, although internal struggles were apparent between elections. It brought into prominence Eduardo Frei, founder of the Christian Democratic party, who garnered a respectable 21 percent of the votes. And it presaged a growing tendency of the Chilean electorate to opt for increasingly liberal positions. Adding together the votes for the Christian Democratic party and the coalition of the Left, both of which criticized capitalism and looked for alternatives, more than 50 percent of the Chilean population had voted for new economic and social arrangements.

Yet the winner was conservative Jorge Alessandri, who was to try his own brand of capitalism to deal with the badly wrecked economy he had inherited. Inflation had been reduced to 25 percent, but only at the expense of destroying the independent labor unions and increasing the social misery of the urban and rural masses. Unemployment hovered around 10 percent, and much of the industrial capacity of the factories lay unused.[14] Alessandri called in a group of economists with a different theory of economics and set to work to remedy these problems. This school of economists believed that inflation was due to an undersupply, not an overdemand, of goods. Thus what was needed were incentives for industry to produce more. The borders of Chile were thrown open to foreign capital and foreign imports under the belief that these would force Chilean industry to compete and therefore to lower its costs and prices. Taxes on domestic and foreign investments were reduced. Profits were permitted to be withdrawn (repatriated) from the country by foreign-owned firms at any time. This laissez-faire, free-enterprise attitude was applied to the labor sector also, with unions once again getting the go-ahead to organize and strike for economic demands.

Labor responded quickly by striking to recoup past losses. Strikes more than doubled from 1958 to 1961 and doubled again between 1961 and 1964.[15] Alessandri's advisers were undaunted. They were certain that a freely competitive economy would adjust to healthy levels. But once again the Chilean economy refused to respond more than intermittently to superficial solutions to deep-rooted problems. The dam burst in 1961, and by 1963 inflation was up almost to the peak levels of the 1950s. Loans and net investment also continued to climb as the Government turned increasingly to foreign sources of revenue to postpone the day of reckoning caused by printing increasingly worthless domestic currency. Net investment and loans rose to $164 million and $171 million respectively, and there was a deficit of almost $300 million in international reserves by the end of Alessandri's term in office.[16]

2

The Frei Years–
The End of
Liberalism

*Years ago the people supported at the polls forces
opposed to the system, forces that were not conservative. But these forces, once in power, became administrators of the system. That isn't the solution. The
government of Frei was the last possible attempt to
modernize capitalism without reverting openly to economic, social, and political dictatorship.*

— Spokesman for the Popular Unity
Coalition, November 1970

The 1964 election again dealt the Left a cruel blow. In
1958 the last-minute candidacy of a defrocked priest had
robbed them of victory. In 1964 it was a different sort of
historical accident. Early that year there was a by-election
in the small town of Curico, an election that the conserva-

31

tive candidate was supposed to win easily. Instead, the Communist party's nominee won, sending tremors through the business and conservative sectors of Chilean society. The conservatives joined with the Christian Democrats, uniting behind the candidacy of Eduardo Frei, to gain victory by a wide margin.

The 1964 campaign was one of the most bitter in recent Chilean history. The Left, strongly anticipating victory, concentrated on educating the populace to the need for socialism. Huge tomes were published describing in detail exactly what a socialist Government would do every day for the first one hundred days in office. Debates between right- and left-wing economists were held in every city in Chile. But the Opposition did not combat facts with facts. Rather it concentrated its energies on another theme—freedom. "Revolution in liberty" was Frei's campaign slogan. The fear of communism was constantly reinforced. Stalin was resurrected to give the lesson of the Kulaks to the Chileans. The target of this emotional campaign was the Chilean woman, who had only gained the right to vote in 1947 and who had shown herself to be much more conservative than her husband. The theme of the Christian Democrats was that Chilean women would have their children and material possessions taken from them if Allende were victorious. In large part this campaign was underwritten by the United States in Government loans, Alliance for Progress expenditures, and private company funds.* Slick posters in down-

---

* As difficult as some North Americans might find this to believe, it is common knowledge in Chile, admitted to by top U.S. officials, and even conceded by Christian Democrats. For those who need more scholarly documentation, two statements from opposite ends of the ideological spectrum might suffice. The first comes from Senator Ernest Gruening of Alaska, who stated in a report to the Subcommittee on Foreign Aid: "Clearly the 1964 financial assistance package must have been based solely on political considerations—to maintain Chile's current levels of economic activity and investment and to support the balance of payments so that financial deterioration and unemployment would not occur in an

town Santiago decried the dread specter of communism with the name of the Madison Avenue advertising agency that produced it clearly discernible. Everything was thrown into the campaign. The night before the election a tearful plea from Fidel Castro's own sister was broadcast, urging Chileans not to fall for the same hollow promises that Cuba had fallen for.

The Opposition proved themselves better politicians. Once again, as had been happening with regularity, the majority of workingmen voted for Allende. But the vast majority of women voted against him, and the "revolution in liberty" was born.

Eduardo Frei, the "revolution in liberty," and Christian Democracy were the darlings of the Alliance for Progress. Idolized and supported by Washington, a showcase for the Alliance, Christian Democracy was considered by many social scientists and diplomats as a possible wave of the future in Latin America, a middle road between violent Communist revolution and fascistic military dictatorship.

In many respects the Christian Democrats were revolutionary. As one Brazilian acquaintance of mine, now living in Chile, explained: "Many Christian Democrats in Chile would be in jail if they lived in other Latin American nations." In many respects the members of the new Government team were similar to their New Frontier counterparts in the United States. Cocky, hardworking, and intelligent, they represented the most advanced non-Marxist theories of economic and social systems in Chile. They used the most sophisticated economic tools and learned from the mistakes of former administrations. They discarded the simplistic notions of monetary economics—the superficial solutions of freezing wages or giving industrial incentives.

---

election year." The second comes from the *Engineering and Mining Journal* of November 1964, which states: "Privately, top Washington officials admit Frei's election was greatly helped by the 'serious efforts' of U.S. copper interests aiding the U.S. Information Agency."

They believed that inflation was a complicated structural problem and that the maldistribution of income and land, with its accompanying low levels of purchasing power and agricultural production, was the major cause of Chilean misery. The vast majority of the population had no money to spend even on necessities. The very rich took their money out of the economy and placed it securely in foreign banks or invested it in industries that concentrated on the production of luxury items purchased by only a tiny slice of the population.

The tragedy of Frei and his administration is that he and his advisers understood the problems so well and yet refused to embrace the methods necessary to solve them. Partly this was a result of the election. Frei had won with strong right-wing support, and although he was not personally inclined to compromise, it was politically advisable to water down certain proposals and postpone others in order to maintain maximum leverage in Congress. Although he had won a majority of the popular vote, he was faced in Congress with a strong left-wing minority that voted against his liberal programs out of political motivations and a strong right-wing minority that voted against them out of conviction.

Yet his refusal to embrace the measures necessary for the radical alteration of Chilean society was in part a result of the vagueness of his own philosophy. His "revolution in liberty" was supposed to be a middle path, a path that would avoid the pitfalls of both capitalism and communism. In both systems, Frei said, the tendency is to take man's liberty away:

Both principal systems do this, in one way or another—capitalism by dehumanizing him, by making his work the over-powering feature in his life, and communism, by making the good of the state superior to the good of the individual. A life of liberty is immutable. No society has the right to deny me the right to be myself.[1]

Of course, such an ideology fit conservative as well as radical teachings, and both gathered for a while under the umbrella of Christian Democracy, giving the Frei administration a tension and dynamic that North American academicians prematurely presumed to be evidence of revolutionary actions. Frei was the man in the middle, and as the situation at home worsened, he leaned further and further to the right.

Frei's regime was caught in the inflexible terms of its own ideology. Having broken with the sterile and rigid dogma of the Catholic Church in the 1930s, Frei found himself unable to adjust to the new lessons of the 1960s. Yet his humanistic rhetoric was as in tune with the struggles of the poor in the 1960s as it had been in the 1930s, and it was the rhetoric of his administration that was his greatest legacy. As one Chilean told me, although the conservatives in Chile threw their support to Frei in order to prevent socialism in Chile, they chose by doing so the only path that would later have permitted socialists to gain power. If the socialists had won in 1964, their victory would probably never have been consummated. Faced with a society almost feudal in many respects, the difficulties of jumping into socialism would probably have been overwhelming. But by permitting Frei to legitimate the concepts of socialism and to begin marching toward a reformation of Chilean society, the socialists by 1970 found much less resistance to their victory.

Frei's rhetoric was socialist, although that word was never mentioned. He attacked the great landowners, the very rich, the elites who had fought against any kind of change, no matter how trivial, over generations. He taught the people that there were enemies other than their own inadequacy, their own disorganization, and their own lack of education. He discussed poverty and repression in social terms and stopped criticizing the individuals who lived in the lowest strata of society as being lazy and ignorant.

Freedom, to Frei and those around him, meant freedom to negotiate. The masses were organized, not to participate in government, but to push against the citadels of power when the decision makers proceeded too slowly. Thus the number of organized peasants rose from five thousand when Frei took office to more than twenty-five times that many in the middle of his term. The repressive Rural Labor Act of 1948, which had put so many conditions on union organizing that it had effectively stopped such organizations from arising, was repealed in 1967 and replaced by a much more permissive statute. Neighborhood centers sprang up, women's centers proliferated, and sports clubs were organized. To Frei, organization meant power. As he once remarked: "When the government doesn't give justice you have to push against the centers of power. My way of doing this is *Promocion Popular*.* This is the key, the backbone, the center of my whole government."

Yet ironically, as the masses began making the very types of demands that Frei had encouraged and, indeed, spawned, internal and international factors limited the Government's will and power to respond. As the masses gained momentum, the "revolution in liberty" lost it. The irony is that the Christian Democrats, who were the spark for revolution, refused to be revolutionary. They could isolate problems but could not tackle them. Redistribution of income, for instance, was considered essential but was never achieved, for it meant pushing against the very powerful business sector of Chile. As the years rolled by, the agrarian reform program bogged down, partly because

---

* *Promocion Popular* was the name given to Eduardo Frei's program of establishing community organizations throughout the country.

the Government decided to pay current market prices for land expropriated, causing a great burden on the budget and an eventual slowdown in the entire program. Housing starts faltered and industrial growth ultimately stagnated.

Much of this was a direct result of the failure of the ideology of Christian Democracy, which holds that all human beings have common interests and need only be made to see that commonality. There are no evil people within this framework, no devils, merely obstacles that need to be overcome. Concentration of income is considered a problem, but the rich are not the enemy. Underutilization of industrial capacity is a problem, but the monopolistic situation of much of Chilean industry is not the enemy. Increasing indebtedness is a problem, but foreign control is not the enemy. Given this ideological framework, it is little wonder that the motivation to confront in possibly violent and certainly unpredictable battle was lacking.

Even as the Christian Democrats were riding the crest of the wave, gaining an unprecedented majority of the popular vote in the municipal elections of 1965, there were murmurs of discontent in their own ranks. One Congressman said: "We have an historical responsibility, but we have done very little for that 85 percent of the Chilean population which voted for a revolution, while we are making continual concessions to an oligarchy and a bureaucratic minority of 15 percent." Perhaps that statement was a bit premature. The Christian Democrats did, to their lasting credit, organize the masses and legitimize revolutionary language. They set in motion a chain of events that was soon to shake the very foundations of Chilean society and split their party itself into fragments. Organization does indeed breed power, as Frei knew, but power often leads to strident demands that become catalysts for social violence if they are not acceded to. And Christian Democrats, like most ruling parties, abhorred violence and instability. Lewis Dieguid, writing in 1967, said:

His [Frei's] desire for order has precluded effective attempts to organize the bypassed masses, a process that is, of course, disorderly.

Dieguid went on to elaborate:

For [the] critics, the Revolution . . . while it was to have been in relative liberty, was bound to be disruptive, if not violent, to the upper classes from which had to come the means for bettering the lot of the lower ones. The critics now look about them and say that the old order has not changed. Peasant wages have doubled from nearly nothing, and the upper classes are paying significant amounts of taxes, for the first time, yet the old patterns of economic and social, and to a lesser extent, political power, remain the same. The voice of the technocrat is heard in the land, and the same social revolutionaries have lost the President's attention.[2]

As the imagination behind Christian Democracy wavered, the people of Chile pressed forward. From 1964 to 1966 the number of unions increased from 1,863 to 2,870. The number of strikes rose from 584 to 1,073 during the same period.[3] Demands that at first dealt merely with higher wages and union recognition soon broadened to include rehiring of employees who were unjustly fired. Peasants in rural areas, long passive under the yoke of repressive legislation, lack of communication, and patronal violence, began demanding the rapid expropriation of the land under the newly legislated agrarian reform law. When the government still did not move rapidly enough to suit them, small segments of the rural peasantry began occupying the land themselves as a means of pressuring the administration. In 1965 there were 13 land takeovers. In 1966 there were 18. In 1967 the number dropped to 9, but in 1968 it rose to 26, in 1969 to more than 70, and in 1970 to more than 250.[4]

The mushrooming explosion was not only rural; social

protest touched almost all facets of society—some sooner, some later. In the slums that ring Santiago, the residents began organizing. Others seized the land itself as a means of leverage to demand better housing.

Although it might not be entirely accurate, the impression one gets when taking a bus from Santiago down the Pan American highway south is that the city is ringed with concentric circles, each circle containing a community a little worse off than the one before. On the inner rings are the new high-rises, dominating downtown Santiago; farther out are the private suburban homes. As the rings span out the homes become smaller, more untidy. Then the *poblaciones* begin, areas where government-supplied homes sit, two- or three-room shelters in which families of five or six dwell. Each *poblacion* possesses "urbanization," the Chilean word for the conveniences of urban living— water, electricity, plumbing. In the outer ring lie the *campamentos,* those communities which spring up overnight in a takeover of terrain. The takeovers occur after much preparation, usually as a sort of sloppy military maneuver occurring in the middle of the night. The residents live in tents or in homes made of sheet metal or wood with the ubiquitous stones holding the roof in place. There is rarely water, rarely electricity. Plumbing is nonexistent, telephones likewise, and medical care is a long, long bus ride away.

I was sitting in Campamento Metropolitano, in the polyclinic, a two-room wood structure which creaked as the wind whistled through, talking to the Secretary of the Commission of Discipline and the President of the Campamento, when a mother and daughter, both well dressed, came in. The mother wanted to know if there were any more sites available. The Secretary explained patiently, with a sympathetic smile, that they had twenty-five people already on the waiting list and the chances of her getting a site were doubtful because the government had given permission for only four more sites. (It seems that the government, although not approving land takeovers, uses them to make the process of constructing public housing more orderly. Each *campamento* is given a certain number of sites, meaning that the government housing authority has agreed to construct a certain number of houses in another area for that *campamento*. If more than the requisite number of sites are filled when the community finally moves into public housing areas, someone will have to be left out.) The lady stands erect and smiles, her nervousness betrayed only by the constant wringing of her hands and the pinching of her shoulder with her finger, kneading the skin so as not to cry. "We're living in a place half this size," she quietly explains, "me and my five children." She says it matter-of-factly. She adds her name to the waiting list and leaves to try another *campamento*. I asked a friend why she would want to live in this flat dusty hellhole of a place. Two reasons, he told me. One, if they don't become a member of an organized pressure group they might wait years for better housing. Second, they probably would live under better conditions in this *campamento,* where the children would have room to play outdoors rather than in the overcrowded two-room apartment downtown that she is probably sharing with another family and its kids.

Even for those who seized the land the prospects were dim. At great risk the success depended on how many other Chileans one would vault over, as one-third of the population stood in line. The housing authority had promised houses to the Campamento Metropolitano by the thirtieth of July, but that is the middle of the winter in Chile, and even if the houses were ready on time there still would be many deaths before then. But for many Chileans an adequate house was worth fighting and sacrificing for.

Other Chileans began striving for different goals. There were 723 strikes in Chile in 1965 and 1,142 in 1967, culminating in the general strike of November 3, 1967. Chilean society was speeding toward an upheaval. No longer was there enough largess in the society to buy off a few large groups. In 1967 there were 2,447 labor conflicts. And in 1968, during just the first eight months, there were 2,539 conflicts, during which 4.4 million man-days were lost.[5]

These strikes, seizures of factories and land, and student demonstrations evoked two major reactions from Chilean Government personnel. One was an increasing reliance on force. In 1968 slum dwellers, in an effort to persuade the Government to construct the promised housing, took over unoccupied but privately owned land near the southern city of Puerto Montt. Several were killed as the police came to dislodge them. Ironically, the man who in 1962, after shantytown dwellers were murdered by Alessandri's police, had said "When the humble act, there are always bullets for them," found himslf caught as President in the same contradictions that underdevelopment and organized masses thrust on even the finest statesman.

A council for national defense was established. United States military aid to Chile, which was pouring in at a greater per capita rate than anywhere in the world except South Vietnam, was increasingly oriented toward counterinsurgency and riot control. Beginning in 1967, the last quarter of the Chilean cadet's schooling took place in Fort Gulick, in the Panama Canal Zone, under U.S. supervision. A tactical riot squad called the Grupo Movil was created.

The second reaction by Frei and his counselors, as the economic situation worsened and the masses began demanding more, was to rely with increasing regularity on foreign investment, hoping that foreign capital and loans would tide the economy over until it could somehow right itself. The hope was that copper production would double by 1970 and that the immense investment in agriculture would begin yielding profits by then. But the rhythm of foreign investment and debt carried a dynamic all its own.

Foreign Investment in Chile: The Vicious Circle

Foreign investment in Chile, as in the rest of Latin America, has been seen as a necessary evil. The theory put forward by North American economists and accepted until quite recently by their Latin American counterparts goes something like this: Latin America is starved for capital. It cannot break out of its underdevelopment until it gets sufficient capital necessary to build national industries. Once these national industries are established they will employ an increasing percentage of the population, a growing group of people who will then have more money to spend on consumption since they will be receiving salaries. Once the consumer market has grown to a significant size it creates its own dynamic. Employment rises as production rises. Wages rise as profits go up, and money begins to be saved in banking institutions, where it can be easily channeled into national investment funds.

In Chile this theory was only fully embraced in the 1960s. As Chile opened its borders to foreign capital, its tiny national industries were quickly taken over. A 1968 study by the National Development Corporation (CORFO) found that one-third of all Chilean capital was foreign controlled. Foreign capital tended to enter the largest Chilean firms. Of the industrial enterprises that were controlled from outside the country, "86.4 percent of the enterprises . . . have control of the market they supply."[6] Of the one hundred largest businesses in Chile, sixty-one had foreign participation, and in forty of these that participation was large enough to be considered controlling.[7] By 1968 foreign interests—mainly North American—controlled 60 percent of the industrial chemical and metal products industries, 100 percent of petroleum distribution, 100 percent of tobacco production, 44 percent of shoe production, and 100 percent of rubber production.[8]

Tales of foreign penetration during this period abound. In 1967 Ralston-Purina entered the fish and poultry industry, despite an August 1966 report by the Bureau of Agriculture and Fish, which had warned: "This department believes that the request [of Ralston-Purina] cannot be accepted with the terms proposed . . . without doing danger to the stability of the national industry." Scarcely six months later the deal went through as proposed. The company's terms that the bureau found so offensive were: freedom from import duties on equipment, tools, and machinery necessary for its business; the freezing of all taxes in such a manner that future national tax increases would not affect it; the opportunity to amortize its assets in as little as five years; and the right to revalue company assets from year to year without paying higher taxes.

With such incentives it is easy to understand how foreign firms in Chile could make huge profits. The net return on their capital doubled during the decade of the 1960s, increasing from 11 percent in 1959 to 23 percent in 1969. (That figure, incidentally, was double the net profit percentage gained by such firms in other Latin American countries.)[9]

These huge profits were not plowed back into internal investment or industrial expansion, as the economic theories promised. Rather they were remitted, taken out of the country. The outflow of exchange due to amortizations and depreciation of foreign capital grew from $25 million in 1950 to $272 million in 1963, to a high of $284 million in 1968. Amortization and depreciation of foreign capital, which had only represented 7.6 percent of income on current account in 1950, zoomed to the almost unbelievable figure of 47.8 percent in 1967. Direct investment in the period from 1950 to 1967 totaled $450 million, but profits, dividends, and such were equivalent to four times the net amount of income.[10]

As foreign interests gained control of Chilean industry, contracts for advanced technology rose, even though Chile, with its high levels of unemployment and high debt payments, did not need capital intensive equipment. Nevertheless, Chile paid out more than a third of a million dollars in royalties in 1963—a figure that jumped to $3.5 million in 1964 and doubled to $7.4 million in 1968.[11] As one worker at a small factory explained to me, pointing to a Coca-Cola bottle: "We pay a couple of cents for the use of the bottle, and some more for the use of the name, and the money leaves Chile, not benefiting us at all." What he grasped at the most basic level was becoming obvious to the most sophisticated economists by the end of the 1960s.

Perhaps most irritating to Chileans who had accepted the thesis that their capital-starved economy needed an input of foreign capital was the knowledge that most foreign investors were using Latin American sources of capital. Orlando Caputo and Roberto Pizarro, two Chilean economists, have estimated that of the total resources utilized by North American capitalists, only 11.8 percent represented funds coming from the United States; the remaining 88.2 percent came from Latin America. And 14.1 percent of that total came from the internal savings of Latin America, domestic savings put into banks or savings and loan associations.[12] Although this fact of international economic life has only recently been discovered by many Latin Americans, North American businessmen have been boasting for years of how they managed to make a profit without taking a risk. Fredric G. Donner, at the time Chairman of the Board of General Motors, once informed his public:

Let me summarize our overseas record during the past 15 years in terms of some objective measure of business accomplishment. At the end of 1950, the value of General Motors net working capital and fixed assets overseas was about $180 million. . . . By the close of 1965, this investment had increased to about $1.1 billion. . . . This expansion was accomplished almost entirely from financial resources generated through General Motors operations overseas and through local borrowings which could be repaid through local earnings. As a result . . . our overseas subsidiaries remitted about two-thirds of their earnings to the United States.[13]

The dynamic of foreign control never stopped. At first the largest corporations were taken over—a simple task when one considers the size of the Chilean market. In automobile production, for example, the entire output per year was only thirty thousand cars (in the United States, General Motors alone produces that many every few days). As the large corporations succumbed, foreign financial institutions began to move in. Utilizing a country's domestic savings is much easier when one has a branch bank in that country, connected to international liquidity reserves. As one economist discovered:

At the end of 1962, three foreign banks had 3.4 percent of the reserves of private banking sectors, 13.2 percent of the sight deposits, and 5.2 percent of the term deposits. By the end of 1967, as a consequence of the appearance of the Bank of America, and the acquisition of a minority part of the Banco Osorno y LA Union by the Deutsche Südamerikanische Bank, the percentages increased, respectively, to 15.7 percent, 28 percent, and 20 percent.[14]

Probably the most important effect of this increase in foreign ownership of Chilean capital was its tendency to increase the indebtedness of the Chilean economy. Foreign corporations which have an unlimited right to exchange local currency such as Chilean escudos for dollars, called the right of convertibility, often utilize this right to remit dollars to the host country. Yet Chile has only a limited supply of dollars. It earns them only by selling something to industrialized countries. Its main source of revenue has for decades been copper. And copper during Frei's administration was controlled by foreign corporations. As more copper was sold, more dollars were remitted by the very industry that was needed to generate enough dollars to give to other North American corporations. The resulting deficit was covered by resorting to loans.

But loans also have a very nasty dynamic. Economist Harry Magdoff, in *Age of Imperialism,* describes this situation using a hypothetical example that is quite applicable to the Chilean case:

> To appreciate what the continuous growth in debt means, an exercise in simple arithmetic is helpful. If a country borrows, say, $1,000 a year every year, before long the service payments on the debt will be larger than the inflow of money each year. . . . Take a typical loan: $1,000 is loaned to a country at five percent interest, to be repaid in equal installments over 20 years. We assume further that a similar loan is made each year. . . . during the 5th year of such aid almost half of the money coming in has to be used to service the past debt. In the 10th year almost 90 percent of the new money is needed for debt service. By the 15th year the capital outflow is larger than the capital inflow. In the 20th year, the borrower is paying out more than $1.50 on past debt for every $1.00 of new money he borrows.[15]

In 1970 almost $700 million of the $2.8 billion Chile owed various international financial agencies had not even been received![16]

When a nation reaches this level of indebtedness it usually requests a renegotiation of the terms of the debt. The debtor nation can ask that the debt be temporarily postponed or that the interest charges be lowered. The only leverage the debtor nation has is its threat to plead bankruptcy and not repay any of the money. That, however, is a most drastic step, for it is the prelude to massive internal dislocations and possibly a slow strangulation of the economy. Poor nations must pay their debts regularly in order to keep their standing among underdeveloped countries. Even renegotiation, which in the Chilean case occurred in 1967, merely postpones the inevitable, for at some future date a new administration must confront the economic "beggar" status. In addition, renegotiation brings with it certain conditions, depending on the weakness of the requesting country. In some cases these conditions include a severe austerity program. Often the conditions reinforce the very basis for the dilemma (for example, by permitting the unlimited repatriation of profits by foreign corporations).

Some economists respond to these observations by asserting that debtor nations should be able to use the borrowed money to develop industries that would eventually become profitable enough to pay off the debts. Magdoff answers that argument this way:

We have to appreciate the difference between an internal and an external debt. When a businessman borrows internally and has to repay the debt, the procedure is very simple: As his business grows, with the help of the borrowed money, he uses his profits to repay the debt with the same kind of currency he borrowed. But if a businessman or a government borrows from a foreign source, he can only repay the debt in the currency of the foreign nation. So that even if the borrowed money helps to create internal growth, the debt cannot be repaid unless there are sufficient exports to get the needed foreign currency. If exports are not sufficient to pay for the debt and buy the needed imports, then the pressure exists to make further loans. When this process comes to a head, the bankers reschedule the loans—provided the recipient country behaves like a good boy.

Economists Caputo and Pizarro, in a recent book on foreign capital in Chile, agree:

> Given on the one hand the restricted nature of exports, and, on the other, a growing rate of exchange necessary in order to pay servicing, we are enclosed in a vicious circle that cannot find a solution within its own terms.[17]

By 1970 all the various threads were becoming interwoven. An overview portrayed an economy in Chile controlled by the very few (and those with strong ties to foreign interests), an economy that was taxing the lower classes in order to pay off the foreign corporations, which were consistently taking more out of the country than they were putting in. By 1970 17 percent of the corporations held 78 percent of the total assets. A total of 284 corporations controlled every one of the sectors and subsectors of economic activity in Chile. Within each corporation the concentration was even more pronounced. Among the largest 161 corporations, excluding banks and insurance companies, the ten largest stockholders controlled more than 90 percent of the stock capital.[18] As America Zorrilla, now Minister of the Treasury, notes: "And if to this we add the many cases in which the same person owns stock in different enterprises, we will be able to explain in what measure the Chilean economy is controlled by a handful of great monopolists."

By the end of the 1960s, no more than 500 of the 2,034 corporations existing in Chile dominated 80 percent of all production there. And these 500 were in turn controlled by the one hundred supergiants among them. Yet it was precisely those one hundred that were tied into foreign multinational corporations.[19] Agustin Edwards, reputed to be the richest man in Chile, owned 25 percent of the stock of the Ralston-Purina branch in Chile. The Yarur family, one of the five most powerful clans in Chile and controllers of banks, radio stations, and textile companies, were partners with Chase Manhattan Bank in many ventures. The First National City Bank of New York had close ties with Anaconda and its affiliates. In 1968 the Bank of America assumed control of the Banco Italiano, having opened eight branches of its own in Chile in the early 1960s. The Bank of London was the principal stockholder in 1966 of Textile FIAP and Cemento Melon, huge corporations which dominated their respective industries.

Concentration of corporate ownership was mirrored in financial concentration. In 1969 sixty-six debtors in Chile garnered 26.5 percent of the credit, and 200 gained almost half of the total credit disbursed.[20] Banks were linked to family economic groupings. The Yarur family, for example, controlled the Banco del Credito e Inversiones. That bank in turn gave 30 percent of its credit to five enterprises in the late 1960s, all of them controlled by the Yarur family. In that particular bank there were over 100,000 depositors, but only thirty stockholders controlled the stock and therefore the election of bank officers and the direction of bank policy.[21]

This concentration, plus the links to foreign enterprises, gave the rich in Chile several tax advantages. In 1967 Chilean enterprises not tied to foreign capital (which were usually the medium-sized and small businesses) paid an average of 40 percent of their profits in taxes. Two and a half million wage earners paid an average of 20 percent in taxes. But the one hundred firms connected to foreign firms paid out only between 2 and 6 percent of their profits in taxes.[22]

The Chilean State and Foreign Investment: The Creation of Mixed Enterprises

Although the foregoing material gives a good idea of the extent of foreign penetration into the Chilean economy by the late 1960s, the interrelationship of foreign capital and domestic politics went still further. As the Chilean state began playing an increasingly powerful role in the economy—a role that was initiated during the depression with the creation of CORFO—and foreign investment began flooding into the country, it seemed almost natural that a partnership of sorts would be formed between the large corporations and government officials.

CORFO, although established to spark national industrial development, actually acted as a sort of catalyst for transferring public money into private hands. Kurt Drekmann, CORFO vice president, describes this process in an interview in *El Siglo:*

Traditionally CORFO has done everything for the private businessman. It did technical studies, prepared plans, and finally induced the businessmen to invest. The fishing industry is an enlightening example. CORFO spent millions and millions of escudos in developing this activity and encouraged the private sector to join. CORFO started supporting 75 percent of each fishing business, and the private sector supported 25 percent, and that not even in new money, but rather by promising later profits. The business failed, and CORFO had to absorb the losses. At the same time CORFO prepared very profitable businesses, which later were given over to the private sector, frustrating therefore the traditional role that should have been played by that organization in the Chilean economy.

Sometimes the Chilean Government acted directly on behalf of foreign businesses. For example, it borrowed millions of dollars from the Export-Import Bank, which by United States congressional directive can only give loans to be used to aid U.S. export industries. These loans thus went directly to U.S.-controlled or U.S.-owned industries, yet added to Chile's already high debt burden.

Increasingly, the very personnel of the Government came from sectors linked with business. Of twenty-seven ministers of state named by Alessandri and Frei, twenty were lawyers connected with large corporations, or managers, or rich agriculturalists, or rich businessmen. The rest were professors, doctors, and other professionals not directly related with big business.[23] Moreover, the distinction between public and private sectors was breaking down. Ministers alternated between big business and public office so often that Joaquin Undurraga, at the time Director of the National Planning Office, commented in 1965 at a meeting of corporation executives:

It surprises me when in the meetings of businessmen we speak of public and private sectors, in circumstances where a year ago I was in the private sector, and, on the other hand, many of the businessmen here were in the public sector. We have changed our shirts, but in no way changed our thinking.

This increasing intimacy in personnel, reflected indirectly by financial subsidies, was made explicit during the later Frei years with the creation of a new type of industry, the mixed enterprise, wherein the Chilean state and foreign capital became partners in business operations. The best and most controversial example of this type of enterprise occurred in the copper sector. Under Frei, Chile bought over 50 percent of the stock in the copper companies but permitted them to retain control over production and sales.

To discuss the copper industry at all, it is necessary to trace its history at least briefly. United States investors entered the lucrative copper fields in 1905, when the Braden Copper Company initially invested $2.5 million. Shortly thereafter, Anaconda and Kennecott came in. Copper became a political issue only as the profits of the companies mounted. It was a major issue in 1938, when for the first time the Popular Front Government taxed the companies to assure a revenue from their profits over and above import and export duties. Between 1922 and 1931 the copper companies had exported $592 million in copper, and $445 million of that sum had never returned to Chile in any form. Taxes paid by the enterprises during that period represented less than 1 percent of their liquid profits. The Popular Front imposed a 12 percent tax on profits, as well as additional levies.[24]

Although through taxes Chile managed to siphon off a trickle of the flood of profits the copper companies were making, her lack of control over either the production or the sale of this precious metal caused problems. During World War II, for example, although sentiment in Chile was pro-German, the copper companies as their part of the war effort held down the price of copper sold to the United States. During the Korean War the companies froze the price at 24.5 cents a pound, losing Chile some $300 million, since the world market price was much higher. In 1951 an agreement was finally negotiated which gave the Chilean state some leverage in the sale and distribution of copper. It was permitted to sell on its own account 20 percent of the copper produced by the largest mines in the country. But conditions were placed even on this concession. Chile could not sell to socialist countries. She had to promise to revise her tax system to benefit the Anaconda holdings. She was permitted to sell only at the price of 27.5 cents per pound, even though the London metal market's price, usually used as the official indicator of copper values, was at the time about 35 cents a pound.[25]

The next year Salvador Allende, then a Senator, presented a bill in Congress asking for the nationalization of copper—a proposal that was rejected by Congress but strongly supported by the copper miners. Even though it was rejected, the popular fervor engendered in the national debate forced the Government to raise the selling price of copper so that it would be in line with the London price.

During the 1950s, partially as a result of the Klein-Saks recommendations, Ibanez gave back the concessions gained by Chile in the 1951 agreement, restoring to Anaconda the right to retail copper throughout the world, even to the Chilean Government itself, and giving even more financial incentives to the copper companies.

By the time Frei assumed office copper had become the major national issue in Chile, with agrarian reform second in importance. The statisticians of the Left had compiled a record of the almost unbelievable profits made by the copper companies during recent Chilean history and at every opportunity publicized the figures. A dissertation by Mario Viera, Professor of Statistics and Econometrics at the University of Chile, showed that by 1928 the companies had taken $300 million from Chile. From 1928 to 1950 another $1.23 billion had left the country, and between 1950 and 1960 $770 million had been remitted. In 1960 alone, almost $140 million was remitted abroad. The process was speeding up. "To this must be added," Viera explained, "the losses that were signified by the freeze of the market price at 11.5 cents a pound during the Second World War, a loss that has been estimated at $500 million."

In 1961 a popular magazine published by the Socialist party and edited by many who were to become Ministers in the 1970 Government declared:

If these enterprises had been Chilean or if legislation that affected them had been enacted in the national interest, we could have more than multiplied by five times the investments that the steel, ENDESA, and ENAP industries have so painfully realized. We could have five *huachipatos* [huge steel refineries], five times the hydroelectric complexes, and five times the oil pumps and the exploration of oil that today we possess. And that could have been done without begging loans, without subjecting ourselves to the demands of international financial agencies, nor of Wall Street bankers.[26]

Perhaps the most painful aspect of this process to Chilean leftists and nationalists alike was the worsening of the situation even as the revelations became more numer-

ous. As a result of the enactment of recommendations by
the Klein-Saks Commission in the mid-1950s, taxes on
copper were reduced. Thus the tax income received by the
Government from copper sources totaled $163 million in
1955 but dropped to $126 million in 1956 and to only
$52.2 million in 1958, rising only slightly to around $70
million by 1961—even though production in foreign-
owned copper mines rose from 390,000 metric tons to
500,000 metric tons during the same period. Another way
of putting this is to say that the state received $415 per ton
in 1955 and only $142 in 1961.[27] Who paid the differ-
ence? The wage freeze and worsening living conditions of
the poorer classes in Chile have already been noted. In
addition, taxes paid by the large mines in 1955 accounted
for 24.7 percent of the total fiscal income, and indirect
taxes that year came to 55 percent. In 1959 copper revenues totaled only 12 percent of the national revenue and
indirect taxation rose to 67 percent. As the burden of sales
taxes increased, net return on invested capital rose to 20
percent for copper companies by 1960.[28]

There are profits to be made from the mere mining of
copper, but even more to be made from the subsequent
stages of refining and fabrication. As a Federal Trade Commission report noted after World War II, "reports of companies which fabricate as well as mine the copper show
that . . . the greater part of the profits come from the
fabrication division of operations." But fabrication in Chile,
being controlled by foreign markets and dependent on
foreign companies, varies according to external factors.
Thus the number of metric tons produced in Chile has
fluctuated wildly, from 3,525 in 1957 to 32,415 in 1959,
from 4,953 in 1960 to 49,729 in 1964 to 5,578 in 1969.[29]
As Andy Zimbalist writes: "It is certain that this experience
has not made Chile's attempt to develop a copper fabricat-
ing industry easier."

The lack of control over this industry has produced

other profits for the foreign companies. One is the profit from recycled copper. Chile, exporting virtually all of its production, does not partake in this recycling, which accounts for between 25 and 35 percent of each year's consumption of copper. "We may estimate," writes Zimbalist, "as a consequence, that Chile loses an additional 30 percent of potential 'returned value.' "

With 25 percent of the world's known reserves, Chile was producing only 12.7 percent of the world's copper in 1966, in spite of her production costs, which were lower than elsewhere. And the situation was again worsening; Chile's share of the world market had been 19.6 percent in 1946. Moreover, the 1.6 percent annual growth in copper production between 1946 and 1966 occurred mainly in the small- and medium-scale mines. The large mines increased their output at less than a .5 percent compound rate annually.[30]

The percentage of all exports refined also declined, from 81 percent in 1951 to 45 percent in 1962, recovering slightly to 63 percent in 1968.[31] Both Anaconda and Kennecott, the two giants in Chilean copper, had built electrolytic refineries in the United States to process blister copper from their Chilean subsidiaries during the postwar period.

The American companies have preferred production of blister because it involves a smaller foreign investment per final ton produced, centralization of refining capacity in the U.S., smaller taxation, and control of the destiny of the final output. It is likely, that in the view of the foreign firms' multi-plant and multi-country operations, the optimum export mix for them leads to a less than optimum mix from Chile's point of view.[32]

This was the situation Frei faced when he took office in 1964. Among his campaign promises was one to return to Chile control of her natural resources. His solution was not outright nationalization, which he felt was foolhardy, but "Chileanization," a mixed partnership with the copper companies. Yet leftists noticed that although Frei was calling his Chileanization program a great step forward, the copper companies themselves were willingly acquiescing in this new move. The *Engineering and Mining Journal* in November 1964, the month Frei took office, cleared up some of the mystery:

> Washington remains hopeful of getting along well in Chile with the new moderate-leftist Frei government even though problems are apt to crop up. The feeling is that any problems created will probably be minor compared to those that would have resulted if the Marxist Allende had won. . . . Privately, top Washington officials admit Frei's election was greatly helped by the "serious efforts" of U.S. copper interests aiding the U.S. Information Agency.

The Chileanization legislation passed Congress in 1967. Nearly everyone outside the Left in Chile seemed ecstatic over this example of international cooperation. Kennecott was especially proud, reporting in its 1967 annual report to stockholders: "Kennecott voluntarily and enthusiastically entered into an agreement with the Chilean government. . . . This partnership arrangement will be mutually advantageous to the Chilean government and Kennecott."

Others, however, thought the copper companies were winning hands down. For example, one analyst found that the Braden mine, which was valued at $160 million for purposes of equity transactions, had a book value of only $65.7 million. Griffin writes:

> At every point in the negotiations—from the value placed upon the Braden Copper Company, to the level of taxation on the profits of the nation's richest resource—foreign companies were favored. Even today, after four years of a government [ded-

icated] to a "revolution in liberty," the foreign-owned copper companies are given privileges not enjoyed by Chilean businessmen; e.g., the right to import equipment duty free. The nascent entrepreneurial groups in Chile are not given protection from foreign businessmen; they are not even allowed to compete on equal terms; instead, they are placed at a disadvantage and subjected to unequal competition.[33]

Another observer, Teresa Hayter, who at the time was working for the Inter-American Development Bank, said: " 'Chileanization' meant basically that the Chilean Government put up most of the capital for expansion."

Although Chile now owned 51 percent of the stock, the Government had no more control than before. In fact, in 1969 the Anaconda Copper Company was fined for its refusal to sell copper to the Chilean army. Yet during the Vietnam War the companies had been selling copper to the United States at prices far below the London market price. Only in 1969 did the Chilean Government move in to change this practice.

As for company profits, they zoomed skyward. Braden obtained $62 million in profits between 1960 and 1964, but in the next five years its profits totaled $156 million. The El Salvador mine earned $9.5 million from 1960 to 1964 and then $71 million in the next five years. Adding all the profits together, the large copper interests gained about $213 million between 1960 and 1964 and $552 million from 1965 to 1970.[34] Although they promised to increase production substantially in return for lower taxes, the copper companies in fact increased it only minimally. And even that minimal increase had to be accomplished through the negotiation of huge loans, which the Government of Chile would have to pay back. The disadvantages of being a silent partner became clear when Allende took office and his Minister of Mines found that the Anaconda Company owed millions of dollars in back taxes. Anaconda's response was that it was only a minority interest, that it was the *Government* that owed the Government those taxes.

Allende, in his first major speech in office, noted the "good business deal" that Anaconda had made. In 1969, from all its far-flung international operations, Anaconda made $99 million, of which $79 million came from Chile. Investing only 16 percent of its world-wide capital in Chile, it took more than 80 percent of its world-wide profits from that tiny country.[35] In other words, for every five dollars Anaconda invested world-wide, only one dollar went to Chile; but for every five dollars Anaconda earned world-wide, four dollars came from Chile. To make matters even worse, Anaconda took those remitted dollars and invested them in plants for extracting aluminum in the Caribbean, knowing that aluminum was the chief competitor of copper.

As the handwriting became obvious and the copper companies realized by the late 1960s that eventually even the conservatives in Chile would ask for complete nationalization, they began de-investing capital. Equipment was left in so dilapidated a state that the common saying in Chile was that the copper companies took their wealth and left only big holes in the ground. An independent group of French technicians, looking at the huge Chuquicamata mine in mid-1971, concluded: "The actual owners have inherited a situation so bad that they see themselves confronted with all problems simultaneously." Machinery was broken down, repair parts had not been ordered, converters were obsolete, furnaces were falling apart. It was the legacy of fifty years of plunder.

Reaction: The End of Liberalism

As Chile began to fall ever more under the control of foreign capital, a dispute broke out within the Christian Democratic party over the entire issue of foreign investment. The youth wing especially, which saw the state becoming a silent partner to foreign corporations and utilizing uneven taxation to pay off foreign interests, began to complain. In a speech in early 1967, Eduardo Frei responded to these youthful critics with a pragmatism born of leadership:

To renounce foreign investment would lead fatally to economic stagnation and would create for ourselves a condition of inferiority vis-à-vis the rest of the countries of the world. It is a fact, furthermore, that external capital resources are not unlimited, and, therefore, all developed and underdeveloped countries make a considerable effort to attract these investments. It is a world competition. To remain outside would be fatal for our country.

The radical section of his own party responded vaguely: "The capitalists should understand that the state will regulate the use of financial resources in accordance with the national development program, and that this will not be determined by the interests of distinct economic pressure groups." Furthermore, they added, trying desperately to stretch the party's ideological underpinnings to embrace an anticapitalist thrust:

We, Christian Democrats, want an economic growth that will place us at some distance from capitalist criteria rather than commit us to them. . . . We want progress, but we also want the great effort of the nation to benefit the majority and not to serve to consolidate the power of certain economic groups. Therefore, we will never measure the success of our policies with simple statistical criteria: more houses, more roads, more schools, more industry, more jobs. All this interests us, but we add a further requirement: that the dominant beneficiaries of the development process should be the workers, the peasants, and the middle class of the country.[36]

These words went unheeded, but soon other voices were joining in as the effects of foreign intervention began harming larger and broader segments of the population. By the late 1960s even the large landholders were beginning to complain as United States programs and investments poured into that sector. In 1969 Pedro Opaso Cousino, a conservative member of the National Agricultural Association, outraged by what he felt were harmful favors given to foreign investors at the expense of domestic landholders, exclaimed:

> In whose interest is there a devaluation of our money every 15 days? Why are the trucks that the mines acquire 15,000 escudos, yet for agriculture they cost 80,000? Why are agricultural prices not fixed with the same criteria with which they fix the price of iron? Why aren't equal guarantees for capital and agricultural profits given that are given to capital and profits of the telephone company?

And, he added, in language unfamiliar to a middle-class landholder in Chile:

> It is an undeniable fact that Chile is today less independent than in 1810. Then our country supplied its own food and had control of its own money, things that are not true today. . . . Today this money is controlled by a foreign organization that is called the International Monetary Fund. . . . The recognition of the bad influence of the United States in Chilean life is in the subconscious of the majority of Chileans, but we are afraid to say it through fear of being called pro-communists. . . .[37]

Agriculturalists had a special gripe with the United States. It centered around the U.S. Food for Peace programs, initiated in the mid-1950s and greatly expanded and formally named under John Kennedy. There were eight separate contracts with Chile between 1955 and 1969, varying in amount from $17 million to $30 million annually, the latter occurring in 1969. The conditions of the agreements were enough to make even the richest landowner scream. Payment consisted of 50 percent in U.S. dollars and the rest in national currency. The part paid in national currency was based not on the banking exchange rate, the usual rate taken as parity for all current imports, but on the current rate of exchange on the market for dollars. Thus products purchased through this plan were on the average about 20 percent more expensive than they were at the world market price. It was also obligatory that 50 percent of the surplus foods be transported in North American ships and assured with North American companies. All the credits paid interest. Finally, in a classic example of how charity and self-interest intertwine to become imperialism, a certain percentage of the domestic currency reserves were to be used to develop an "increase in the consumption by the national markets of North American products." Thus, by leaning on these aid programs as temporary props, Frei's Government not only increased Chile's debt by paying dollars for food it could have purchased in exchange for saltpeter or other goods from Argentina or Uruguay, but also encouraged importation of United States luxury foods at the expense of domestic production.

Professionals in Chile were angered by aid programs that included restrictions creating unemployment in their ranks while utilizing Chilean credits to gain jobs for North American professionals. Rodrigo Flores Alvarez, President of Chile's Association of Consulting Engineers, described the situation in early 1971. He explained that in the period from 1965 to 1969 investment in industrial sectors and public works provided the equivalent of 4,300 jobs for engineers, and that the proposed investment in these areas for the period from 1970 to 1973 placed the number of engineers to be employed at around 5,700. In Chile there was no scarcity of skilled people available for such employment. The number of graduates from engineering schools rose by 46 percent between 1965 and 1969, and graduates from technical schools rose by some 200 percent in the same period. But, Flores Alvarez lamented, during those four years almost 90 percent of industrial expansion projects were contracted outside the country and 50 percent of infrastructure public works projects were also contracted with foreign firms. North American companies and consulting firms were used.

This created not only unemployment—these firms naturally used their own engineers—but more subtle problems as well. Foreign engineers who designed the projects often did not have adequate knowledge of the materials available in Chile. Thus designs often needed to be revised after completion, raising the cost of the final project. Also, foreign engineers charged from one and a half to three times what Chilean consultants charged, and they had to be paid in dollars. Finally, when foreigners designed projects they naturally made use of materials with which they were most familiar—that is, North American construction materials. Alvarez cited a study of ten projects, five designed by Chileans and five by foreigners. In the five Chilean-designed projects, twenty-two thousand tons of Chilean steel and four thousand tons of imported steel were used; the figures for the five foreign-designed projects were almost exactly the reverse.

In the cities, owners of small and medium-sized businesses also were beginning to complain. They had to deal simultaneously with concentration at home, liberal taxing and pricing incentives for foreign corporations, and tiny national markets. Their problems were serious, for like their counterparts throughout the world, Chilean entrepreneurs operate on very low margins of profit. In May 1966, for example, the margins of profit for prime necessities were as follows: soap, 2.9 percent; cheese, 1.8 percent; matches, 2.9 percent; coffee, 1.07 percent; rice, 0.12 percent. For some items, such as butter, milk, and sugar, there were moderate losses during that time.[38]

Thus, as the 1960s faded, more and more Chileans were finding their interests threatened by the liberal policies of the Christian Democrats. As Pedro Vuskovic, Minister of Economy under Allende, wrote in a prescient and panoramic view before taking office:

Certainly the process of concentration is affecting increasingly broader interests. For example, the concentration of the distribution of services, with the large supermarkets, affects an important and growing number of small merchants who would always find it difficult to reorient their work into different activities. In similar manner the small and medium industrialists are seeing themselves dominated by the growing concentration in large corporations and the increasingly greater degree of monopolization of production. The improvement of the relative position of the middle sectors, made up of white collar workers in public and private sectors, which since the decade of the forties had as its counterpart a relative deterioration in the position of the manual workers, is now approaching its limits, limits that cannot be surpassed within the existing system; on the contrary, inasmuch as the groups of foreign and national interests that today receive the benefits of concentration are not affected, the middle sectors see themselves confronted by increasingly burdensome tax pressures and they find other mechanisms which in the past facilitated their upward mobility to be less effective, as for example what is happening in education. To the small proportion of workers who have access to activities within the modern sector—where they obtain remunerations absolutely greater than the general average—increasingly it is more difficult for them to defend their levels of real income, in the face of the growing indices of unemployment and marginality, that is being registered in the rest of the population.[39]

Although it was the small businessmen, represented in the Radical and Independent parties, who would tip the electoral balance in favor of the Left in 1970, it was the workers who were faring the worst during the 1960s. That, of course, was not a new experience for Chile's millions of laborers. For decades the vast majority that have been politically unorganized, although linked with political parties, have not been able to raise their living standard. Although Frei claimed to have aided the workers, and probably did somewhat increase the living wage of peasants, the plight of those living in and around the metropolitan areas actually worsened. The best illustration of this is simply the amount of time a worker must work to buy necessary items. In 1956 the average worker had to work one hour to buy a kilo of green vegetables, a kilo of sugar, and a liter of milk. In 1965 he had to work a little longer than two hours to purchase the same amount. Four years later he had to work more than three hours. In 1965 a worker earning an average wage in Chile and having a wife and an eight-year-old child spent 66.8 percent of his earnings on food. In 1969 the same man spent 82.3 percent on food, if he used the standard minimum diet established by the United Nations.[40] Of course, that presumes the impossible—that Chilean families were spending almost all their money on food. Instead, bread and a mixture of flour and water substituted for more nutritious fare. The result was massive malnutrition, which in working-class areas was often so severe as to cause brain damage.

Laborers in Chile live, in the best of circumstances, at or near subsistence level. In 1969 forty-four of every one hundred workers earned less than the poverty-level income (according to an index that underestimates the necessities of life and their cost as much as its counterpart in the United States does), while twenty-seven more earned barely above that. Yet, at the other end of the pyramidal income distribution, seven out of every one hundred earned twenty-three times that much monthly. The pyramidal structure became even more pointed in the last years of Frei's tenure in office. In 1965 51.6 percent of the employed population was below or near the poverty level; by 1967 this percentage had risen to 71.2.[41]

Jorge Pinto is young, no more than ten years old, but he looks fifty. He earns a living hopping on and off buses, selling his wares to preoccupied and sweating passengers who more often than not simply ignore his shouts. "Buttons, buttons, thirty-six for two escudos, pretty white buttons," he screams, holding up the sheets of uniform buttons to prove his declaration. Two escudos, enough for a copy of the daily newspaper, or two bus trips. It's a dead-end street for Jorge Pinto, a little cash for his family or an occasional Coke or movie, but no future. When he grows older he might still be seen peddling his wares on buses then as old as he is, selling combs or buttons, or singing pathetic songs, passing the hat around afterwards. There is almost no begging in Chile. Pride prevents it. But Jorge Pinto is only a step above that.

On September 21, 1970, just three weeks after Salvador Allende won on a wave of working-class sentiment, Jesus Ortiz shot himself through the mouth, dying instantly. He was one of those who couldn't wait any longer, no matter how short a wait it might be. He was fifty-three years old. He had worked twenty-four years in a flour mill but had been fired earlier in the day because of a need to "renew personnel." He had been earning, after twenty-four years, the equivalent of a dollar a day.

And still we have not seen the lowest levels of the society. There remain the armies of unemployed, the *lumpenproletariat,* as the Left in Chile calls them, who are ignored by mostly everybody. The Marxists consider them close to unredeemable; the Conservatives treat them as individual cases of laziness, as peculiarities in an economic system otherwise running fairly well. In 1967 the rate of both unemployed and underemployed people throughout the country was hovering around 27 percent.[42] And this in a society where, as we have seen, even full-time work bought nothing more than a little filling bread. As economic opportunities disappeared, the number of people who continued to seek employment also fell. Between 1952 and 1960 the percentage of working women dropped from 25.5 to 20.9 percent; among men the decline was from 81.1 to 77.9 percent.[43]

People often point to Chile as an example of a country with advanced social legislation. In fact, through decades of struggle the working class in Chile has managed to gain a number of excellent laws. There is welfare, unemployment insurance, and a labor court system whereby a worker who feels he has been unjustly fired can appeal to the specified tribunals. Yet the reality belies both the theory and the grand pretensions of the law. The courts for workers are few in number and enormously understaffed, and there is a real question as to how objective the judges are. Cases wend their way through courts for years, during which time the worker is without a source of income. Usually disputes are settled out of court for a paltry sum. In 1966 a law was passed stating that if a person is dismissed and the labor tribunal finds no cause for dismissal, the person must get his or her job back or be paid by the employer one month's salary for every year worked, in no case receiving less than six months' pay. A study completed in 1968 found that of 3,844 complaints, 459 were settled in behalf of the complainant, 775 went against him, and 2,610 were settled out of court or abandoned.[44]

Chile's labor court system obviously had glaring loopholes. The major one was Article 10, which said that people could be dismissed when the "necessities of the functioning of the enterprise recommend it." The independent Chilean Labor Institute reported in 1970:

If the enterprise is obligated to prove the pre-eminence of this cause it is enough to get a report from some professional or even some dependent of the firm that indicates that the reduction of personnel is owed to reasons of great validity (bad economic situation, acquisition of new machinery, etc.).

The provision that the employees could be sacked in order to introduce new machinery was used extensively. For example, the Ready Mix Cement Company, a U.S.-owned firm, announced that it had been having difficulties inducing construction teams to buy cement that was being prepared mechanically and distributed in special trucks. But after the above-cited law was passed, construction firms began purchasing the item (although unemployment in the construction industry in Greater Santiago was at the time 17.3 percent).

For the unemployed, the welfare system offered little. During 1968 six months of unemployment insurance was paid to 15,383 laborers throughout the country, while in Greater Santiago alone there were 32,100 unemployed workers.[45]

As the workers' plight worsened, they looked with mounting bitterness at the wealth of the top 2 percent of the Chilean population. Between 1967 and 1968, while workers' wages were falling, profits increased by 68 percent. Between October 1964 and October 1969 the average salary in Santiago rose by 217.8 percent, but the price of the dollar rose by 304.1 percent—a factor that helped increase profits in foreign-owned and export industries.[46] In 1964, when Frei took office, foreign business remitted profits of $165 million from Chile, but in 1968 these had almost doubled to $320.3 million. Coca Cola, a latecomer to Chile, declared a profit of 63,300 escudos in 1967, but a year later its profits had risen to a breathtaking 1.3 million escudos. American Screw Company in 1967 declared profits of 487,000 escudos and twelve months later saw this figure rise to over two million.[47]

No wonder workers began to echo the sentiments of

the 15 percent who were already organized and who were represented in the national Confederation of Trade Unions (CUT). The leadership of most Chilean unions has always been in the hands of communists and socialists (although Christian Democrats have a respectable minority sentiment). In 1962 the Confederation of Trade Unions declared:

The social injustice and misery which oppress the national majority have as their cause the chronic incapacity of the capitalist regime, which, based on private property in land and the instruments and means of production, divides society into antagonistic classes—workers and employers, exploited and exploiters.

By the late 1960s the rank-and-file workers were expressing these same sentiments, although ironically, as the economic and social crisis became more pronounced the Confederation of Trade Unions found itself incapable of translating into action the revolutionary rhetoric that so long had been its stock in trade.

As Chile careened toward a crisis, rifts in the parties themselves began to show up. In July 1967, the youth and radical wings of the Christian Democrat party managed briefly to wrest control of the party from the older moderates. However, in so doing they confronted Frei, the party leader, with an anomalous situation. In Chile Presidents are also heads of their parties, ruling in a semiparliamentary manner and depending heavily on straight and unwavering party support. As one observer noted, with the election of a slate of radicals to the party leadership "the ensuing relationship between the party and the Government tried the boundaries of their autonomy and interdependence."

At the end of 1967 Frei, whose options were becoming severely circumscribed by increasing indebtedness, proposed a forced savings plan whereby the wage readjustment (for many decades, the Government has each year re-adjusted everyone's salary upward to reflect approximately the cost of living—conservative Governments readjust to somewhat less than the cost of living, liberal Governments to somewhat more) for the coming year would equal the cost of living rise, but 5 percent of that amount would be in Government bonds or public investment bonds, another 5 percent would be in bonds contributed by the employers toward worker bondholdings, and 15 percent would be in cash. The rest would be take-home pay. Along with this proposal was a companion one that would have prohibited strikes for the coming year. The youth wing clearly opposed the bill, as did most of labor. The lines were drawn. Colin Bradford, writing of that period, notes:

The President was forced to specify regulations requiring members of the executive branch to resign who held views contrary to those of the Government and who wanted to express them in public. Finally, in an all-night meeting of the national assembly of the Christian Democrat party in January 1968 Frei forced the party to determine whether it was with the Government or with the Opposition. The result was the defeat of the party directorate headed by Rafael Gumicio and its replacement by a new directorate headed by "oficialistas" and party ideologue Jaime Castillo. The principle of mutual autonomy between party and Government had been strained to its limit, and Frei was forced to impose his will upon a divided party.[48]

The bitterness was only papered over. As 1968 dawned, all of Chile was confronted with a massive breakdown of political institutions and massive signs of unrest. In March the Vice President of the Government party, surveying the social and political landscape, declared: "I think that there is truly a crisis of confidence; no one believes in anyone." Early in the year the cabinet was reshuffled and Jacques Chonchol, architect of the agrarian reform program and vocal critic of that same program in its later years, was forced out. That summer the newly elected president of the Christian Democrats' youth wing was disciplined and nearly expelled from the party for his "extremist" views and criticism of the Government. Early in 1969 the president of the party accused the youth wing of teaching guerrilla tactics at its summer camp.

Simultaneously there was a growing relationship between workers and students and a rising militance among the peasants. The first ventures in rank-and-file actions began in 1968. They were disavowed by the traditional trade union hierarchy, however, who increasingly defended and maintained the political and social system as the 1970 elections approached.

On January 4, 1968, the workers of SABA, a small electronics plant, presented a list of their demands. One hundred and sixty-five workers asked for an increase in salaries which for the most part had remained at about the equivalent of a dollar a day. By June 11 the employers still had not negotiated in good faith, according to the workers, and on that day the union called a strike. This carried the conflict to the Minister of Labor. On June 15 the professionals—seventy white-collar workers—joined the strike. One week later, in order to prevent the employer from taking material from the factory and setting up operations in another part of the country, the workers occupied the factory, setting off shock waves throughout the Chilean business community. The Confederation of Production and Commerce spoke of a "national plan of subversion to destroy some productive resources in the country." The Association of Electronic Industries expressed its outrage at what it considered "this criminal act . . . [which] demands an energetic and opportune action on the part of the authorities in the face of the excesses of some groups that, under the pretext of labor conflicts, take over industries by force."

The employer turned to the Minister of Interior, who

promptly sent in the police to dislodge the squatters. The police lofted tear gas grenades into the factory, which according to several plant workers caused a small fire. According to the authorities, however, the fire was set by the workers themselves to prevent the employer from re-occupying the building. Dozens of workers were arrested, held incommunicado for over a month, and released on bail only after a long hunger strike by wives, sweethearts, mothers and sisters. They were released on bail in May 1969, almost a year after having seized the factory. In October of that year the Visiting Minister handed down jail sentences that ranged from seventeen years for the leader to between eleven and fifteen years for others charged with setting the fire. Several more were given two- to three-year sentences for trespassing.

The SABA strike and arrests were the catalyst for beginning links between students and workers. Students at the University of Concepcion began aiding the workers in their struggles. Later in 1969, when the Revolutionary Left Movement (MIR), a student guerrilla organization, was forced underground, thirteen of the SABA workers who had been sentenced to more than five years in jail joined the underground network.

There was ferment in the educational system also. The university reform movement was initiated and spearheaded by the Christian Democrats as part of their policy of rationalizing and modernizing the entire society. Universities in Chile were grossly inefficient, with few people gaining access to classrooms and fewer still graduating after many years of attending boring, irrelevant classes. Schools were ruled by a few old professors who were given life tenure. Teachers were underpaid and usually worked part-time, finding a second job where available. Thousands who wanted to enter the university were not permitted to do so because of lack of space. The Christian Democrats led the movement to expand educational facilities and to modernize both the facilities and the administration of the colleges and universities.

But in so doing—they were quite successful in expanding and establishing a new norm for education in at least parts of the country—the Christian Democrats opened a Pandora's box of student agitation. Students in Chile, like their counterparts throughout the world, are verbal, incredibly romantic, and middle- or upper-class in origin and ideology. But the martyrdom of Che in nearby Bolivia and the wild tortures in other Latin American nations caused these students to be more active and less rhetorical than their brethren in the United States. At the University of Concepcion the MIR movement arose first out of issues of student power in universities; its linking up with worker and peasant groups came later. The MIRistas were forced underground because in mid-1969 they were allegedly involved in the beating of a well-known and highly sensationalistic journalist, who was left tied, semiconscious and naked, to the large gates of the university. One MIRista with whom I spoke conceded the error: "We made a mistake. We did not realize the full power of journalists."

However, historical mistakes often force new directions. In this case the Government invaded the previously holy sanctums of the university, searching students and their rooms indiscriminately. This action led to national protests, for in Latin America universities had traditionally been considered inviolate, even to the reach of the state. Once underground, the leaders of MIR were forced to break with their middle-class backgrounds and lead new lives as revolutionaries—lives that caused them to mature their concepts of revolution and temper their idealism and romanticism with street experience. MIR moved off the campus, strengthening nascent links with workers. In late 1969 and early 1970 it moved into the *poblaciones,* the shantytowns that ring Santiago, establishing a network under the leadership of Victor Toro, himself a slum dweller. Later they moved into the rural areas, forming popular militias and creating revolutionary peasant movements in the farm belt of southern and central Chile.

Unrest spread. The first national peasant strike occurred in mid-1969. MIR and student demonstrations and worker takeovers caused the state to rely increasingly on force. The Grupo Movil was reinforced. The National Defense Council was established a year later. The results of this increasing militarization of Chilean society, a society that had been extraordinarily free from repression until that time, became quickly apparent. On March 9, 1969, police fired on squatters in Puerto Montt and killed nine. In May 1969 the police surrounded School Number Ten of the farm El Vinculo in order to dislodge the mothers of students who had taken over the building to demand more classrooms. On May 30 a high school student leader accused the Grupo Movil of coming into the school cafeteria and beating students. In June, Carlos Molina, leader of the Federation of Industrial Students, was hit in the leg with a tear gas bomb and needed a cast. On August 29 a worker was killed with a gas pellet fired by the police. On September 10 a policeman fired into a group of high school students and killed one nineteen-year-old. By late 1969 the police had invaded the University of Concepcion, the student body president and vice president were under arrest, and a state of siege had been declared throughout the country.

The political and social ferment was rising. It seemed like the perfect time for radical leadership. But where were the Socialist and Communist parties, which had so long been predicting just such a crisis?

The Socialist party meandered through the 1960s, splitting into two vague groups. There were the party bureaucrats who had been fighting in elections for decades and who had come so close to victory in 1958 that they were addicted to the electoral process. And there were the middle- and upper-class socialists whose intellectual insights enabled them to theorize on the impossibility of using elections to overturn entrenched economic interests but whose background and inclinations told them to stick it out at least one more time—always one more time. The youth wing of the party was becoming increasingly restless in the face of this dualism. The far left magazine *Punto Final* criticized the party's Hamletian timidity in early December 1968, saying:

> One cannot speak to the people in two different languages. It is not correct to tell them, on the one hand, that universal suffrage will get them nowhere . . . that power can only be gained through armed confrontation; and, at the same time, induce them to vote, to trust in electoral results, in the efforts of the parliamentarians, in their speeches in Congress, in the legal initiatives or amendments which they propose.

To the left wing of the party the disintegration of social institutions was not to be mourned; it represented a great opportunity. Chaos, after all, had long been predicted and should be utilized, not avoided.

The Communist party in Chile has an image among members of the Left and Right alike that borders on the comic. Communists are considered dogmatic, ideological, incredibly well organized and disciplined, and above all, terribly boring. In Chile, where a sense of humor is not only an asset but almost a congenital trait, this last is perhaps the most damning. The widespread joke in Chile is that the worst fate—worse than death itself—would be to have to sit through a fiesta given by the Communists.

But beneath this prejudice lies envy and fear. Both the Right and the Left fear the well-organized cadres of the Communist party, for different reasons. Banished in 1948 for a decade, the party came back in full strength when it was legalized by Ibanez. Its political chests are full, for its members pay dues and the representatives who win office on the party ticket are paid according to their needs, the rest of their salaries going to party coffers for other battles. Communist support is widespread among the organized elites of labor. Although many years ago the party was led by workers, by the 1960s the leadership was made up mostly of intellectuals.

The Communist and Socialist parties have maintained an uneasy friendship, a marriage of convenience consummated only at election time. In 1958 their forces combined and almost won. In the early 1960s the rhetorical battles between the Socialist party, which supported Fidel (especially Allende, who publicly supported Che and Mao) and the Communist party, which bought the Moscow line unwaveringly, even at the expense of common sense, are legendary. But in 1964 the parties were back together, with Allende at the helm. In the late 1960s the battles raged once more, stoked by Allende when he personally went to the Chilean-Bolivian border to welcome the survivors of Che's heroic band, much to the consternation not only of the Communist party but of many of his own party, who called it a personal testament that could only lose votes. In 1968 the Communist party, alone of any Latin American group, supported the Russian invasion of Czechoslovakia.

But perhaps the most meaningful confrontation occurred in the late 1960s—between those who argued for armed revolution, pointing to the debacle of 1964 and the repression of 1968 and 1969, and those who espoused the peaceful road to socialism, a view cited often by Luis Corvalan, Secretary General of the Communist party. Increasingly, the youth and workers, and finally the peasants and slum dwellers, saw this belief in nonviolent means of revolution as a cover-up for a deep fear of disorder and an addiction to the electoral process. History proved them at least partially correct. By 1968 and 1969 the Communist party in particular found itself willing to compromise any of its principles in order to participate in one more election.

And it appeared that there would be only one more election, for as the Secretary General admitted shortly before the voting, this would be the last peaceful election in Chile, since even the Communist party was finding it more and more difficult to maintain discipline among the younger segments of the organization.

As social unrest escalated and the parties began dividing, it was a natural step for Eduardo Frei to begin discussing the possibility of forsaking a political system that was not flexible enough to deal with the major problems of the era. In early 1968 Congress, mainly as a result of a block vote by the left-wing members, refused Frei permission to leave the country to visit the United States, a visit that would have added greatly to his prestige. He was furious at what he deemed infantile opposition when he had won a clear majority at the polls in the municipal elections shortly before. In July 1968 he declared publicly:

It is necessary that this country undertake constitutional reforms that would permit an authentic expression of the people —the plebiscite, and, if not the plebiscite, a dissolution of Congress for a single time. This road is indispensable. The Government must be given the tools it needs. Because if Congress itself has accepted national planning—which is not totalitarian planning but a democratic one—it cannot destroy it in such a manner as to make it impossible to achieve a systematic, coordinated, and coherent direction of the national economy.

Frei, democrat at heart, planner by orientation, by late 1967 was putting economic planning ahead of that most cherished of all Chilean assets, the multiparty system. He explained:

I think the solution of a one-party Government responds better than the multifarious combination of parties in this hour when countries must program and plan their economies and maintain stability in direction and a coherent orientation unified in all its actions.

Congress did, in fact, pass a constitutional reform giving the President the power to go directly to the people in cases of a dispute with Congress.

José Antonio Viera Gallo, later Undersecretary of Justice under Allende, presented a somewhat long analysis of this tendency toward a stronger, dictatorial state. To him, as to most socialists in Chile, democracy was merely an extension of a certain form of economic system. He predicted that as Chile's economic system began to break down, antidemocratic as well as fully democratic tendencies would arise:

Industrialization has arrived at the dead end. Import substitution cannot continue in the same manner as it has during the past decades. It appears necessary to initiate a new era of industrialization characterized by the installation of industrial complexes which produce capital goods. But that requires the support of foreign capital (if the present system is maintained). Seen from that perspective it is interesting to verify if we are approaching an accentuation of a new form of dependence, and, at the same time, the internal exhaustion of the economic scheme of the last years. This situation seems to be having repercussions at the political level with the appearance of the first serious cracks inside the politics of compromise. The social contract has lost its base of support and the fight for power is tending to become increasingly antagonistic. The state has suffered the impact of this break in its base of legitimacy and all the contradictions that previously were hidden have now appeared: the existence of a vacillating, inefficient state, tied to private interests, including foreign interests, that has lost its very justification.

With respect to democracy, it is important to see until what point this situation is translated into the impossibility of continuing the existence of a formally democratic state within a society that is authoritarian, whose fundamental institutions exclude the public from power (business enterprises, communications media, educational system, etc.). It would appear that the presence of a formally democratic state within an authoritarian society can only exist if at the same time there exists a growing and self-sustaining economic accumulation, that would permit the establishment on a solid foundation of a politics of consensus. Such a situation occurs, for example, in the developed capitalist societies. But in situations like ours, the continuing authoritarian-democratic continuum tends to break down. There are those who in the name of democracy would not fear to sacrifice formal democracy in order to assure the basic authoritarianism of the society; and, on the other hand, there are those who fight to extend democracy into all the sectors of our national life.[49]

Four years before, Julio Silva Solar, then a Christian Democrat, had presciently told Congress that "the pressures of the masses are so strong and so deep, that for Latin American governments during the next ten years there will be only two alternatives: revolution or repression." Viera Gallo reinforced this theory, emphasizing the fragile nature of Chile's economic system.

Yet it was not until October 1969 that a series of events, still mostly unexplained, illustrated just how delicate was the politics of compromise in Chile, just how close Chile, with its strong tradition of democracy, had come to social dictatorship. That series of events came to be known as the *Tacnazo*—named after the military barracks in the town of Tacna, which were seized by a group of officers under the leadership of General Roberto Viaux Marambio.

The military in Chile has traditionally been considered apolitical. When even the finest scholars are questioned as to the reason for this unique attribute among Latin American nations (except for Costa Rica), the invariable answer is: "Because there is a tradition of noninterventionism." And around the circle we go. Yet there may be a couple of reasons external to national character that have contributed to this relative isolation of the military from domestic political affairs. First, during the nineteenth century the army had a function and purpose separate from domestic political meddling. In the middle of that century it was sent south to fight and subdue the Indians. In 1879, in the War of the Pacific, Chile beat the combined forces of Bolivia and Peru and wrested from the latter country the southern third of her territory, lending great prestige to the army. Second, the upper-class interests in Chile—industrial, agricultural, merchant—did not have to use the military as a tool to intervene in governmental affairs because the state had a source of revenue separate from the various domestic income groups. In most other Latin American nations the military was supported by separate factions within the country, and numerous coups resulted from the struggle for power. In Chile such struggles, which did occur before 1833, quickly died down and were replaced by a consensus of the ruling classes. Such agreement was possible partly because the state did not have to choose among various revenue-producing sources. Since most of the natural resources of Chile have been owned by foreign interests—first British, then North American—since their first utilization as exports, there was an independent source of revenue. Through import duties and fees the Chilean Government could amass most of its public revenue, permitting the consensus among ruling classes to go on fairly uninterrupted for decades.

The prestige of the armed forces in Chile is enormous. Most people, especially those in the lower classes, see them as the true protectors of the Constitution. Politicians are corrupt and suspect. The police are controlled by the Minister of Interior and therefore are quasipolitical. But the military is above politics. Cadets are prohibited from belonging to any political party and cannot vote. They are not even supposed to read political journals or newspapers, which isolates them from the political machinations of daily Chilean life. In a survey taken in the early 1960s, a majority of the lower-class people interviewed declared their faith that if the military did have to intervene it would be on behalf of the lower classes to protect them from an unstable or chaotic administration.

Within the military itself, however, there were increasing complaints beginning in the early 1960s, particularly among the higher-ranking officers, concerning the declining and changing role of the armed forces. Their budget had been reduced substantially under Alessandri. Their function had been changed from protecting the frontiers to conducting civic action programs. Many military generals were paid less than teachers or public service bureaucrats and felt slighted. Others looked enviously to neighboring Peru, Argentina, Brazil, and Bolivia, where militarists not only were gaining national power, but were also earning international recognition for their leadership in coping with social problems.

By 1969, however, the middle and upper classes were beginning to call for strong government. Unrest in the streets seemed to portend social rebellion. Economic planning, some felt, could not take place until there was a unified government with a stable society. "What this country needs is an Ongania," one Chilean exclaimed in 1969, referring to the military dictator in Argentina. Into this breach stepped General Roberto Viaux Marambio, handsome, charismatic military leader who would be a catalyst for a political crisis of major proportion.

On October 16 General Viaux was asked to retire from his office within twenty-four hours. The reasons have never been entirely clear, but many felt that his growing popularity among the younger officers was viewed with alarm by Frei. The twenty-four-hour time period was extraordinary; usually such dismissals take months. The next day Viaux told news reporters: "They have asked for my retirement because they think I have too much influence on my subordinates. . . . They told me that they do not want a leader in the army." In the streets of Antofagasta, a medium-sized city on the northern coast of Chile, there were demonstrations in his favor. On the eighteenth, Viaux's replacement arrived and took over command despite Viaux's absence—highly irregular procedure. Viaux at that time began portraying himself as a leader of a middle military sector against a "small group of generals." This highly insubordinate statement brought a call for him to come to Santiago to explain his conduct. On the twentieth he arrived in Santiago, declaring: "I certainly have not handed over my command of Division I."

That statement, certainly seditious, did not lead to his arrest, however. Rather, the Minister of Defense tendered his own resignation as a sign that Viaux had more power than he. The next day Viaux traveled to Tacna and led the seizure of the barracks with the full support of the soldiers stationed there. He explained that he was leading a movement of soldiers and demanded the dismissal of the Minister of Defense and the Commander in Chief of the Army, along with an increase in salary for both positions and improvement of equipment. He made clear that the *Tacnazo* was not a coup d'état, but a pressure tactic.

President Frei responded immediately by imposing strict censorship on the entire country, using national television and radio stations to enlist popular support for his Government. He called the *Tacnazo* an intended coup and played on peoples' fears of military dictatorship. Yet his calls fell on deaf ears; he had little support on this issue. Army units called out to arrest Viaux refused to do so. The military was no longer loyal to its civilian leader.

This crisis caused some strange permutations in the existing political coalition. The sole supporter of Frei was the Communist party and, through it, the CUT. Both called for a general strike in support of the Government (or, rather, against a possible coup). The next day Viaux, in a conciliatory gesture, agreed to submit to military justice if his demands were met. The Commander in Chief and the Minister of Defense resigned and huge salary increases were granted. The crisis ended, but its repercussions continued. Huge wage increases were then demanded by and granted to other powerful sectors of the economy, spurring upward the inflationary spiral. Viaux was thrust onto the national stage, a not unwelcome figure to many who believed that the whole civil system was weak. He was to intervene once again a year later in a more serious and critical manner (ironically, the new Commander in Chief appointed as a result of Viaux's demands was René Schneider, who would be assassinated by Viaux in the tragic events of the following year).

The Communist party and its Confederation of Trade Unions were also caught in the rush of history. After having based their recent activities on the possibility of gaining power through electoral politics, they were forced to shore up a social system in its moment of crisis to try to keep it together until the upcoming elections. Yet such compromising actions were occurring while the rank and file's wages were constantly dwindling, and while in several instances workers and students joined in street demonstrations and factory takeovers.

As mentioned above, in 1967 Frei had tried to get through Congress a forced savings plan. The Communist party, like most other leftist and labor groups, opposed this, stating: "To vote in favor is to give the green light to regressive politics." But in 1968 the Communist party voted for a similar plan, giving as its reason that the annual readjustment of wages had been delayed too long and the workers were willing to compromise to get their money. Some outsiders saw this as a reversal based more on a fear of anarchy than on practical judgments about workers' desires. Osvaldo Sunkel, a Chilean social scientist, has written that leftist parties and unions in Chile have been

increasingly incorporated into the political establishment and . . . their existence and influence depend on the maintenance of this system. The political influence of some of their leaders and their respective bureaucracies would probably vanish if these parties and trade unions were to be turned into real popular mass movements.

With Chilean institutions in disarray and the economic system near bankruptcy, hanging on only through increased favors to foreign corporations and increased indebtedness, and with the masses beginning to mobilize themselves, the Communist party was fighting for its life as a political agent of change by maintaining close contact with parliamentary modes of decision making.

When the *Tacnazo* occurred, Luis Corvalan declared: "The professional necessities of the armed forces also should be attended to. In this respect the Communist party will do everything it can." Leftists pointed to an almost simultaneous editorial in the *Washington Post* which lamented the lack of money and arms the Chilean army was getting because it was "not capable of fulfilling its internal police functions." Others were just disgusted with the Communist party conservatism. Manuel Cabieses, a MIRista, asked:

Why should the life of an establishment that employs the jail for children and young people accused of "terrorism" or shoots workers and women each time their protests offend the ears of the ruling class be protected? Why avoid problems with a yankee imperialism that is in the background of all governmental measures of parliamentary actions? What happened with the forces of the left, like the Communist Party with respect to the readjustment bill, is painful. But it is only an episode that is quite revealing. The principal conclusion to be learned from it is that in the game of "rascals" the bourgeoisie always triumphs. Consequently, we believe, now is the time that the sector of the new left, which undeniably is arising in Chile, in the same manner as it is arising in other Latin American countries and Europe, should take seriously its role and should organize itself to fill a vacuum that would be a tragedy and a betrayal to leave abandoned.[50]

But the Communist party and CUT were willing to go still further to bolster up the system. Just before Christmas of 1969 CUT, for the first time in history, signed an agreement with the Government on wage increases, an agreement that elicited murmurs of approval from the ranks of conservatives and howls of outrage from the Far Left. The new wage agreement, the Far Left maintained, still recognized the difference in the amount of family allowance for white-collar workers as opposed to blue-collar workers. It accepted a minimum daily wage of twelve escudos—about a dollar a day—that would affect about two million Chilean urban and rural laborers. The Far Left pointed to recent studies by the Chilean National Health Service which indicated that a family of four (two children) in Chile would have to spend at least twenty escudos a day on food just to maintain minimum standards. Others cited statements by Luis Figueros, head of CUT, who had said on October 20: "If we want the minimum salary to return to the value it had in 1953 the readjustment should be approximately 84 percent." But in December CUT was willing to settle for 28 percent. What intervened? The *Tacnazo*.

The day after the agreement *El Siglo,* the Communist party newspaper, happily exclaimed: "The worker salary of twelve escudos is equivalent in real money to the minimum worker salary of 1953, the highest that has existed in Chile." The Right also cooed happily, although from a somewhat different perspective. *El Mercurio* said:

At other times we have been able to accuse the union leaders of intransigence and even of acting with the clear proposition of blocking governmental action. . . . In this occasion the directive of CUT has contributed to avoiding the climate of agitation that normally is incited when discussing the bill concerning readjustments. It is certain that it has obtained the greater part of what it has asked for, but also it is true that the original demands were more realistic than others of other years, and that it has been flexible in some important respects. . . . For our part we applaud the example given by CUT in this opportunity to other sectors . . . it constitutes a first step toward constructive participation of unions in the elaboration of responsible wage and salary policies.

El Diario Ilustrado, a conservative newspaper, commented that CUT seemed so much more flexible than the "rigid demands of public employees," and added: "It could signify a type of 'entente' between the Government and CUT." Patricio Rojas, Minister of Interior, noted: "It is an example for many other sectors which haven't had the appropriate understanding in the difficult moments we have lived." He congratulated CUT on its "responsibility and sobriety." The Minister of Economy, Carlos Figueroa (no relation to Luis) noted that the number of days lost in strikes dropped from three million in 1968 to only 60,000 in 1969. He thought he saw a relationship between CUT's actions and this reduction in labor strife. "I believe that this situation of social tranquillity, of good judgment on the part of the working sectors, manifested in the readiness of CUT to arrive at an agreement with respect to remunerations, is giving the lie to the belief that a situation of disorder exists in the country."

These public accolades, of course, were only temporary. CUT had called a general strike the year before and would call another the year after. But at this critical juncture in Chilean history an uneasy detente between Government and Communist opposition was apparent. Nevertheless, the economic situation in Chile actually worsened. The only real increase in economic activity that occurred in 1968 and 1969 occurred because of the renegotiation of foreign debts, which postponed the huge debt payments until the next administration took office. Even the factors in this economic growth were transitory. New machinery increased output but also probably increased unemployment. Eighty-one percent of this machinery was imported, adding to a debt burden already onerous. A drought in 1968 and 1969 caused a decline in food production and gave landowners an excuse to begin a reign of terror on employees. The Government's enthusiasm for agrarian reform declined at the same time as the increase in mechanization and the commensurate increase in unemployment exacerbated tensions in these areas.

Finally, the delicate coalition that was the Christian Democratic party split. The issue, one that would cause the party to split again more than a year later, was whether the party would open up a dialogue with the Left or ally itself with the conservatives.

On May 6, 1969, Senator Agustin Gumucio resigned from the party, saying:

The last party congress revealed the invincible resistance of those forces that dominate the party to search for an understanding with the Left in order to produce a solidarity in the people. . . . This brings me to the conclusion that in our party forces have been consolidated that have nothing in common with what I believe. The resolution of the Congress reveals a truly alarming indifference to the serious possibility that the Right will return to the Government and with this a very deep refusal to seek conditions that could bring us closer to the Left.[51]

According to the Constitution, Frei would not be permitted to succeed himself, and many in the Christian Democrat party were wary of the Right coming back into power. To them a detente with the Left was more appropriate. Their superiors felt differently.

Gumucio, putting his finger on the pulse of the Catholic movement, found the Christian Democrats a heartbeat behind. "The most advanced current of Christian thought no longer is picked up by us and in fact, rather than an instrument of revolutionary change, we are an instrument of the status quo, an administrator of the system, guaranteer of the established order." The new heroes in the young Catholic pantheon were men like Camilo Torres, a young Colombian priest who finally laid his vestments aside and picked up a gun, explaining: "A true Christian must do what he can to help the people." On May 4, coincidentally just two days before Gumucio and many others split from the party, during the consecration of Bishop Errazuriz Gandarillas in the Church of El Bosque, the Young Church Movement was born. Younger members of the community stood up during the service and questioned the antidemocratic and therefore, to them, anti-Christian nature of the ceremony. They were physically attacked. Clotario Blest, an old trade union organizer, explained the new attitude of younger segments of the Church in this manner:

> We, say the Young Church, will arm justice in the measure that they arm their injustice. Christ is not only a lamb, but also a lion. And as a lion he will come today with us. If Christ should descend today to the earth, to a world like this one, what do you think he would be wearing on his shoulders? A cross? No, he would carry a machine gun.[52]

From the Christian Democratic party was born a new group, at first a community action movement, later a political party—the Popular Action Movement (MAPU). The group did not have many adherents, but it was particularly important in the Chilean context, for it became the vehicle for the gradual cooperation between Marxists and Christians in the next governmental coalition. In fact, as one Chilean explained to me, when MAPU resigned from the Government, the "mystics" left. The Government looked older and more traditional without their fervor for revolution.

As 1970 began, social violence was becoming a commonplace in Chile. In late February eight MIRistas robbed a branch of the National Labor Bank and took 275,000 escudos, later donating 5,000 to the struggles of a recently seized *campamento,* the "Twenty-sixth of January." In May this *campamento* was the scene of a score of injuries as police and residents fought over possession of the land. On May 15 thirty-six students were arrested in street demonstrations. On May 19 seven policemen were wounded during street demonstrations. On May 21 army forces discovered a guerrilla cache containing ammunition, rifles, and literature. On June 2 another branch of the Labor Bank was robbed (the Chilean Left calls it "expropriation" and even the conservatives use the word). On June 11 MIRistas, to revenge and compensate for the army raid on their offices, invaded the Italian Armory and took guns and munitions. On June 22 at Farm Filuco four peasants were seriously wounded in a struggle to take over land. On June 26 a Socialist student leader was killed by a police bullet, resulting in a temporary "zone of emergency" being designated in Santiago. On July 8 there was a nationwide strike called by CUT in which one Communist student leader was killed during street struggles. On July 29 a peasant was killed by the owner of a farm in Chillian. On August 4 the police searched a garage in Santiago and uncovered a small arsenal of arms, vehicles, and literature supposedly belonging to MIR. The same day two MIRistas were sentenced to seven years in jail for robbing a supermarket a year before. On August 7 more than five hundred slum dwellers paraded through Santiago protesting the fact that they hadn't yet received housing from the Minister of Housing. They were armed with poles, chains, and slingshots. On August 12 forty workers, some with firearms, took over a small factory on the outskirts of Santiago.

It was in this environment that the elections of September 1970 took place. The Frei administration, increasingly bereft of ideas and moral leadership, became more and more ambiguous in confronting a reality partially of its own making. On August 31, only days before the polls opened, Eduardo Frei still repeated the formula he had espoused since 1964—that there were no real enemies, that the problem was that people were not willing to accept practical solutions. Concerning inflation, he explained: "The remedies, from the technical point of view, are known, and, I would say, recognized by all the specialists. But what happens is that the patient calls the doctor and doesn't want to take the medicine himself. It is substantially a political problem."

Everyone knew that the 1970 elections were critical. The young Socialists and even young Communists were gaining the upper hand with their theories of violent revolution. But the veteran politicians did not give up so easily. Trained in decades of political infighting and external politicking, they once again huddled to decide who would be standard-bearer. After much internal wrangling they finally decided on the perennial candidate, Salvador Allende, who would be running for his fourth time.

If we look at the election results we can perhaps see, with hindsight, that the Radical party was the deciding factor. It supported Alessandri in 1958, it went with Frei in 1964, and then it joined the coalition under Allende in 1970. Although not one of the larger parties, by 1970 it represented the one clear group of middle-class Chileans and small businessmen in the coalition, negating the Right's argument that it was a coalition that would snuff out liberty and the small businessman if it won.

The Left had learned much from its previous campaigns. The Right, it seemed, had learned little. Or maybe that too is merely historical hindsight. Radomiro Tomic, the Christian Democrat candidate, was to the left of Frei, and by the end of the campaign he would be more revolutionary, at least in rhetoric, than Allende. The Right decided to go it alone, thinking that it need not align with the moderates to win. Their candidate was Jorge Alessandri, aged, venerable, a perfect father figure, a businessman, a conservative, previously President before Frei. Their posters concentrated on the Left, portraying tanks in the middle of Santiago in reference to the well-known support the Communist party gave to the Russian invasion of Czechoslovakia.

The Left had learned. It knew that the women had defeated Allende in 1958 and again in 1964. Posters were plastered all over Santiago showing a sort of Joan of Arc figure looking to the heavens, with the inscription: "We depend on you." Allende's wife and daughters campaigned extensively for him. Students put together a rough but quite intelligent mimeographed cartoon series, handed out to workers and their wives, which concentrated on the major attacks the Right was making on the Left (such as the statement that if the Communists won, babies would be taken from their mothers).

But perhaps the best strokes were the most obvious. In 1964, as one campaigner told me: "We tried to educate the people. We had a program hundreds of pages long. We showed exactly what we would do, and why, in our first hundred days in office. This time we played to win." A summarized version of the program, with special emphasis on the first forty measures, was widely distributed.

As the campaign shaped up, it was obvious that to win the Left would have to divide the moderate vote. Just a few weeks before the election, victory for Alessandri seemed certain. One observer told me: "The question was not who would win, but by how much Alessandri would win." The

Left thus concentrated on building up an illusion of major support for Tomic.

In Chile, going back to the time when there was no television and no radio, candidates had followed the practice of having huge demonstrations in downtown Santiago to display publicly their popular strength. Hundreds of thousands of people would parade down the main and side streets screaming approval of their man. Local political organizing committees would get the people out and party newspapers would dutifully report the spectacle. The year 1970 was no exception. When Radomiro Tomic called his rally, the Left coalition prodded its hundreds of local organizing groups to get the word out that people should go into the streets and swell the rolls of Tomic supporters. When Tomic surveyed the vast throngs he felt, perhaps for the first time, that he was going to win. Many in the rest of the country agreed. So the millions who went to the polls, instead of voting for Alessandri, a compromise candidate for many liberals, cast their ballots for Tomic, thinking he stood a good chance of winning.

On September 4, 1970, Chile went to the polls. Late that night the verdict was in. Out of almost four million votes cast, Allende had won by a margin of forty thousand. Maybe it proved that God is, after all, a Marxist. In any case, in the wee hours of the next morning Salvador Allende stood as President-elect on the balcony of the student-union building and addressed the thousands of workers, students, and party loyalists who had persevered for years, and in some cases decades, supporting the Left and usually Allende himself. The slogan of the MAPU group had been: "We shall win the Government in order to win the power in order to make socialism." The election was won, but Allende still had to take office.

3

Transition

To win is difficult, but not impossible. We won within the rules of the game. Our tactic was correct; theirs was wrong. But I told the people: Between the third of September and the fourth of November Chile is going to be thrown around more than a soccer ball kicked by Pele.

—Salvador Allende, in an interview with French journalist Regis Debray

For the second time in the history of the Western Hemisphere a nation had democratically gone to the polls and voted into office a socialist candidate. Moreover, this candidate had run with the strong support of the Communist party! For the little more than one-third of the country who voted for Salvador Allende it was a dream come true, the fruition of decades of steady and at times tumultuous struggle. Some members of the lower classes refused to wait any longer. Workers took over thousands of downtown apartments still in the process of construction; almost overnight a small city of thousands of Chileans sprang up on the dusty way to the airport. Peasants in rural Chile, emboldened by the election results, began taking over farms by the score.

For the middle and upper classes it was another kind of dream come true. Having increasingly dehumanized the Left in their election propaganda during the past two decades, they had come to believe their own exaggerations and distortions. To them the Marxist's victory meant Stalinist tyranny, not democratic liberty. With this vision of the newly elected Government (to be fair, this was the vision they had of the Communist party, not of the President, although the propaganda had been so distorted both at home and abroad that most thought of the two as synonymous by the time election night came), they laid their plans accordingly. Those who had posters in their windows or slogans painted on their walls in support of Alessandri went out and painted over or hid such public signs of support, hoping to avoid what they thought would be the inevitable witch hunt.

Señor Gurstein has a number branded on his arm, a number that is seared into his memory as well as his skin, a reminder of another era when one man promised much, and did much more. Señor Gurstein and his wife ran El Ideal, a super laundromat with some seventy employees, and it was a good business. On the Friday following Allende's narrow victory the Gurstein family told the maid that they were going to their summer home on the shore, a traditional escape spot for weekend excursions. Sunday night the maid dutifully set the table and awaited her patrons. And waited. When Monday and the mail arrived her questions were answered. The Gursteins had quietly left the country liquidating what they could and leaving in carefully sealed envelopes the salaries owed to their employees plus a small bonus. Because separation wages in Chile are so high it was cheaper for the employer to leave all his machinery behind rather than try to sell his business. The employees, faced with a business that was mostly mechanized and not having any managing nor accounting skills, accepted a lawyer's proposal that they auction off the machines and divide up the money. To Señor Gurstein that was the price he had to pay for making a mistake twice in his life of living in the wrong country at the wrong time.

However, it was the state of the economy that worried the incoming Government the most. The stock market plummeted. As people began hedging their bets on the future, money flowed out of the country. Some Chileans began spending vacations abroad, examining possible living alternatives. Usually Chileans spend about $8 million on trips abroad in September, but this September the amount more than doubled, reaching $17 million, and in October it continued the record pace, reaching $13 million. Banks for a time printed nothing but the largest possible denomination—one hundred escudos.

Three weeks after the election the Minister of Treasury dramatically described the situation: "After the election the comportment of the economy has changed radically, creating a situation that completely alters the advance of the different economic sectors." Outlining the economic situation, he went on to say:

Certain firms have proceeded to suspend their plans for expansion and even to paralyze those that were already in progress. . . . The textile, clothing, and footwear sectors have suffered drops in sales of around 30 percent. . . . Sales of durable goods, like articles for the home, televisions, radios, furniture, have dropped . . . 50–80 percent according to sector.

He then added, ominously:

The financing necessary for the next three months won't be
able to come from higher taxes, and therefore, the only road
would be to resort to the monetary system, which, because of its
own afflictions, will have to make use of inorganic emissions
(paper money not backed by any productive capacity) of such
magnitude that it would threaten the very basis of the economy.

El Mercurio, the largest newspaper chain in Chile,
owned by Agustin Edwards, the richest man in the country
and a prime target of Allende throughout the campaign,
saw the economic chaos as a sort of second election return:

In this emergency situation, which shortly will have dramatic effects for many thousands of homes, the political sector
continues on as if we were in full normality. Many of our public
figures appear not to know that the panic is also a form of
democratic expression, since it constitutes the means by which
the great masses of moneyholders are reacting before the risks
that they believe inherent in a Marxist solution.

Members of the Popular Unity coalition didn't see it
that way. To them the Minister of Treasury's statement was
an exaggeration of short-term effects designed to produce
the impression that somehow Allende was causing the economic problems. *El Siglo,* the newspaper of the Communist
party, blamed others. "The National Textiles Federation,"
it explained, "announced on September 23rd that the
monopolies Yarur, Said, and Sumar were boycotting the
supply of primary materials and that the factories Ananias,
Monarch, Deik, and others have shortened their work day
and dropped their overtime." They were more than a little
suspicious of the decision by Ralston-Purina's subsidiary in
Chile to close down its plant coincident with the election,

supposedly because of an outbreak of disease among the fowls.

The charges and countercharges were by no means limited to the economic sector. To many the fact that a socialist was President was the merest technicality. The election had been a victory of the Communist party, and everyone knew that Communists never allowed free elections once in office. Many argued that the election had been a fluke. Two-thirds of the people voted against communism, they said, pointing to the combined totals of the Christian Democrats and the right-wing parties. The Left responded by combining the totals won by Tomic, whose rhetoric by the end of the campaign had been more radical than Allende's, to the total won by the Popular Unity coalition, in order to say that a majority of the people had voted for socialism. The conservatives, clinging to their analysis of the election results, decided that there was still time to act. Congress had yet to approve the electoral results, and there was nothing in the Constitution that precluded that body from ratifying the second highest vote getter rather than the first.

Only ten days after the election a leader of a pro-Alessandri group, Enrique Ortizar, began criticizing Allende for making statements as if he were already President.[1] "The candidate of the Popular Unity," he declared, "cannot attribute to himself the quality of President-elect since that would place him outside the Constitution." Two weeks later Pablo Rodriguez Grez, head of a newly formed group called Fatherland and Liberty, told thousands gathered in the Chilean Stadium:

For us the anguish of the electoral defeat has been transformed into a fighting fervor and this fighting fervor will be carried to its ultimate consequences. . . . Those who think that we are carrying Chile into a Civil War think that because they are afraid to exercise the rights that the democratic system gives them.

He was speaking, of course, of Congress' right to ratify the election results. Yet, he continued defiantly: "If they [the Left] want Civil War, they will find us here, ready. . . . We warn them that we will re-establish order in Chile, and we will use force if it is necessary in order to accomplish this."

Even the Christian Democrats, whose candidate during the last few weeks of the term had out-lefted Allende, were not immune to this hysteria, although theirs took an appropriately religious slant. The President of the Student Federation of the Catholic University called on young Catholics everywhere to:

. . . awaken your religious consciences and ask God—with deep and public faith—that his providence should intercede to save Chile from Marxism . . . Marxism is about to take over the country. . . . When the essence is about to succumb, when the Fatherland itself is in danger, with all the moral, spiritual, and human values of its history, no one can refrain from assuming his personal and collective responsibility.

Allende himself felt that he would be threatened and perhaps killed. He had asked for police protection during the campaign, but Frei delayed in giving it, so Allende fashioned a bodyguard out of young MIRistas—a bodyguard that he was to rely upon even after winning the Presidency, bypassing the more traditional secret service agencies. He changed his sleeping habits, using two houses and two beds so no one could know exactly where he would be sleeping at any given time. Allende explained some of the things that were happening then in an extended interview with Regis Debray. In his words: "From the fourth of September, the day in which I was elected President, until the third of November, the date in which I took office, I was not a man who was preparing to take office, but rather I was practically a Director of Investigations." He explained:

Naturally there was a General Director of Investigations, but he had no interest in protecting the kind of legality that had given the government to the Popular Unity. I notified him at the correct time that a powerful textile industrialist had prepared an attempt on himself which consisted of having a bomb explode in his home so as to justify his departure with Chilean capital. The police chief took no measures to prevent it and the bomb exploded. The persons responsible were arrested afterwards because of our protests and public denunciations, but the magistrate in charge allowed them to go free, and these people, members of an ultrareactionary political party, fled from Chile.

To Allende, the panic itself was manufactured, part of a brilliantly conceived conspiracy. The first phase in that conspiracy was to make it seem as if the economy were collapsing. Thus, although money was indeed flowing out of the country, the Frei Government was doing little to stop it. The second phase, according to Allende, consisted of "explosive attempts against public buildings and work houses, offices, and so forth. The international airport was on the point of being closed down." He continued:

What I am telling you is only the beginning. An organization was invented in order to attribute to it these attempts; of course it was presented as a revolutionary organization. They tried to blame us for the attempts. Elements of this reactionary conspiracy assassinated a uniformed policeman who was on guard at a public building and shot another seriously who was guarding the entrance of a foreign embassy. Two times they made attempts against my life but they were not successful because of the devotion and zeal of my personal guard of revolutionary comrades.

As the Right, either in rhetoric or action, united against the still-to-be-inaugurated Government, the Far

Left was divided on its opinion of the electoral victory. The Tupumaros of Uruguay declared their solidarity with MIR and characterized the Popular Unity as "collaborationists with all bourgeoisie regimes that had used the people for their own gains." MIR was not as sure as its brothers and sisters half a continent away. The organization had matured greatly in its short public life and had gained great respect from a wide segment of the lower classes in the period from 1969 to 1970. Perhaps out of respect for Allende as a person, perhaps because of their political theory which supposed that the Government would be defeated once again and would then have to join with MIR, the group had agreed to be quiescent during the political campaign in order not to be an embarrassment to Allende. Although they did not participate in the elections directly, they did do some community organizing and building of peoples' militias.

With electoral victory the prestige of the Communist party rose and that of MIR fell. Bitterness between the two groups, always present, seemed to grow worse as victory came between them. The Communist party seemed vindicated in its reliance on electoral politics to achieve socialism. The MIRistas responded this way:

The supporters of the peaceful road have only demonstrated—with the support of those who disagree—that a coalition of the Left can win an election by proposing a program to initiate the construction of socialism. Granted. They were right in the Chilean case (nevertheless, that possibility never was placed in doubt by the revolutionary Left). If they are looking for a theoretical laurel, conceded.

Luis Vitales, a MIR sympathizer, took a longer-range view in a hastily written but brilliant manifesto published in October, entitled "After the Fourth, What?":

The Communist party suggests the possibility of achieving socialism through the peaceful road. While socialism is not installed in Chile through that route, although the Left wins elections, we have all the right of reaffirming the thesis of the founders of Marxism, that the only manner of achieving socialism is to defeat the bourgeoisie and its repressive forces, through armed struggle, through the armed revolution of the workers and peasants.

These two powerful organizations had already been divided by a generational attitude spawned by the international tumult in Latin America in the 1960s and its worsening economic crisis. The Communist party, which had begun as a workers' party, had gradually evolved by the late 1960s into a worker-based organization with a directorship composed mainly of intellectuals. At about that time the MIR group was born, based at first among students and intellectuals, but then spinning off into the slums, worker neighborhoods, and farms of Chile. The election sharpened the polarity. With a Communist Minister of Housing and Minister of Treasury, and with a Communist- and socialist-controlled Confederation of Trade Unions, a dream was close to fulfillment for the Communist party. But revolution to the MIR did not mean the consolidation of control by one organization, no matter how revolutionary. Rather, it meant the decentralization of power and the democratization of factories, banks, and so on. MIR pushed for people power. "Up front with the masses" was their slogan. The Communist party pushed for revolution from the top. The two partially overlapped. Undoubtedly the programs of the Communist party, which emanated from the organized sectors of labor, correlated strongly with the goals of MIR. But there were significant differences. I remember one conversation with a young MIRista who had come from Colombia after being exiled as a student protest leader there. He was critical of the Communist party. "Did you see the headline in *El Siglo* yesterday?" he asked. "The Communists think we now control copper merely because the President says we should in a speech. But we don't, we still don't own it." In another instance, in the winter of 1970, just before the elections, the MIR had organized the Jefatura Provincial Revolucionaria in the shantytowns, and this organization in turn had helped slum residents organize to take over land, university buildings, crowded boulevards, anything to dramatize their plight and create pressure for their demands. To the head of the Comando Provincial, the MIRistas were only "political adventurers," romantic revolutionaries who stirred up trouble without bringing results. "They are turbulent in the streets but offer no solutions," declared the president of the Communist group. One MIRista responded to me: "While the traditional parties often take four years to give the people what they need, we get it for them in four months, by organizing the people to take action."

After the elections any street actions were considered sacrilegious. The Communist party was sure that the Right was attempting to create an illusion of instability so that the army would intervene. MIR actions such as encouraging takeovers of apartment houses or farms would, in its opinion, feed right into this conspiracy. The intergroup hatred reached such levels of verbal intensity that at one point the Communist party leadership was calling MIRistas agents of the CIA. On December 2, 1970, rhetoric exploded into action. During the student election at the University of Concepcion, where the MIR movement had been born in 1967, a MIRista student leader was shot and killed by Communist students, allegedly because the MIRista was taking down political posters. That death sobered the Left. Perhaps for the first time they realized that the road to socialism was a long, hard one, that both Communists and MIRistas could—must—work together at least part of the way, that the immediate enemies could only laugh at the dissension in the ranks of the Marxist Left. Chastened, the leadership of both groups agreed to work together in future student elections and against the corporate and foreign interests that both felt were the immediate threat. They agreed to reserve their organizational and theoretical differences. MIR continued to concentrate on people's militias and community organization while the Communist party concentrated on governmental matters and organized labor, but their pact was honored for many months.

While all of this was occurring outside the Government at the same time that the economy was seemingly on the verge of bankruptcy and the Right was organizing conspiracies aimed at coups or parliamentary obstacles, the new Government had to choose its own team members. It then consisted of six separate parties, ranging from the Christian-oriented MAPU to the Marxist Socialist party to the liberal Radical party. In terms of longevity and clearness of principles, the groups compared this way: The Socialist party was created in the 1930s and had been fairly consistent in refusing to compromise and take part in a Government not to its liking; the Radical party, older than the Socialist or Communist parties, had for the past four elections always gone to the winning candidate, throwing in their lot with candidates as disparate and diverse as Ibanez, Alessandri, Frei, and Allende; the MAPU party had been born out of conflict over agrarian reform in 1969 and was the link between Christianity and Marxism.

No one in Chile expected such a coalition to work harmoniously for any period of time. Party members themselves recognized that problem beforehand; thus some of the internal wrangling that might have occurred after the election took place the year before, when the parties got together to hammer out a platform. That platform became a very detailed program which espoused not only a clear socialist basis for future reforms, but clear measures upon which all participating parties agreed before joining the coalition. Even with that agreement, however, the task of dividing up political offices among the different groups was not an easy one. The method used was a combination of what Ambassador to the United States Domingo Santa-Maria called "vertical and horizontal integration." Thus, for example, the Minister of Economy might be Marxist, but then the Undersecretary would have to come from another party, and the Secretary below him from still another party. On the other hand, if the Minister of Economy were an Independent, then the Minister of Education might be a Radical, the Minister of Agriculture a MAPU adherent, the Minister of Work a Communist, and so on. Yet the members of the coalition also had to take into account the varying strengths of the different groups. The Communist and Socialist parties had the most strength and thus got the most important offices. MAPU was given the agricultural portfolio mainly because of Jacques Chonchol. The Radical party was put in the Ministry of Defense partly to assuage an armed force whose members might have balked at being under the control of a Communist or Socialist. It was a delicate and time-consuming process. Pedro Vuskovic, the Minister of Economy, admitted in late December that one of the major problems of the Government was that it had set up its work teams a little late and therefore could not move into high gear as quickly as it might have desired.

The Chilean cabinet under Allende faithfully reflected the various facets of the Marxist Left. In many cases it was a classic example of the outlaws of society coming to power. That is a hard concept, perhaps, for North Americans to grasp. In this country the "ins" and the "outs" are usually very similar in policy, training, and background. None have been arrested; none have struggled in underground movements; few, if any, have held beliefs so dearly that they have suffered personal anguish as a result. In Chile, however, the election was much more than a change in personnel. The outlaws were suddenly the Government. Some had had their training in revolutionary Cuba during the 1960s. The new President of the State Bank, Alban Lataste Hoffer, had worked in Cuba as Director of Industrial Planning in the Ministry of Industry. He had also been Director of Investments and Construction Planning in the Central Planning Committee of Cuba and for seven years had been Vice President of National Planning. Alberto Martinez Echeverria is now head of the Bureau of Industry and Commerce, an agency overseeing price and quality controls. He had been Vice Minister of the Central Planning Committee of Cuba and Professor of Economy and Planning at the University of Havana.

Others had received their training in the factories of Chile. Carlos Cortez Diaz, almost sixty years old and a copper miner, had joined the Socialist party in 1937 and in 1964 had become an officer of the Trade Union Confederation. He tells the story of his proudest day. "I said to my wife, 'I received a great honor, dear. The President designated me Minister.' " "I don't believe you," she retorted. His wife added: "Many times I have heard him say, 'I would take the *momios** from their mansions and put them in the place of the common people who at times remain for months without water. Then they would feel the impact.' "

Americo Zorrilla, the Minister of Treasury, is a Communist party member and former linotype worker. It is refreshing and fascinating to visit a country where a worker rather than a banker is in charge of financial affairs. Only vaguely conversant in the complexities of economic high finance, Americo Zorrilla has a very good experiential grasp of the problems of society and their solution. As one

---

* The word *momios* is widely used in Chile. Roughly it means "mummies," describing those who have not been able to change with the times, whose conservatism harkens back to an era when there were masters and slaves. It is a derogatory term but is used even among the upper classes to describe each other.

economist working at the United Nations (which has a branch in Santiago) told me: "The Ministers need only direct the global program. It is the technicians who will carry out the details." It is better to have a Minister who feels with his heart the general outlines of an economic program than a technocrat who knows by heart the details of such a program but has little political or existential understanding of why such a program is necessary. Zorilla is sixty years old, and for thirty-one years he has been a militant Communist. He remembers the days of early labor struggles not as the good old days, but as the time of the first faltering steps that led to the current victory. Recalling the 1920s, he notes: "The union movement was very divided . . . in their speeches the unions didn't attack the bosses, but rather other union groups." Blacklists were common. Zorrilla remembers being fired from *La Nacion,* a leading newspaper, for leading a strike. But he notes with satisfaction another episode later on, when another employer, an avowed Fascist, approached him one day and told him: "I am a Fascist and you are a Communist. We cannot work together. One of us must leave. Naturally it will be you." But Zorrilla had spent years organizing a union within that newspaper and now benefited from its support, staying on for another two years until the Communist party told him to go to Santiago, where he was designated the head of *El Siglo,* the party newspaper, in 1940. After World War II the Communist party was outlawed, unions were purged of Communist officials, and Zorrilla and *El Siglo* went underground. The goods of the party were confiscated, but its members managed to hide the printing presses. Zorrilla was picked up by the police and tortured in order to get him to reveal the hiding place of the printing presses. Electric cathodes were attached to his sex organs in an unsuccessful attempt to make him talk. He was separated from his family for four years, unemployed and blacklisted after his release, and then imprisoned once more for another six months.

When he looks back on that period, however, it is with stoicism, with the feeling that he was, despite all the difficulties, luckier than some others. "There were others who suffered more. Like companion Galo Gonzalez who died." In 1958 he was called to reorganize *El Siglo*. Now he is Minister of the Treasury.

At perhaps the opposite end of the social spectrum stands Jacques Chonchol Chait, forty-four years old, who had studied in London and at the Sorbonne and who for the past decade had been one of the world's leading experts on agrarian reform. He was in Cuba during the beginning of its agrarian reform work, studied the reform experiment in Peru in the mid-1960s, worked for the Food and Agricultural Organization overseeing agrarian reform in Latin America, and was finally chosen in 1964 by Eduardo Frei to head the Chilean agrarian reform program. Perhaps his most striking characteristic is his consistency. Even his most ardent enemies respect the fact that during his seven years in and out of public office he has not compromised his theories of economic development. When, in 1968, it seemed that Frei's Government no longer was giving agrarian reform the priority Chonchol deemed essential, he resigned from his post. Breaking away with him were the younger and peasant sections who later formed MAPU and joined the Government coalition. He is now Minister of Agriculture. Perhaps the best comment I heard about Chonchol came from an opponent, conservative Senator Ibanez who, when rural Chile seemed to be exploding in the spring of 1971, rebuked his colleagues for blaming Chonchol, describing him as "one of the few politicians in Chile who has precise goals, clear, frank ideas, and the opportunity to express them, the tenacity to realize them, and an absolute consistency in all his actions." The Senator asked: "What is he doing as Minister of the Popular Unity?" He answered his own query: "Exactly the same that he did as Vice President of INDAP, the same that he did in Cuba, the same that he did as functionary of FAO charged with preparing agrarian reform for Latin America. He has proceeded with an unobjectionable consistency." He concluded by saying: "No one can feel deceived by the actions of Mr. Chonchol, and he who says he is, is deceived only because he wants to deceive himself. Mr. Chonchol has been clear, and will continue to act in the same manner in which he has always acted."

At the helm stands Salvador Allende, statesman par excellence. Born in 1908 in the coastal city of Valparaiso, Allende entered politics while still in high school—not an abnormal occurrence in this highly politicized country—and continued his political activities at the University of Chile, where he attended the School of Medicine. In 1926 he was elected President of the Student Center of the Medical School and later became Vice President of the Student Federation of the University of Chile. In 1932 he was arrested during protests after General Marmaduke Grove's short-lived socialist republic was overthrown. In that same year he and several colleagues created the Socialist party. He was selected deputy on the party slate in 1937. He became Minister of Health in 1939, under President Aguirre Cerda's Popular Front Government, and continued in that office for some years. A doctor by avocation and profession, Allende has all his life been preoccupied with the desire to know and understand the conditions of the poor and to lift them out of their misery. His doctor's thesis concerned "Mental Health and Delinquency." While Minister of Health, he helped establish the National Health Service and tried to promote the idea of national distribution of milk to combat the chronic problem of malnutrition. Rebuffed in his attempts to do this, he joined with several associates in a business enterprise (which, he is quick to point out, he got out of in short order) to distribute milk bars, a candy bar with milk additives which, it was felt, would provide some nutrition for the lower classes. During the late 1940s he wrote a book entitled *Social and Medical Reality of Chile*. In 1942 he became Secretary General of the Socialist party and in 1945 was elected Senator from the Southern Province.

A man of keen humor, Allende looks and acts every inch the President of Chile. Indeed, for almost half his political life he has been trying to attain that office. He jokingly says that before the 1970 election he had requested that if he should die he wanted his tombstone to be inscribed with these words: "Here lies the future President of Chile." He had run—and lost—in 1952, 1958, and 1964.

He is a magnificent speaker, who explains the complex in simple ways, using illustrations that the common men and women can understand, emphasizing and repeating major themes. When, for example, he talked of taking over the copper mines, he translated the amount of money the copper companies had taken from Chile into a pair of shoes and a school book for each Chilean child. The people could understand this; they could not understand adequately the complexities of international finance. He is not the great teacher Fidel Castro is, but he is much more the statesman, working behind the scenes when need be, maneuvering events, taking advantage of historical accidents.

The Far Left looks on Allende as the best of the worst and grudgingly credits him with a good heart. One MIRista with whom I spoke answered my question about his attitude toward *el compañero presidente* like this: "That depends on which Allende you mean. Allende the man we like and respect. Allende the President of Chile, we are not sure." When Allende first took office, the Far Left asked him to move the presidential headquarters into the slum areas in order to maintain contact with the poor. Allende, well-known for his middle-class proclivities, refused, indicating that for him love of the lower class and an earnest desire to help had been formed during decades of struggle and would not be affected by his place of residence. It was an important psychological and symbolic confrontation. Allende seemed to be indicating by his dress and manner the difference between the Cuban and the Chilean revolutions. Fidel came out of the mountains with guns and took over a country that had been bankrupted and corrupted through generations of North American rule. According to Edward Boorstein, who worked in the Ministry of Economics in Cuba during the early years, the three major sources of revenue in Cuba before the revolution were sugar (owned entirely by North American banks), prostitution, and gambling. Fidel, wearing old army uniforms and sleeping in one-room houses, showed his people that in a poor society poverty would be spread equally, with the leaders shouldering the worst conditions. Allende, with his ties and jackets, living in the presidential mansion, was saying, in effect, this is a revolution made within the law, within the rules of the game. I don't have to hide in a slum. The country is rich enough so that the lower class can be made middle class instead of the middle class having to reduce its standard of living.

These differences in style and philosophy between Allende and the Far Left, although not apparently significant at the time, were to take on great importance within the next year and a half.

With the selection of at least the top cabinet members completed and the inauguration coming up, the Government began amassing its forces and hammering out its strategy for the coming months. To be sure, there was a detailed program that outlined exactly what the new administration would attempt to do in its first few months. But exactly how to go about it was another matter. Allende's strategy was simple. Although they were playing by the rules of the game, there was no reason why they should not take advantage of the rules themselves. Lawyers of the Popular Unity group were sent to uncover old decrees, dusty legislation, old Supreme Court decisions that could be used to expand the powers of the President, regulations that could be utilized to restructure the economy, and agencies that had previously not utilized powers of regulation. Allende wanted to know how far the powers of the President could be stretched. What was the spirit of the law, rather than the letter of the law? What about subsidy power of the state government? And so on.

As the new Government tried to find out just what powers it had, the Christian Democrat opposition was trying to formulate agreements that would restrict certain governmental powers. The Christian Democrats had a great deal of leverage during this period. They were the largest party in Chile, and they held the balance of power in the Congress. Upon their acquiescence depended the ratification of Allende's victory at the polls. Already, in early October, Alessandri's backers were coming up with a unique "solution" to the dilemma of a minority Marxist President. Alessandri would promise that if the Congress ratified him he would resign, thus forcing another election where only the Christian Democrat and Popular Unity candidates would face each other. It would be 1964 all over again, and probably with the same results. The Christian Democrats refused this offer, but only if the Government would agree to certain promises concerning its future policies. Although to an outside observer these conditions may seem reasonable, one should understand that for many Chileans the election victory was a mandate for revolutionary change, and revolutionary change usually means a radical restructuring of the society. Yet one of the provisions was that the armed forces would not only continue to exist, but:

This demands that the organic structures and hierarchies of the Armed Forces and *Carabineros* [police] be respected, the systems of selection, prerequisites, and disciplinary norms now existing; that these groups be assured of adequate equipment for their mission as watchmen of the national security, and that their work on national development not be used to reroute their specific functions, nor compromise their budgets, nor create armed organizations parallel to the Armed Forces and Carabineros.

Socialists, familiar with Lenin's dictum that a revolution can only succeed after the military is effectively neutralized, blanched at this provision but accepted it reluctantly.

In addition, many laws were rushed through Congress just days before the ratification vote. These laws, too, seem reasonable until one considers the context. On October 24 Congress passed legislation concerning the safeguards of freedom of speech, university autonomy, and control of the media. This was done partially to protect freedoms that many in Chile felt might be threatened by the Communist membership in Government. But the new laws tended to freeze the existing standards for defining those freedoms. For example, although the attitude that politics and education should not mix, that the university should be protected against the intrusion of vested societal interests, is laudable, it stems from a certain way of viewing education. Fidel Castro, in a 1970 speech concerning education and university autonomy, explained:

The definitive solution is not to create more universities but rather to convert the country into a university. The industrial, agricultural and education centers, etc., will be workshops where students will realize their productive tasks and investigation projects directed by a professor who at the same time will impart the necessary theoretical knowledge.

Or, as he put it more simply: "The development of the universities leads to the disappearance of the universities; in other words, the institution's own maximum development will lead to its disappearance." How can one who accepts such a theory of education also accept the principle of university autonomy?

In the case of freedom of the media, one again runs into an ideological predisposition, a certain world view which colors the subject. It is, of course, easy to sidestep the issue by saying that freedom of the press means freedom for anyone to write anything he wants. But the real question is, who is doing the writing, and who has the resources to publish the journal or magazine or newspaper in which it appears? Or, even more basically, for whom is there freedom? For the man who puts up the money but does not gather the news, write the stories, or publish the paper? For the journalists who actually write the stories? For the people who read them? In Chile up until this time, freedom of the press meant basically freedom of those with sufficient capital to establish a newspaper and print what they saw fit. Those with sufficient capital naturally tended to be those with capitalist viewpoints. Thus, although there was a great diversity of opinion in Chile, the circulation of left-wing newspapers and journals was pitifully small. Outside Santiago and Valparaiso there was almost no newspaper that was leftist in orientation. Yet the concept of freedom concerns not only content and circulation, but also control. Many Government supporters thought there would be more freedom if workers controlled the newspapers they printed and distributed. Yet by freezing the concept of freedom at a given time, the Opposition was making it difficult for alternatives based on different philosophies to spring up.

The newly passed laws covered television also. Opposition parties were given the right to reply to attacks on television and to have equal response on the air. The law provided:

All intervention by government through television in order to express ideas, proposals, or successes, will give the right to

reply to political parties of the opposition with equal scheduling
and time. The time given to reply will be divided by the opposition parties in proportion to the parliamentary representatives
that they have.

A National Television Council was established, charged
with "general orientation, vigilance and control" of the
medium. The president of the council was to be nominated
by the President of Chile, although his nomination would
have to be ratified by Congress. Also, each channel would
have an advisory council of programming, consisting of a
psychologist, a professor, a sociologist, a lawyer, and a doctor, to approve movies. The Congress also gave the University of Chile and the Catholic University the right to
establish together a network that would cover the entire
country, thus creating a competitor to the current state
monopoly on national television broadcasting.

Most of the legal provisions concerning television
were directed at guaranteeing democracy in Chile. The
Chilean Left, however, raised the question of why such
provisions, which had been proposed in Congress after the
last election, had never been passed. The answer was obvious. Still, better that good things be done for bad reasons
than that no good things be done.

The Christian Democrats did more than safeguard
their own concepts of freedom and of the roles of the military and the media. A law was passed giving job protection
to all civil servants beneath the ministerial levels. Thus
none of the bureaucrats who had come to office during the
Christian Democrats' reign could be fired when the new
Government took office. The Left had to start with an
unsympathetic and at times hostile bureaucracy over which
it had only partial control. Any time an employee was
dismissed the Opposition would quickly scream about
political reprisals and the "injured" bureaucrat would take
the case to court, win, and be reinstated.

Allende was correct. Between the fourth of September and the fourth of November Chile was kicked around more than a soccer ball. Economic chaos, threats on Allende's life, political maneuverings in Congress, forced agreements that tied the Government's hands, internal bickering over distribution of offices—all this was part of the scene in Chile during this short period. But there was still one more event that would take place before Allende was finally permitted to take office. And this one was perhaps the worst of all: On October 22 the Commander in Chief of the Armed Forces, René Schneider, was assassinated.

Chile has no tradition of political assassination. As a matter of fact, Chileans look on the United States, with its intermittent assassinations of Presidents and presidential aspirants, as a quite unstable nation. The last political assassination in Chile had happened many decades before 1970. The actual murder of the Commander in Chief remains blurry. Not much is known about the maneuverings before or after the event. But the murder itself was transparently clear. General Viaux, who led the *Tacnazo* in late 1969, was the leader of a small group of people who planned to kidnap the Commander in Chief in order to get the armed forces to intervene. The climate had been prepared by the destruction through bombings of several public buildings, which was blamed on a mythical leftist organization. The conspirators' belief was that the kidnapping of Schneider would inevitably lead to intervention by the army. Their attempt occurred only two days before Congress was to vote on the election results, when it had become clear that Allende would be ratified. The kidnapping plot became an assassination by accident. Four cars closed in on Schneider's vehicle in downtown Santiago, in broad daylight. The conspirators were so sure of themselves that they dressed in their regular street clothes and used their own cars. Schneider, however, refused to play by the rules. He drew his pistol and was killed.

Allende immediately called for a state of emergency, even though he was technically not yet President. Relying heavily on the intelligence network of the MIR, within hours he knew the perpetrators of the crime and could notify Frei of that fact. The army patrolled the streets of Santiago, and as Congress voted, a curfew was imposed on the entire country.

The assassination, as it turned out, was a tragic and desperate mistake by the Right. Maybe it could have worked. Salvador Allende surely thinks so. But most of the army was as much caught up in the myth of its own neutrality as anyone else was. And everyone knew that if once the army did intervene, it would be difficult to put the pieces of Chilean democracy back together again. In retrospect, the assassination actually helped Allende during the first few months of his regime. Whenever he had the opportunity, he pointed out to the country that the Opposition had said Marxists would deprive the people of liberty but had itself chosen not to play by the democratic rules by first picking up the gun.

Two days after René Schneider's assassination, amid rumors of impending economic catastrophe, Congress voted to ratify the results of the September election. The Right abstained, but the Christian Democrats, honoring the agreement, voted for Allende. And so a second impossibility had been achieved. Socialists had won the election and had been permitted to take office. Ahead lay their most difficult task. As the newly inaugurated President outlined it:

The difficulties that confront us lay in the extraordinary complexity of the tasks that await us; to initiate the political road towards socialism, and to achieve this beginning with the present situation, a society depleted through its backwardness and its poverty, properties of dependence and underdevelopment; to break with the causative factors of retardation and at the same time construct a new socioeconomic structure capable of providing for the prosperity of the community.

And, he promised, all this would be done within the existing
law, within the existing institutions, abiding by the rulings
handed down by the existing judicial bodies. Allende was
proposing to create a new system using the rules of the old
one. It promised to be a fascinating experiment. Already
the former Colombian President Lleras Restrepo was calling Chile a "political laboratory." *Newsweek* magazine
perhaps summed it up best in its November 4 statement:

Whatever the measures that he utilizes, the victory of
Salvador Allende in Chile has been the most important political
happening in Latin America since Fidel Castro triumphantly
entered Havana more than a decade ago.

4

The First Few Months

We must make haste—slowly.
—Salvador Allende

After November 4, different segments of the population reacted differently to the fact of victory. Among the powerful there was acceptance of the probability of radical change. Acceptance of electoral results was so ingrained among Chileans—or, as some leftists insist, the myth of democratic elections had become so widespread—that even the election of Communists and Socialists was more or less accepted after ratification by Congress. Among the masses, or more specifically, among those who had previously made up the membership in the hundreds of local political committees of the Popular Unity coalition, there was stagnation and apathy. These committees folded like so many evening flowers, sinking back into lethargy and moribundness, either because they sensed that all would come easily now or because they honestly did not know what to do. Some

119

thought that with the new Government it was only a matter of time until fresh meat would be on the table, electricity would run to the front door, and the children would march off to school with free school books tucked under their arms. Others wanted to integrate themselves into the process of change but didn't know how. Among the rural peasantry there was still another reaction to the inauguration. A small but quite public and vocal group called the Revolutionary Peasant Movement (MCR), an offshoot of MIR, began organizing and encouraging farm takeovers.

The Opposition waited, pondering what the new Government would actually do. It was by no means rare for politicians in Chile to promise much and deliver little. No one was sure whether the Government would have the courage to enact the measures promised in its campaign platform. Some were not even sure that the fragile coalition would hold together in the coming months of struggle. The Opposition was at first conciliatory. *El Mercurio,* the business newspaper, tacitly supported the coalition in the first few months, always making the distinction between Allende and the Communist party, since it felt the latter was up to no good. The Christian Democrats were busy establishing their own newspaper, called *La Prensa,* since they had been stripped of the governmental newspaper when they left office. The president of Chile's influential and conservative National Society of Agriculturalists, Benjamin Matte, went so far as to travel to Cuba, returning to explain, to no one's satisfaction, that Cuba's revolution was not exportable to Chile. He noted with surprise but obvious glee that much of Cuba's land remained in private hands, and he accepted Fidel's statement that "We make the rules of the game and they [private interests] must conform." The powerful in Chile seemed willing to accept some restructuring of the economy. They seemed willing to accept the Government's outlining broad requirements or guidelines while capitalists retained control of the economy. One head of a medium-sized textile industry explained it to me in this manner: "The state is too inefficient for the task of running businesses. The best system would be to have the socialists, those with strong social conscience, regulating the capitalists, who would, with their strong profit motive, and expertise and initiative, produce the goods and services necessary in the most efficient manner possible." The efficiency of capitalism would be tempered by the humanity of socialism.

This was also a waiting period for the masses. The vow of the Young Socialists to "win the Government in order to win the power in order to make socialism" had been carried out. But for many, electoral victory provided only the means for that construction, not the solutions of how to go about it. The disintegration of the local political committees was a source of worry. However, this worry stemmed from different concepts of the role the masses should play in the new Government. For the major portion of the coalition, it was extremely important to have mass support. The Opposition controlled the wealth, the foreign news services, and the domestic media, so that in order to stop rampant rumors of economic disorder the Left had to rely at first on the various local groups whose members could provide face-to-face communication with their neighbors. Most people recognized that any progressive steps the Government might take could come about only if it had the active support, encouragement, and participation of the masses.

To the Far Left (especially MIR, which was not part of the coalition but supported Allende) the participation of the masses was also extremely important, but for different reasons. To them only with the masses as the cutting edge of revolution could the Government escape falling into the morass of state capitalism and bureaucratization. MIR believed that the Government, no matter how revolutionary in theory, was bourgeois in practice and in life style, and that when push came to shove these leaders would succumb to the obsessions middle-class people have with stability and with power.

In the beginning these two concepts merged as both groups agreed to call for the reactivation of the local committees and the integration of the masses into government. *El Amigo,* a rural Communist newspaper, perhaps put it best when it tried to explain to its readers the situation shortly after the inauguration:

We are in power now, say our friends . . . it is said we are a majority. But it happens that we are becoming disorganized, becoming isolated, and are only waiting for the *compañero presidente.* . . . Why such indifference? We are achieving our program, say others. We opened relations with Cuba and Vietnam. But the banks are still here, copper is still here, the consortiums, the great industrial concerns, the large farms, and parliament is still here. We are in the government, that is true, but not in power. The oligarchy and bureaucracy have not been touched. What will happen tomorrow when we confront these problems? Do you think the right wing will remain so quiet?

Even during the first few months another conflict within the Left could be discerned, although it would take a year to flame into a full-fledged crisis. This was the conflict between those who wanted socialism and those who wanted a type of state capitalism. The program of the Popular Unity coalition was not designed to introduce socialism into Chile, no matter what the North American press has written. Rather, it was meant to construct the preconditions for a transition to socialism. Such preconditions included a restructured economy, to be achieved by breaking up the monopolies and ending Chile's dependence on foreign investment and loans. As Allende said in a speech early in the campaign, only 2 percent of Chile had anything to worry about—the 2 percent of the population owning most of the economy, gaining most of the credit, and controlling most of the wealth. The Far Left, however, wanted the Government to break quickly and completely with capitalism, a step that would entail considerable instability but that would also by its very nature be irreversible. That meant the installation of a "dictatorship of the proletariat," a phrase the Left was not at all embarrassed to use. It meant attacking the concept of private property. It meant attacking the middle-class values that a majority of Chileans, even the poorest, embraced. (By middle-class values, the Left meant an aping of the values of the upper classes—a deep belief in the more political forms of democracy, that is, democracy in the voting booths rather than in the schools or the factories or the homes, and a belief in gradualism.) The tension between those who wanted to move toward socialism slowly, regulating and attacking only a very small portion of the population, and those who wanted to move much more quickly, attacking and undermining the values of a much larger part of the society, was keenly felt.

Although these differences in ideology eventually became prominent, in the first few months the euphoria of victory and the rapid achievement of many planks of the platform created a genuine unity among the six parties and disparate philosophies in the Government. Even in the first few weeks, before the governmental teams were ready to move rapidly in a coherent strategy, there were signs that the Government was eager to change traditional ways of thinking. As one of his first acts of office Allende rerouted the subway that was still under construction. The original route would have gone from downtown to the wealthy suburbs; now it would go from a downtown working-class area to a factory suburb. I asked a businessman who lived in Los Dominicos, the first proposed destination of the subway, what he thought. He had voted for Alessandri but responded: "It was a good thing. We have cars. There is no need for subways." Yet he thought that the original plan was conceived in good faith. "I don't think there was a plot involved. That's just the way things are usually done." It was a sign of the changing times in Chile. A revolution, when one gets right down to it, is doing traditional things in nontraditional ways, uncovering long-buried biases, and using creative energies to deal with difficult problems. Subways usually connect downtown shopping areas with wealthy suburbs in order to get more people downtown to buy things, aiding businessmen in the area. The theory is that increased business means increased sales revenues, adding to a general revenue fund for the city, which can in turn be used to provide better bus service. Isn't it simpler to put a subway between where the workers live and where they work?

Another of Allende's measures, promised in the program, was to disband the hated Grupo Movil, which had become a symbol for worker, student, and slum dweller alike of state police power intervening in political demonstrations. A cartoon in a left-wing comic book noted with joy after the Government's initiative: "The Grupo Movil dissolved faster than the new margarine." Water hoses which had previously been used to drench social protesters were redirected into the shanty towns that surrounded Santiago to quench the thirst of the residents as summer approached.

Of course, as in every period of rapid change, there were the quixotic measures that are taken when premature enthusiasm overwhelms nascent organization. Allende promised three million pairs of shoes for Chilean children by Christmas. The problem was, the Government didn't have the industrial capacity to produce three million pairs of shoes. It had to rely on donations from the citizenry. Within weeks the failure became so evident that the Government made a special plea on television for donations of large-sized shoes, since previous donations had mostly been for smaller ones. In one city tens of thousands of children crammed into a local soccer stadium on Christmas day only to discover that their gifts had not arrived. Dismayed and angered, they rioted through the streets, causing the mayor to apologize and to promise to do better next time. But such incidents were surprisingly few in number.

During the first few months, Allende's major steps were defensive in nature, reactions to the closing of dozens of important plants and factories by the wealthy in Chile who were fearful of socialists in power. Companies such as Ralston-Purina, which had closed their doors within days of the election, had put thousands of workers out of jobs. Using a 1943 law, Allende intervened to reopen the plants. Later, to intervene in the textile industry, he used a 1953 decree stating that establishments dedicated to the production and distribution of articles of prime necessity were public utilities and authorizing the President to expropriate such establishments when they were closed and their workers were unpaid. Allende reasoned that the textile products were the basis for the clothing industry and therefore were part of the process of producing items indispensable to the nation's welfare. On December 2 he expropriated the large textile factory owned by Teofilo Yarur.

By late December the pace quickened. The Government teams were ready and the economic game plan was publicized. It was an economics strictly Keynesian in concept. The state's powers would be expanded and actively used to right the economy. Deficit spending would be heavily relied upon. But there were noncapitalistic aspects also. The powers of the state would be expanded in order to redistribute income. Salaries were raised enough to surpass the cost of living increase. The lowest salaries were raised the most. A ceiling on salaries in public industries was set, with the highest-paid person receiving only twenty times the amount of the average worker. Family allowances for blue-collar and white-collar workers were equalized, and Allende promised that those for rural and urban workers would also be within a year. Daily pints of milk were delivered free to pregnant mothers, nursing mothers, and every child under fifteen years of age. Bus fares were reduced and equalized. Rents in public housing were frozen. So were utility rates.

The economic program was based on three major assumptions. One was that the heavy malconcentration of income in Chile was one of the root causes of poverty and misery. Because of it, the vast proportion of the society had little money to spend on anything but necessities and had almost no savings. The small percentage of people with a lot of money bought luxury goods, causing new investments to come into these highly profitable industries and cutting off savings and capital that could have been used to help the lower classes gain housing, food, and transportation. Pedro Vuskovic, Minister of Economy, outlined the economic program as follows:

In its essence, the strategy could be characterized as an attempt to drastically modify the concentration of poverty and income; in order to reorient the productive energies towards fulfilling the basic necessities of the population, not assigning new resources to the production of luxury items, and even reconverting in those cases where it is possible the installed capacity to other ends; to raise the productivity of the most backward sectors, through the extension of resources that tend to modify the sectoral and regional disparities with respect to modernization and efficiency, and adjust a new politics that would be quite selective of new development, oriented principally to the production of capital goods, basic equipment, or determined export products.[1]

The second assumption in this plan was that the state should become the major actor in the national economic scene in order to accomplish the above goals. As a March 1970 CORFO study paper had recommended:

The role of the state . . . should not be restricted to the function of tax collector, of financier, of normalizer of economic activity, but rather it should be even more a businessman, a negotiator, a trader of products, an investigator, an agent that stimulates and orients the development of these activities in the country in a quick and expeditious manner.

After the elections the Undersecretary of the Economy, Oscar Garreton, supported this view, writing:

It is difficult, if not impossible, to redistribute income in a stable manner while the monopolist sector of the economy is not directed in planned form in behalf of the interests of the majority of the country. This . . . will result only in the measure that the monopolist sector passes into the hands of the state.

The leaders understood clearly that the major obstacle to an efficient and productive redistribution of income lay in the inflation that seemed endemic to Chile. During Frei's administration there was a freeze on prices of food and other necessities, but it was quite ineffective. The new Government believed that that failure had resulted from the Government's lack of power—either surveillance power or economic power—to actually make such rules stick. Garreton explained:

In order to control prices effectively it is a fundamental requirement that the state enter the monopoly sector and have there a decision-making power, in such a manner that the state is the one regulating prices.

The third assumption was that all this was possible within the present Chilean economic system. This assumption was based on several pieces of information. One was the profit margin of the largest corporations, especially the copper companies. The Government felt that these industries could be run by the state and that prices could be frozen without causing a shortage of goods or economic problems because the profit margins were so large. In addition, the average Chilean factory was running at from 50 to 75 percent capacity, and it was felt that with a redistribution of income the lower classes would buy more, causing the industries to operate at a much higher level of efficiency. Thus prices could be frozen while wages rose because of the low level of operating capacity and the high level of profits.

The Opposition, of course, had other ideas about such a program. Some feared the increase of state power by Socialists and Communists and especially by the young leftists who constantly evoked the image of a dictatorship of the proletariat. Jaime Castillo, chief ideologue for the Christian Democratic party, pursued as a theme of his articles in *La Prensa* in late January the notion that centralized control leads to stagnation. He went on to explain:

Upon exercising its economic function the state has a tendency to deprive the economy of its internal motor force. When these tendencies become strong the state can transform itself into a factor for stagnation and retardation of social development, and an obstacle to the social mechanisms called to organize the development of socialism.

But most of the opposition was predicated on economic arguments. *La Prensa* and *El Mercurio* began printing articles about the weak underpinnings of the Chilean economy. *La Prensa,* in a series of articles called "The Bomb of the Salaries," examined the various facets of the economic plan and saw contradictions. According to these articles, the rise in salaries was disjointed, credit and fiscal spending appeared to be unrestrained, and there was an unbalanced and unfinanced budget, a lack of capitalization, and what the Christian Democrats called "a lack of a work and discipline mystique."

The result of the high readjustment is the increased consumer pressure, without relation to productivity or to the increase in the national product. Sooner or later it will have to translate itself into an inflationary pressure (at least that eliminates the reserves of foreign exchange because of the importing of food and other articles) or we shall fall into the odious system of rationing and bread lines, of such sad memory and already forgotten by Chileans [there was rationing during the Second World War].

The Government responded by proposing to cover the increased spending on health, housing, and welfare with a capitalization fund raised by levying a 15 percent tax on the incomes of corporations whose capital was more than two million escudos. *El Mercurio* argued in turn that this, on top of rising salaries and frozen prices, would lead to widespread bankruptcy.

As the Government began moving into high gear, intervening into broader areas of the economy, the honeymoon period ended and criticism from the Opposition rose measurably. The Government expanded its powers in the economy in three major ways. First, it utilized old decrees or old legislation, as mentioned previously. Second, it proposed new legislation to Congress (as in the case of the nationalization of the copper companies). Third, it used indirect methods. In the banking sector, for example, Government officials believed that state control of credit was vital. Two percent of the creditors were receiving over 50 percent of the credit in 1970. Pedro Jeftanovic, a Chilean economist, discovered in a 1961 investigation that "for the most part credit was going into the hands of the stockholders that, generally, are directors of the banks." Once that credit was obtained, he further discovered, it was loaned out again at higher interest rates. Jeftanovic calculated that "the transference of credit sometimes occurs five times and the interest rate by the last time is 60 percent." By late Janauary 1971, even the director of the private sector of the Central Bank of Chile had to admit: "The banks do not have a good image in Chile. That seems undeniable." Allende, in a major speech in early January, declared his intention to nationalize all banks. He expressed his desire to do this through Congress, explaining that he would send a bill to Congress within two weeks. In the meantime, he said, all those who had stock in the banks might want to take advantage of a good deal. Those who sold their stocks right away would get a higher than market price, and the payments would be readjustable with the cost of living. Those who waited until the bill came out of Congress would receive a much lower compensation, which would not be readjustable (that is, the bonds given out would not be readjustable every year). In a country with a 20 to 35 percent rate of inflation, that was an ominous proposition. Even so, people were slow to sell their stocks, and the Government dragged its heels in sending the proposed bill to Congress. Months afterward, the deadline for people to sell their stocks directly to the Government was still being postponed, and several of the banks had already become state owned. Although the methods were direct, the actions were not. Banks, as a friend of mine who worked in the United Nations noted, have very liquid assets. "If you are going to nationalize banks," he told me, "you don't tell them six months in advance what you are going to do. You march in one day, put a gun to the bank president's head, and say 'get out.'" Allende did not do exactly that, but at the time he made his announcement concerning banks he put intervenors into each bank, allegedly to act as auditors but really to act as overseers of bank transactions, approving each loan over a certain amount in order to control the amount of money going out of the country.

There were other indirect methods of establishing

Government control over private sectors. In the publishing industry, the workers of the largest publishing house, Zig-Zag, struck for a huge wage increase. When Zig-Zag refused, arbitration was called and the Government sided with the workers. Zig-Zag did not have the money to pay the increased wages of the workers and was forced to get a loan from the Government, with the terms being that the Government in return got the use of 50 percent of the house's printing facilities. The Opposition parties (Christian Democratic party and National party) noted gloomily that the union was controlled by Communists, that the Minister of Labor was a Communist, and that the Minister of Treasury was a Communist—and charged conspiracy. The same process occurred in the cement industry, where the largest producer was put under Government control through the use of loans to bail it out after a prolonged strike for huge wage increases.

As state power grew, other questions became important. One was the question of decentralization. That concept had been the goal of many Chilean administrations. Everyone—liberal, conservative, Marxist—understood that in a country almost 2,700 miles long, with a population spread throughout the length of it, and with only one rail line and little air travel from one end to the other, decentralization was absolutely essential. Each administration, however, had failed to achieve it. The socialists made their promises as their predecessors had. In an interview published in *El Siglo,* Kurt Drekmann, Vice President of CORFO, explained how his organization would change its nature to become a central fulcrum in the socialization of the economy:

We will not go to a centralization that is rigid, nor anything like that, but the anarchy has to end. All the branches of CORFO will be grouped by productive branches. A Committee of Sectoral Development will concern itself with each branch.

The Committee will coordinate all the grouped enterprises. It will be charged with making the plans of production, the financial problems, cost studies, rates, etc. The Committee will be, therefore, the first level of planning of the productive branches. This initial plan will go to the Committee of Planning of CORFO, that will be the organization that will finally plan the productive branches of development. Then all that plan will go to the office of national planning, which will coordinate it with the rest of the economy.

Only time will tell the results of this elaborate scheme.

Besides decentralization, which everyone agreed was a problem that would take years to resolve, the question of the role of the masses, especially the working force, became increasingly important. The Government realized early that the only way it could actually change policies was by having representatives from entirely different sectors of the population gain power instead of asking old delegates to change their policies. With the control of banks, for example, interest rates were reduced for cooperatives, small businesses, and agricultural small holdings. But to ensure the continuity of this policy, different bank directors were named. The President of the Association of Small and Medium Businesses, Carlos Devino, was named Director of the Bank O'Higgins. He expressed his satisfaction at the turn of events, exclaiming: "The norms that the traditional bank used were not obtainable for the small proprietors. . . . Credit was directed to the great industrialists. In spite of the fact that the producers of small industry . . . reached 30 percent of the market they only received 8 percent of the credit." This Government, possibly because of the representation of the Radical party but mainly because small businessmen were never considered the enemy in any of the polemics written by political leaders, relied heavily on small business participation. The real question, however, was the role of the white- and blue-collar workers. Since the Government had won on the shoulders of the working class, and since its parties' rank and file was composed mostly of workers, this was both a philosophical and a political question.

There were many reasons for wanting workers to participate in running the factories and institutions that affected their lives. For example, it was felt that the efficiency of business would increase if workers had a feeling of ownership or participation. Thus a CORFO bulletin published in mid-1970 discussed the advantages of worker participation in this manner:

> The present businesses have serious deficiencies in their property structure, but more important, they are characterized by an internal structure of concentrated power, with scarce participation from the workers. The level of internal tension in these enterprises is growing. The worker finds himself many times marginalized and alienated in his work, since business organization is not adapted to giving a certain responsibility to the worker in his own area of action. . . . The enterprise should look for its social legitimacy and to find it it should find new formulas of participation and new forms of business.

There was also a need to have workers oversee plant production during this transitionary phase in order to stop sabotage and watch for opposition plots of conspiracy. Rumors told of deals being made between some workers and rich Chileans to raise the level of absenteeism or to sabotage production in return for favors.

But perhaps the most important argument used by many of the political leaders was that effective participation by the workers in the factories and elsewhere meant a redistribution of power in Chilean society and a genuine revolution; that an irreversible revolution comes about only when power is taken from the hands of the few and given into the hands of the many. It was this question of power that would later split the coalition into those who favored participation and those who favored ownership.

During the first few months the Government moved rapidly to place workers and professionals into positions of power. Later in the year the Confederation of Trade Unions was given juridical status, which meant that it could negotiate on behalf of the worker on a par with Government, and each worker was forced to pay a few cents a week into the organization. Workers participated in all major economic organizations, including CORFO, ODEPLAN, and the newly created National Development Council. The latter was made up of most of the Ministers of Government, as well as the vice president of a copper corporation, six representatives of the workers, six representatives of the small- and medium-sized businesses, a representative of the Professional College, and two representatives of youth—all chosen by the President through lists proposed by the corresponding organizations. The groups' functions were to examine, recommend, render opinions on, and generally be aware of, the planning programs. In the pension funds and the welfare agencies, as well as in the social security trusts, the workers, or rather those who either paid into the fund or ran it, participated in decisions such as where the money would be invested. In the Social Security Service, for example, the administrative council was composed as follows: three representatives of the Peasant Confederation, two pensioners elected by their national associations, two from CUT elected by the Executive Council, one representative of the staff of the fund elected by direct and secret vote, and five workers elected by direct and secret vote by the directors of those industrial and professional unions having more than fifty members. In other funds equivalent representation occurred. Usually the counselors held office for three years and could be re-elected only once. They could be removed from their offices by a simple majority of their respective constituencies. It was a move away from trust funds being run by bankers or accountants toward putting decisions about allocation of resources into the hands of representatives of popular organizations.

With respect to worker participation in the factories (which will be examined more fully in the next chapter), the Government moved just as strongly in a more democratic direction. The strongest group was in favor of worker participation but not outright control. One leader of the MAPU party explained to me the reasoning behind this desire: "The miners in the north do not yet have a clear idea of how their work affects the peasants in the south. The unemployed in Santiago and the construction worker in Valparaiso cannot yet have the political sophistication to run the economy." Oscar Garreton, Undersecretary of the Economy, put it another way. He felt that the workers of any particular industry represent only a small section of the population, whereas the state represents a broad section, and that the state should therefore be the final arbiter of where resources are allocated and what production levels should be. Garreton was answered by a professor at the University of Chile who saw the ongoing process in the early months of 1971 as state capitalism. To her, state capitalism could indeed be a step toward socialism, but only if it were directed by the workers themselves. She wrote: "But if that revolutionary class is not at the head of controls, state capitalism is converted into a tool for the consolidation of power by the bourgeoisie and for fortifying the capitalist system." In most of the large industries taken over by the state, the directorships were made up of five representatives of the workers and six representatives of the state. That would seem to have given the state a majority vote, but it probably didn't because many times, given the close interrelationships of the political parties, the political leaders, and the worker organizations, at least one of the state representatives is also a representative of the workers.

With respect to worker participation in factories, the situation remains quite fluid. Pedro Vuskovic has said:

"The model of transition has specific structural characteristics that do not fit in with our understanding of the problems of capitalism, nor of socialism, as now constituted." Oscar Garreton explained at the same time that the Government was learning by doing—that theories were fine up to a point, but that since Chile had no models applicable to her situation, her experiences would indicate "to us our errors and our successes, the forms that should be adopted, the criteria that should be used, etc."

There was another reason for mass participation—it would help the Government in local areas to enforce statutes controlling prices and quality. Garreton had said that the state must be a dominant power in the economy in order to control prices. That was one of two conditions he thought necessary:

> The second condition is the conduct of the people, the mobilization of the workers and the fight to maintain the prices in the neighborhood juntas, and in the organizations. It is fundamental that we not base ourselves so much on legal norms, which are limited, and begin developing decisions at the level of production and the mobilization of the workers.

This theory became very important in the first few months of 1971. For example, there were rent controls, but landlords consistently evaded the law, asking a tenant to pay one rate and sign an agreement for another. This was patently illegal, and anyone with a lawyer around knew it, but it was so common and housing was so scarce that everyone acquiesced to the practice. The Government needed neighborhood groups to see that the regulations were followed—that is, to become the eyes that would act as enforcers. For another example, when Allende took office the price of bread was regulated and lowered, and many breadmakers responded by simply undercooking the bread, making it weigh more and therefore overcharging.

Although the Government publicized its efforts to curb this practice by showing pictures in the newspapers of merchants being awakened in the night and escorted to the bread kitchens to check on conditions there, the success of the project depended primarily on the vigilance of local groups.

Salvador Allende's role in the turbulent events of the first few months of his administration was not an enviable one. He had to effect radical changes quickly, but without violence. He had the Far Left asking for direct participation of workers and peasants in decision making, the Communist party asking that these masses be represented by organizations of trade unions, and the Radical party asking for calm and gradual expropriation of large farmholdings. Meanwhile, peasants in southern Chile were arming themselves and thousands were taking over apartments in Santiago. The middle class was alarmed, the upper class was leaving, and the lower class was expecting improvement overnight.

To respond to the different pressures and to cope with the gigantic problems of underdevelopment, the new administration had to weave in and out of the legal framework, now skirting anarchy, now embracing force, now moving so rapidly that the Constitution was casually ignored. Allende in his speeches did not paint rosy pictures; he did not speak of the "new man" who was so common a theme in Fidel Castro's speeches. He did not see himself as the creator of a vision of a future moneyless and cooperative society. Possibly this was because he knew that in a few short years he would leave office. Possibly it was because he was not elected on such a platform, although the rhetoric of the campaign might have made it seem so. As he has said repeatedly: "I was not elected to effect socialism. I was elected to accomplish the program of the Popular Unity." He speaks of revolution, but is quick to add that "revolution does not come overnight," and then emphasizes what became sort of an unofficial slogan: "We must make haste—slowly."

After the first ninety days in office, it was obvious that the new Government was moving faster than most people expected. I remember one business student running into his professor's office while I was there, saying unhappily but with a trace of admiration: "We expected this Government to try to bring about socialism within six years. But at the rate it is going, it will do it in six months." Of course, his definition of socialism was state control and ruination of private enterprise, not mass rule. Yet by anybody's definition the Government was indeed moving quickly. The banks had begun to be indirectly expropriated, the textile industries had been half intervened, legislation to nationalize the copper companies had been introduced in Congress, the concept of popular tribunals was being debated openly, prices were more or less frozen, rents were frozen, and so on. Almost daily there was another announcement of a new Government measure. As the momentum continued, however, and as the ease with which the Government seemed to be radically transforming the society became apparent, some began pushing for still faster progress. And as the Government began to explore the possibility of changing not only the economic basis of society, but also the legal system, the media, and the banks, the right-wing and the moderate segments of the Opposition began slowly moving together in a process that within six months would show the first signs of a tenuous coalition and within a year would show fairly solid unity.

A debate broke out over mass participation. The feeling on the part of many in the new Government was that if the leadership could change the society so quickly without major participation by the masses, it might be possible for future reactionary leadership to change it right back. Others said no, that giving land to a peasant was quite a different matter from taking it away from the same peasant at a future date. In any case, the Far Left wanted the parties to act as educators and representatives of the lower classes. The Popular Socialist party, which had broken off from Allende's group in 1967, is now headed by Raul Ampero, a brilliant theoretician. In late January 1971 he evaluated the Government's program with respect to the masses and found only the newly created peasant councils truly revolutionary. In a public policy document he declared:

> To take the right road, and not a tangent, to realize the hopes of the people and not frustrate them, to establish socialism on our soil and not let it become a type of state capitalism, we need a new type of party at the head of the people. Until now, an egoistic spirit has predominated in them, the obsessive conviction that each one is the exclusive and authentic vanguard, such that their ecclesiastical structure has carried them to divide the world rigidly, into angels and devils.

He concluded by warning that when a party "portrays itself as the incarnation of destiny it usurps the role of the working class in history." Although this criticism was directed primarily at the Communist party with its compact hierarchical structure, its validity is general, for all Chilean parties are elitist in character. As one laborer in a worker-controlled plant put it: "All the governments are the same. They are all middle-class intellectuals who don't know the reality of the workingman."

Allende asked for a different concept of mass participation. He asked for mass solidarity with the Popular Unity coalition so that the coalition could be used as a "battering ram" pushed by the "aggressive mobilization of the masses."

After four months in office the Political Commission of MAPU added its voice to the growing debate, declaring in a party document:

The masses have not had sufficient presence in what the Government has done. . . . We have the impression that we have spent, from the election to this day, a period not only of demobilization of the masses, but of dismantlement of the unifying structures. We are worried that the Popular Unity would let itself be absorbed by the government and lose all of its mass vitality and its political autonomy. . . . The Committees of the Popular Unity have much to do in this respect. They are not meant to replace the mass organizations (e.g., neighborhood groups, Mothers Centers, etc.) but they should constitute the locus of activity, and its political direction. The Committees of the Popular Unity are the best communication links between the Government and the masses.

The document concluded by saying: "If our united organization immobilizes its base, the fight of the masses loses direction and takes on a purely spontaneous organization, something that doesn't always coincide with the interests and perspectives expressed in the Government, as we have been able to verify by so many crazy takeovers during these days." This last comment concerned the rising number of farm takeovers in Chile, especially in the southern central part of the country. These "crazy takeovers," or spontaneous uprisings, worried MAPU almost as much as did widespread apathy and passivity. In fact, it seemed that spontaneity might well be viewed as the other side of the coin of passivity. Apathy could lead to misdirected and counterproductive activity. The two were seen to be interconnected. According to MAPU, when the masses lack political leadership, immediate demands tend to supersede political programs, causing difficulties for the Government. Not suprisingly, *El Mercurio,* the conservative newspaper and MAPU's arch rival, agreed. It said in an editorial only a few days before the MAPU document was published: "No totalitarian government has thought or deliberately desired to be totalitarian. It is the force of the masses, inflexible, violent, resistant to dialogue or reason, moved more by emotional slogans; this is what pushed men, and regimes, to totalitarianism."

The takeovers were not restricted to rural areas. When Allende took office there was an eruption of apartment takeovers. By early spring of the following year the low level of construction activity was blamed by the Chilean Chamber of Construction on the occupation by squatters of some five thousand apartments. Allende partially agreed, but refused to send in the police to evict the squatters. Immediately upon gaining office he went to one uncompleted housing development that had been occupied and talked with the squatters, explaining that he understood their plight but that those very houses were meant for other workers, not for the rich, and that those workers had also been waiting for years and would now have to wait much longer. His emphasis on class worked and the people agreed to leave with the understanding that housing would reach them soon. Yet this was not the general reaction. The housing situation was extremely chaotic during the first few months. Owners were afraid that if they left for even a weekend their houses would be seized by some local group. Guards were stationed around unfinished apartment houses. Friends were found to live in houses that would otherwise be empty for a few days. The Minister of Housing kept promising to draft a law that would make the occupancy of a house not one's own a criminal offense; he also continued to foster the impression that the disputes were being gradually resolved. But the Chamber of Construction published ads in the local papers replying that only one hundred of the five thousand such takeovers had been settled and that the bill about "housing crimes" had been in study so long that the Minister's statements lacked credibility. The Corporation of Housing Services (CORHABIT), run by the Government, waded into this argument by generally asking neighborhood groups to denounce "those occupants of housing who have more than one real estate or that with false facts are trying to obtain a benefit that isn't theirs and that thousands of other families are asking for, having the necessary quotas and dependents, but can't obtain because of the illegal occupations." CORHABIT admitted that in some cases the disputes were valid but stated that in other cases opposing political forces "with the desire only of creating problems for the Government" had handed out "keys to apartments and houses . . . in payment for electoral favors" before November 4.

As the socialist Government moved more rapidly, what was happening in Chile became big news internationally. Stories concerning the proposed nationalization of copper, the takeovers of farms, and the apartment takeovers were featured prominently in international newspapers. Chileans loved the attention. Even the most distorted stories—which were usually printed in *Time* or *Newsweek*—were eagerly devoured by them. As every Chilean is quick to agree, it was a time of importance. Every news story, no matter how distorted or how critical, was reprinted in local papers as evidence that this tiny country, with a population smaller than that of New York City, was internationally important. In one classic example, *El Mercurio* faithfully printed a summary of C. L. Sulzberger's story in the *New York Times* summarizing an article written in an Italian magazine by Luis Corvalan, Secretary General of the Communist party in Chile, which outlined the party's formula for success. The formula was a blueprint for subversion, claimed Sulzberger, and could well work in volatile Italy, with its fractured party situation, upending NATO and causing international catastrophe. Chile was ecstatic. Little Chile, on the periphery of world politics, was suddenly in the big league. Allende himself, when visiting a small village in southern Chile, referred to Sulzberger's piece, cheerfully noting that the United States seemed to fear that a free election in Chile would produce the end of NATO and European upheaval. The villagers roared their approval and applauded every comment. Chile was on the map.

However, the international publicity was also a cause for anger. Chilean journalists continually pointed to the distorted nature of the stories going out over AP and UPI. At one point they protested as a group that the AP and UPI stories always referred to President Allende as "Marxist Allende." They felt that the only reason this could be done so consistently was that it was a conspiracy. The word "Marxist" was so laden with emotion for most people outside socialist countries that by its mere mention Allende's character was besmirched. These journalists, of course, didn't think that Allende was *not* a Marxist. Rather, they thought that if political adjectives were to be used to describe people, they should be used consistently. No North American news services referred to the Brazilian leader Medici, who was never elected and is a general, as Military Dictator Medici. Richard Nixon was not being referred to as Capitalist President Nixon. Nor were Brezhnev or Kosygin being called Marxist leaders of Russia. Some Chileans remembered the last popularly elected President these news services had called a Marxist. That was Cheddi Jagan of British Guiana, who was shortly thereafter overthrown in a coup that parts of the U.S. foreign policy apparatus gladly acknowledged having engineered.

There was no way the Chileans could fight back. The protests of their journalists never had much impact. Finally, when for a few days Allende barred UPI from the country, the international press made the action seem as one more step toward state control of the media. In fact, the only time that I saw the Chileans actually enraged by North American reporting was when a spate of articles was published concerning freedom of the press in Chile. When the Inter-American Press Association criticized Allende for strangling freedom of the press, the Chileans finally, as a group, both Left and Right, blew up. As one newspaper noted, Chile was being criticized in a meeting held in Rio de Janeiro, where not only are newspapers censored but journalists who muckrake may well be imprisoned without trial and tortured almost routinely. In contrast, there were the streets of Santiago, where there was a newsstand on every block that displayed newspapers and magazines of every tendency—conservative business dailies, *Playboy,* mimeographed guerrilla newsletters, political party newspapers, right-wing criticisms of the Government, left-wing criticisms of the Government. At one point Allende personally invited journalists from all over the world to witness the political campaign leading to the April municipal elections in order to decide whether freedom of the press or freedom in any sense still existed in Chile. Not many journalists accepted the offer; they were too busy in their offices thousands of miles away writing about the death of freedom in Chile.

Chile Polarizes: The Municipal Elections and Their Aftermath

It became apparent to anyone living in Chile during those first six months that the Christian Democrat party was the key to the future. Although Radomiro Tomic had run a campaign mirroring Allende's, traditional Chilean political rivalries suggested that when it came to getting those same programs through Congress the party might not vote that way. Furthermore, by the early part of 1971 it was not at all certain that Tomic represented the majority of the party. There was a strong group that wanted to undermine the Government, either out of political conviction or in order to regain the Presidency six years later. As Manuel Garreton, previously a member of the party and at the time head of the Center for the Study of the National Reality, part of Catholic University, explained to me: "The Christian Democrats can only become rightists. There is no political future in being left wing. The Government has co-opted that area." Although the Christian Democrats tried halfheartedly to stake out a position on the Left, they became increasingly conservative in orientation, defending the very institutions that the new Government had made the targets of its program (when the Government tried indirectly to nationalize the banks, the Christian Democrats criticized the program because it gave no direct participation in control of credit policy to the bank workers—to which the Government promptly responded that if the Christian Democrats were worried about that, they had had six years to do the same thing).

It was the Right, however, that put out the first feelers. A month before the April municipal elections, Sergio Onofre Jarpa said: "What truly interests the country is the unity of all Chileans disposed to defend liberty and democracy, rather than the theoretical disagreements and the political sectarianism." Radical Democrat Raul Morales Adriasola, who had been the center of controversy when the Supreme Court decided not to lift his congressional immunity and force him to answer questions about his alleged involvement in the assassination of René Schneider, went even further, exploring the potential of a moderate right-wing alliance. As quoted in *Ercilla,* a Christian Democrat magazine:

Forgetting all that has separated us, adding the votes of the Christian Democrat party, the National party, and the Radical party, we have enough votes in the Chamber to suspend from their offices the Ministers and even the President of the Republic. And in the Senate we have the democratic majority necessary, in agreement with the Constitution, so that with the suspension agreed upon in the Chamber, we could proceed not only to the dismissal of the Ministers of State but also, in the cases which the Constitution indicates, of the President of the Republic.

In essence, it was a call to the Christian Democrats to ally with the Right to strip the Government of its powers. But the Christian Democrat party was still split, as it had been in the days of the Frei Government. It seemed that it was always on the verge but always drawing back. In 1967 the leftists had taken control of the party, only to be beaten by Frei in one all-night session. In 1968 the annual convention had refused by a narrow vote to approve the opening to the Left supported by the youth and rural section of the party, causing the party to split. Now the party was split again. Most members wanted to await the outcome of the municipal elections to see where the popular votes were. Congressman Fernando Sanhueza, Vice President of the party, responded to the feelers by saying:

> We are respectful of the constitutional regime, and we believe that the worst favor that we could do for Chile would be to propose things that are planned against the person of President Allende. We can at any moment disagree with him, passing judgment on him politically, but we cannot call for sedition.

The newspaper *La Prensa* said that the proposal for a civic front "deserves to be analyzed with seriousness, because outside of the political intentions that the call would enclose, certainly it responds to the feelings of an important sector of public opinion." It then went on to describe democracy as a system that permits diversity of opinion and stated that it would be a disservice to the Chilean people to cover up divergent philosophies by participating in a popular front under the guise of protecting democracy. But it left the door open for such an alliance by concluding: "No one can doubt that the political groupings of democratic inspiration will be unified in the defense of our institutional system before any menace of transgression on the part of officialdom." Finally, it stated:

The opposing groups thus don't fit into civic fronts. But yes, they should act in a climate of conscious responsibility in order to confront, in common, the defense of the democratic regime when this is necessary. And that responsibility presupposes a climate of respect and the absence of petty sectarianism that makes impossible the necessary coming together in the right hour.

The Christian Democrats were willing to form an alliance to protect the "institutional nature" of democracy. Yet it is this very "bourgeois nature" of democracy, as the leftists describe it, that is a target for socialist politics. In fact, at the very time the Christian Democrats were leaving the door ajar, the young leftists were reviving the theme of the "inevitable confrontation" over exactly the institutional integrity the Christian Democrats vowed to defend. At a Socialist party congress in late January, Secretary General Aniceto Rodriquez, a political organizer who had led the party to electoral victory, was replaced by Senator Carlos Altamirano, the lean, intelligent theoretician who believed and still believes a violent confrontation to be inevitable. Altamirano had spent time in jail under Frei because of a vague law on subversion. The Young Socialists noted in their document passed around at the party congress that "The taking of power by the workers and the destruction of the bourgeois military bureaucratic apparatus are essential conditions to the construction of socialism and the formation of a new type of man." They felt very keenly the need to make the revolution irreversible. They feared that if the inevitable confrontation were not accepted, the enticement of liberal formulas and the lure of state capitalism with its increasingly technocratic solutions to problems would drown the Government's desire for change by impeding program after program—diluting some, sidetracking others. They were upset at what they considered "unifying" talk by Allende, feeling that a revolution is not a task in which all are friends. As they said in the document: "The paternalism and nationalism, especially, coming from the governmental authorities, foments chauvinism in the masses, makes them forget the class contradictions through feelings that 'we are all Chileans' . . ." And further on the document zeroed in again on the possibility that the Government would slowly be overcome by the intellectualizations and rationalizations of bourgeoisie mentality:

The bourgeois institutions are the great historical shackle that the popular government has to deal with in order to develop a revolutionary politics. . . . In the measure that behind the government there does not exist a proletariat with sufficient force to impose its criteria on the fundamental decisions of the government, the president will have to attend to those institutions, with the danger of increasingly assimilating himself into them, and thereby increasingly removing himself from the break, the basic requirement for the entry of workers to power.

With respect to its own party, the Young Socialists were highly critical:

The party is incapable of imposing a consistent revolutionary politics because its direction is eminently social democrat, that is to say, liberal, lifeless; it worships spontaneity, causing in the Socialist party in these times a profound crisis of hierarchy and discipline that has permitted the communists gradually, since way before the presidential campaign, to impose their reformist line, spearheading the political process and leaving us, almost always, with accomplished facts.

The convention accepted this document and defeated Aniceto Rodriquez in the party voting, causing the outgoing Secretary General to comment caustically: "Those who did little or nothing for the success of September now surge forth as the great counselors and administrators of victory." Revolutions, like party politics, devour the young, and party faithfuls are the first to go. Carlos Altamirano hand-picked the Central Committee, promising that the Socialist party would become a serious rival to the Communists and promising to impose "discipline, authority, and work" on party members.

Outside the party there were mixed feelings. Some believed that Allende supported Altamirano; others thought that he preferred the less conspicuous Aniceto. One sociology student at the University of Chile made this observation: "I would rather have somebody in between. Aniceto is unimaginative, but a hard and serious party worker. Altamirano is too theoretical, and has little contact with the masses or practical organizing." Everybody, however, accepted the outcome as further evidence of the progressive dialectic of Chilean politics. As the Opposition tenuously put out feelers for unity, the Far Left was pushing the Government further than it wanted to go. With the victory of Altamirano, the Maoists had a strong foothold in the Government.

Another indication of the changing mood of the country, perhaps, was Allende's acceptance of the advice of the Young Socialists. In a speech shortly after the convention he declared: "I am not the President of all Chileans." The Opposition, horrified at such an unconstitutional declaration, asked him to explain. Allende answered plainly: "I am not the *compañero presidente* of moneychangers, of the large landowners, of those who have denied the land to the workers; I cannot be a companion to speculators . . . I am not the *compañero presidente* of those economic clans who have lived by exploiting Chile. I am the President of those who live by their labor and those who put the national interest before their private interests."

As the municipal elections approached Chile once again was in a gigantic political stew. The Christian Democrats' slogan for this campaign was "Chileans, you are not alone." The assumption was that the average Chilean felt the coming of dictatorship and was afraid to speak out. The Opposition stressed the theme that it was not too late to turn back, to rebuke the Communists who were gaining control at every turn.

But this time such a theme had few advantages for the Opposition. Municipal elections occur only a few months after a new Government takes office—at the end of the honeymoon period, before the disillusionment sets in. There is usually strong support for the party or parties in power. Also, in this particular election the traditional fear of communism was no longer as effective, at least in working-class areas and among women. The campaign literature in 1970 had told housewives that their refrigerators and children would be sacrificed to the god of statism if the Government became Communist. Before and after the elections stories of communal dining halls and communal living arrangements swept Chile. But the effect was mitigated, especially for the lower classes, when instead of losing their children the women were receiving a pint of milk daily. Thus in April 1971 the people went to the polls to vote for or against the Government coalition on the basis of performance rather than on the basis of bestialities committed by Stalin decades before.

Another advantage the Government had in this election was its active record of the previous few months. As one former Christian Democrat explained to me, his party was clearly on the defensive. It was embarrassing to see the new Government move so quickly in so many areas without in fact getting a single new piece of legislation through Congress. Whenever the Christian Democrats complained about the half-heartedness of certain measures, the Government supporters always answered: "But if you have a better way of doing it, why didn't you do so during the six years you were in power?" Frei had always used the excuse during his final years that a recalcitrant majority in Congress had scuttled his programs, but here was a Government with an overwhelming majority against it in Congress and major national and international interests in the Opposition, and it was moving quite rapidly.

Finally, the Government had the advantage of appearing more sure of itself than the Christian Democrat party, which was the largest party in Chile but did not quite know what its ideology was any more. For example, just before the elections ex-President Frei returned to public life, appearing on a local television station to criticize the Government's economic program and predict dire consequences. Yet a week later the party's previous presidential candidate, Radomiro Tomic, published in an Argentinian magazine an interview that was frankly positive of the progress made by the current administration. This ambivalence was finally to explode in late June, at the party convention.

The municipal elections vindicated Allende's prediction that he would capture about 50 percent of the electorate. Altogether, 2.8 million Chileans went to the polls and gave the six-party coalition 50.87 percent of the vote. That was some 14 percent higher than the Popular Unity coalition had in September and was twice that of the Christian Democrats, who garnered 25.62 percent. A significant aspect of the victory was that for the first time a majority of working-class women voted for Allende's coalition. No longer could the Opposition say that the Government represented only one-third of the Chilean population.

On closer analysis, the results were even more of a personal victory for Allende. The Socialist party got 22.38 percent of the vote, becoming the second largest party in Chile and increasing its vote from 12.2 percent in 1969. The Communists, on the other hand, increased their vote marginally, by only 1 percent, to 16.95 percent.

In the months following the municipal elections Chile began to polarize into two major camps. Within the coalition, the Radical party Ministers resigned their posts in a traditional gesture, recognizing that their poor showing in the elections might indicate that they were no longer strong enough to justify two portfolios. Even though the Socialist party leadership discreetly requested that Allende accept these resignations (since, this group felt, if the Radical party were permitted to remain in office during the difficult times ahead, it would act as a drag on the Government's momentum), Allende refused to do so and the party retained its posts.

In the country as a whole, elections during the next few months indicated that the Government had probably hit its high-water mark in terms of popular support. In a by-election in southern Chile to fill Allende's vacant seat, Socialist Adonis Sepulveda won with over 50 percent of the vote. But in another by-election in Valparaiso, where the Government had installed its headquarters during the summer, the Socialist candidate lost by one percentage point to the Opposition's combined forces. In elections in the University of Chile for governing council and rectorship, the Government gained and lost. The candidate of the Christian Democrats, who had opposed the concept of students voting in university government elections in 1968, ran on a platform to keep the university out of politics. His opponent, Eduardo Novoa, asserted that this program was "to insert the university into the processes of social transformation that are occurring in Chile." The Christian Democrat won with 51.42 percent of the vote against 48.24 percent for his opponent. On the council, however, the Left gained a majority of 53 seats and the Opposition won 47.

A by-election in July proved to be the event that broke the Christian Democratic party for the second time in three years. In a convention shortly before the by-election the young members proposed that the party delegates endorse a position whereby the party would under no circumstances form a front with the conservatives. This proposal was denied. The party united with the Right in the by-election, and the Government was defeated by a razor-thin margin. At that point Luis Badilla, the controversial youth president of the party, and others, including eight deputies, left the party and established their own group, calling it the Christian Left. It was a split that had been foreseen as the party moved ever more rapidly to the right. The question was, Which was more dangerous, the Far Left or the Far Right? The youths weren't sure that the Left was dangerous at all, and opted for an opening to them rather than to big business. Older Christian Democrats believed that an alliance with the Right would protect Chilean democracy and also incidentally permit the party to get back into power in 1976. As Bernard-Leighton, a party leader who remained within, exclaimed in responding to the criticism of the self-exiled segment: "If in order to defend democracy we have to ally ourselves with the devil, we will do it." Luis Badilla responded critically but sympathetically: "I know very well what Bernard-Leighton thinks. What he said is not what he really believes. He was overcome by the microphone. It was he who taught us that the 'democracy' in which the Christian Democrats believe is not the same as that of the National party, the Radical party, or the 'Freedom and Fatherland' party [a right-wing group formed after the elections in 1970]."

Not only the young people were leaving the party, however. The religious laity also were beginning to split over the question of Marxism and what they saw as a shift to the right by the party. In the preparty convention in late spring the Christian Democrats had embraced socialism but had called it "communitarian socialism," and many people thought the words probably had a meaning similar to Frei's old "revolution in liberty." The dialogue between Marxists and Christians had been going on since the split of MAPU in early 1969. In the winter of 1971 more and more priests had come to believe that the distinction between Marxists and Christians was less crucial than previously believed. In a meeting in late April eighty priests from working-class parishes expressed their solidarity with the aims of the Popular Unity coalition. The declaration of the priests stated:

As Christians, we see no incompatibility between Christianity and socialism. On the contrary. As the Cardinal of Santiago said this past November, "In socialism there are more evangelical values than in capitalism." In effect, socialism opens up a hope that man can be fuller and therefore more evangelic; that is to say, more conforming to Jesus Christ who came to liberate us all from slavery. In this sense it is necessary to destroy the prejudices and the distrust that exist between Christians and Marxists. To the Marxists we say that true religion is no opiate of the people. On the contrary it is a liberating stimulant for the constant renovation of the world. To the Christians we remind them that our Lord has committed himself to the history of men and in these moments to love thy neighbor means basically to fight so that this world is reshaped as much as possible to the future world that we hope for and that we are constructing.

Twelve theological professors at Catholic University in Santiago warmly responded to this declaration, adding their own comments to the growing schism in religious ranks:

Certainly, it is valid to affirm that everyone is saved by the grace of God, as much the rich as the poor. It is also valid to note that Christian love is universal. We should love our enemies as well as our friends. But this doesn't mean to deny to salvation its character as a historical process. Salvation is realized in history. If Christian love is reduced to a purely "profound" and "universal" dimension, it becomes useless. More than that, such a love could become the cause and justification for many injustices and hatreds. Christian love that is faithful to the Gospel is a strong, liberating force. It should liberate the rich, even with violent love, from their egoism, from their ways of living, consciously or unconsciously, of continuous and at times brutal oppression of the most dispossessed.

With respect to politics, this group noted: "The Christian faith urges a commitment to the oppressed man without indicating a determined political party. Nevertheless, a Christian cannot live a faith that makes real history an abstraction; on the contrary, he must commit himself to those political structures that appear the most coherent and in agreement with the demands of the Gospel."

Thus, after eight months in office, the name of the game was still politics in Chile. The economy had indeed been restructured; agrarian reform moved ahead rapidly; changes had been made in union structures, in legal definitions, and in attitudes in the mass media. But the real question, as Chileans in and out of government understood quite well, was the question of power. The changing panorama of the political scene, as well as the changing vote levels in Congress and in popular elections, was watched closely, for everyone understood that even with the control of the cabinet and the Presidency this Government would last only as long as it had major mass support.

Yet it is not enough merely to scan the political infightings and write off the major changes that the Government had already brought about in other areas of the economy. A revolution is, above all, a process, and it is a process of changing attitudes, of raising consciousness, of educating the people to control and change their own lives. In various areas, in various ways, the Government and the people on the lowest levels pushed against each other to bring about profound changes in attitudes and in institutions in many areas of Chile.

5

Worker Control

The only power in Chile capable of giving justice to the people is not government A or government B. It is the organized people themselves.

—A worker in a factory taken over by fellow workers

Small Industries

On November 13, 1968, the workers of the Industria de Andres Hidalgo, a medium-sized plant on the outskirts of Santiago which manufactures concrete posts, high-tension wires, water well pumps, and motors, went on strike—an action that was not at all uncommon in Chile.

What was uncommon was the mood of the country, the growing belief among workers that they were caught up in a losing proposition. Small industry in Chile, with its low profit margins, was increasingly unable to compete with huge corporations tied in with foreign interests. The larger corporations were introducing new machinery that replaced workers while small businesses were going bankrupt. Coupled with low wages was the phenomenon of an infla-

157

tion whose rate seemed to remain as high as 25 to 35 percent annually. This combination of aggravating circumstances helped push the number of strikes from 120 in 1958 to 1,500 in 1968.[1]

But strikes were not solving the problems. As one welder at the Hidalgo plant told me: "We would strike out of frustration and desperation. Maybe we'd win a little raise. Because of the inflation, we'd be back on the strike line, trying to regain what we had lost during that year."

Chilean labor has always had a deeply political and radical strain. The massacres of the miners in the early twentieth century are still remembered, as are the organizing efforts and birth of the first workers' party. Although only 15 percent of the total labor force is organized and less than one percent of the rural labor force was organized until 1967, the fervor and politicization of the organized workers makes up in part for their small number. The Confederation of Trade Unions has been led, almost uniformly, by Communist and Socialist leaders who believe capitalism is evil. Yet trade unions when tied to the left-wing political parties are often mere political appendages, electoral wings rather than true worker vehicles.

By the late 1960s the small locals, the unorganized workers, and the unemployed began to energize the worker movement with new tactics and new methods. Out of a realization of their plight the workers began exploring new ways of combating the dead-end of labor-employer bargaining in a system with a high rate of inflation.

The spark was ignited in July 1968 when the workers of SABA, after their legal strike of forty-two days during which the employer had responded to none of their complaints, seized the plant.

Chilean commercial circles were screaming for the workers' hides. They wanted the Government to make an example of these left-wing conspirators to prevent the spread of the disease of local control to other vulnerable points. Like all pioneers, the SABA employees suffered the most, but their example was a lesson for others, a model to learn from, to benefit from. The seed had fallen on most fertile ground.

In December 1968 the workers of Industria de Andres Hidalgo, remembering SABA, spent time organizing its community through talks and courses and going to other plants to speak to the workers there. When the employer attempted to dismantle his machinery in order to transfer his plant to another location, vigilant community women watching the plant premises spread the alarm and within minutes hundreds of neighbors stopped the operation.

Spurred on by this initial move by the employer, the employees, in an efficient commando operation (one person got the guard involved in conversation while comrades climbed over the side walls of the factory), took over the plant and awaited the police. But when the police did arrive, replete with tear gas pellets and masks, they found the plant surrounded by students, workers, families, and, in the front lines, several Congressmen and Congresswomen. Unwilling to accept the political consequences of action, the police withdrew, and the first battle of the workers was won.

On January 28, 1969, the first worker-run enterprise in Chile began to function. Two years later I went to the factory to speak with the workers about their successes and problems during that time. They had been hard years. The workers were inexperienced and handicapped by myths of their own inadequacy. One man explained it this way: "Workers are taught so often that they are not capable of being administrators that they believe it themselves." He added angrily: "In a recent survey of labor union leaders in Santiago, 95 percent said workers were incapable of running a factory."

The factory faced difficult times. The Christian Democrat Government, which was the main buyer of its products, boycotted it and denied it credit. Other workers and university groups helped out, but often the weekly paycheck amounted to the equivalent of $2. Family tensions grew. A former line-worker told me: "Our wives didn't understand what we were doing. They only knew that our children couldn't live on $2 a week. Some left their husbands. Many men quit the factory."

As the experiment matured, the vision matured. The wives and sweethearts were invited to participate in the weekly meetings where work problems were discussed and voted on. After a while the factory and its dusty grounds became something of a community center. A free dental clinic and medical station was established for workers, their families, neighborhood residents, and "revolutionaries." Children played in the dirt courtyard. Women worked in the community kitchen while the men worked inside. The family gradually became a source of strength rather than tension.

Within the factory, the changes were dramatic and often surprising. The distinctions between white collar and blue collar were discarded, as were those between manual and intellectual labor. That process was a difficult one, for as one worker indicated, the blue-collar workers "feared they would be overshadowed by white-collar workers who had a higher culture." Yet the white-collar worker "considered that he was going to be put in an inferior position," losing prestige that the old system accorded him. Once the workers were running the factory themselves the old distinctions began to disappear. As one former welder, who is now the accountant for the factory, told me: "The worker could continue to climb the occupation scale (under the old system) but in order to do it he would have to step on the backs of his own brothers."

The factory still has its chiefs and bosses, but they are now popularly elected by a general assembly; they cannot serve consecutive terms, and they are expected to be the hardest and most self-sacrificing of workers. Most salary differentials have been abolished and remuneration is now dependent on hours worked, not on title or professional classification.

Training courses (*capacitacion*) have been set up for teaching the workers to become capable administrators. The goal is not that everyone know everything but that everyone have enough information about factory operations to be able to read the company books and understand them.

Discipline is meted out by a committee or general assembly, depending on the nature of the fault. Lateness is penalized by a strict formula, and chronic lateness can bring suspension. However, since the job of foreman rotates, the individual who this week may be guilty of being late may next week be the foreman in charge of meting out discipline for late workers. By rotating authority, the workers understand why it is important to be punctual and come to take problems of tardiness and absenteeism very seriously.

The new name of the factory is COOTRALACO, and it, like SABA before it, has spawned variations on the theme. There are now over thirty such worker enterprises in Chile, ranging from auto garages to construction companies to movie houses.

Across town from COOTRALACO, standing inconspicuously in a narrow street among closely huddled brick houses, is the SOTRAMET firm. As you walk in the front door it looks like the beginning of an underground parking garage, with a wide walkway turning down and a brightly painted sign, ARDYGAS (SUTRAMET's former name), welcoming visitors. In October 1970 a totally new concept had occurred in this firm. The man who was once owner and president of the firm, René Doggenweiler Setz, became a worker and the thirty-fifth partner, the other thirty-four partners being the work force. An extraordinary individual, Señor Doggenweiler had belonged to a Christian Association of Businessmen and had decided that being a Christian compelled him to practice Christian brotherhood in his business. He began a complicated, gradual plan for instituting a cooperative. The process took four years. In 1966 and 1967 the workers began preparing themselves through a process of self-education. They attended courses in administration given in the cafeteria, a small room off the one-room, two-storied main plant. In April 1970 the second stage was reached: They formed a society of metallurgical workers called SOTRAMET. The group signed a contract with the old society of stockholders, which had consisted of three people. One of these was the former owner and operator, who had owned 70 percent of the stock.

They have painstakingly worked out details concerning the relationship between capital and labor. At present the workers get 80 percent of the profits and the other three get 20 percent, which works out to a pretty even split. The boss explained that some workers were angry, at first, at having to give him a part of the profits because he had capital in the company. But he told them that capital merely means money and that the real question is how that money is earned. In his case, he told them, most of it was earned when he had been a worker and had saved it, and therefore he was entitled to a return on it. They agreed.

The firm manufactures gas heaters. It started with fifteen to twenty workers and now has thirty-seven. In three years the workers have tripled production. They were never supported by the CUT, which also did not support the workers of Andres Hidalgo or of SABA, but the Government's refusal of credits and loans didn't hurt them severely because their market goes to individuals, and the markets remained open while their production increased and profits dropped.

The organization chart of SOTRAMET shows a popular assembly, which meets monthly; since the workers meet together at lunch and pass information over breakfast, there is no need for weekly meetings. But meetings are useful in another way. Doggenweiler relates an interesting anecdote. The chief of production had complained to him that production was dropping because people were attending so many meetings—one in the morning, one in the afternoon, one at night. A commission was created to investigate, and it came up with the rather surprising information that in the sections with the most meetings production was actually higher than in those with the fewest meetings.

Jobs rotate, but there is specialization. The administrator explains: "You have two extremes. The first is that everybody is capable of doing everything. The other is that no one is capable of doing anything but his own job. Neither is good. Everyone has enough knowledge to be able to vote on decisions. That's all." The workers have the power to hire or fire the administrator, to set prices and quality and production standards, and so on. They try to increase employment before buying a new machine, but they also take into account the needs of the firm.

The establishment of worker-run factories in capitalist Chile has created some ironic problems. The main one concerns the legality of such operations. There is no law in Chile that covers them. Doggenweiler turns to Victor Arroyo, a labor organizer recently entered into the work force there, and explains wearily: "You know they told me that there would be trouble if Victor Arroyo came to the factory. Well, the only fight I had was with my lawyer, who told me I couldn't do this."

Especially distressing to the workers is the legal concept of profits. If workers own the enterprise and want to reinvest the money to produce higher wages (since they share in the profits), they must still pay taxes on the money. The entire system of employer taxes makes little sense to them. According to the law, the employer has to pay 44 percent of the white-collar workers' salaries and over 50 percent of the blue-collar workers' salaries into social security funds. It is a way of protecting the worker against unscrupulous employers. But when there is no employer, the bureaucracy that allegedly has been created to protect the worker becomes a burden and a drain on the worker's resources. Once the workers of SOTRAMET began examining the entire area of Government-versus-people policies, it broadened considerably its critique of existing structures. The workers, for example, couldn't understand why, if they were running the factory themselves, they had to pay health insurance to the Government in order to get it back in medical care. The health insurance benefits that Chilean employers are supposed to pay are not usually paid, and employees have little possibility of checking up on this until they go to the hospital and find that their hospital benefits are in arrears. Each employee has a little health booklet, and if it is not up to date the employee gets no medical services. Since so much of the health taxes are used to support a nonmedical bureaucracy, employers usually resort to paying personally the medical bills of their employees instead of complying with national legislation on health insurance taxes. The workers at SOTRAMET are now going one step further. They are asking whether they can set up their own medical clinic in the factory, thereby serving the neighborhood with the money they would have given to the government. The workers under the leadership of Victor Arroyo are coming to understand that in health, as in other areas, the neighborhood concept is most important. A doctor cannot truly understand the nature of a patient's illness without understanding the environment in which the patient lives. Victor Arroyo talks of the difficulties a group therapist has when operating in a neighborhood unfamiliar to him. "The doctor should know that maybe the headache comes from a husband who drinks too much." He speaks of his own battle with bureaucracy. "I was out sixty days, and according to the law, I was sick and should have been paid 66 percent of my salary. After being back to work for two months, I received the check. I needed it when I was broke and sick, not now."

The factory workers are not paid well—they receive about 1,200 escudos monthly ($40.00)—but they earn about a third more than the national average. The administrator gets 2,400 escudos, still an incredibly low wage for owners or chief administrators of factories. People hope that in a few years there will be total equalization except possibly for older people who, because of larger families or failing health, might get a little more.

In these worker-controlled plants there is little politics or theoretical wrangling. As Waldo Leiva, a forty-two-year-old president of COOTRALACO and a former lathe mechanic, says: "Among ourselves we don't ask what party someone belongs to. Our definition is based on whether you are for or against the workers in practice."

The workers are optimistic about the new Government, but cautious. As one worker explained to me, "The only power in Chile capable of giving justice to the people is not government A or government B. It is the organized people themselves."

Still, the newly elected Government is seen with warmth, hope, and optimism. The workers expect a better deal with respect to supplies, credits, and markets, and of course they no longer fear police intervention on behalf of the owners.

But the Government has not been very responsive to their needs during the first year. It worried more about the larger plants, the monopolist industries, leaving the smaller businesses until much later, partially because the latter are not economically important, but mainly because the small businessmen and the middle class in general would be terrified if the Government were to encourage plant take-overs and worker control.

So the workers in small plants have had to do it themselves. Early in 1971 the workers of SOTRAMET, along with some students from Catholic University, initiated a newsletter called *Un Camino Nuevo* ("A New Road"), which is circulated among workers and is a newsy pamphlet about current events in worker-controlled industries. Committees go to other plants that have recently been taken over, explaining to the workers there the difficulties and joys of self-ownership and helping them with technical advice. The SOTRAMET workers agree that along with their change in status has come a change in attitude. Victor Arroyo pointed out with pride that during the previous vacation period seven out of thirty-five workers forsook the traditional visit to the beaches and went voluntarily to other plants to discover new situations and explain what they had accomplished.

Large Industries

The large statue of Jorge Yarur outside the huge textile factory of Industria Manufacturas de Algodones Yarur is now covered with thick ˙burlap. The workers who were forced to donate from their already pitifully small paychecks for its construction have placed a large sign at the entrance of the plant proclaiming: "Yarur: territory free of exploitation." Amador Yarur, the previous owner and a member of the richest family in Chile, is now in Argentina while workers participate in running one of Chile's largest industries.

But bitter memories from the recent past still linger. One textile worker described the medieval hiring procedures that had been used. Ushered into a room lined with long, black curtains, each job applicant was made to stand before a statue of the Virgin Mary, with a Bible and a skull on a nearby table. Amid these symbols of God and death, the cowed applicant would swear fealty before a Chilean flag, promising not to participate in strikes. A seamstress in the factory summed up the results: "For a long time we had company unions, and no one said anything."

Even when people did try to say things, they soon discovered that Yarur's power extended far beyond the walls of the factory. In the 1950s the mere creation of a union caused the resignation of no less powerful a person than the Minister of Labor because he refused to bow to pressures to withhold union recognition. In 1962 a worker strike was on the verge of success when the Minister of Interior sent troops to break up worker resistance. Of 3,800 workers at that time, some 2,600 were fired, ushering in an eight-year period of not unexpected, but unprecedented, labor peace in the industry.

Many miles from Amador Yarur's plant, on the beautiful coast, in the small town of Bellavista (which means "beautiful view" in Spanish), Amador's brother Teofilo Yarur ruled over the textile factory of Bellavista-Tome. Surrounding the plant are the blue-collar workers' houses— dark, dank, one- and two-room structures. Six toilets provide sanitation for the three hundred men, women, and children who dwell there. Nearby, the houses of the white-collar workers reflect their higher status. They are relatively new and are two stories high, with patios. A swimming pool and recreation hall are within the complex.

José Massa Caro, the young Government-appointed intervenor, explains his reactions when first coming to the plant: "I never imagined that in the twentieth century, in the year 1970, there could exist in Chile an enterprise with the feudal structure and with the reign of terror that existed here. All the people living here in Bellavista depend on the factory. The private school in the area depends on it; the church choir, the sports club, too—practically all facets of one's life. According to whether one behaved well or badly, in the judgment of the administrators, the privileges or punishments were meted out, in their homes, in their social clubs, in neighborhood groups, everywhere. The white-collar employees who behaved poorly or who were not efficient had to move to worse housing."

The Yarur family was one of the five powerful group-ings that had controlled Chile before the election of Salva-dor Allende. Its domination stretched far beyond textiles. Amador Yarur was Director of the Banco del Credito e Inversiones. Nicolas Yarur was Director of the Banco Con-tinental. Jorge Yarur was Director of the Banco Español. The family controlled one of the largest radio stations in Chile, Radio Balmaceda.

Within the textile industry, control was shared with one or two other familial groups. In the cotton sector, for example, three businessmen in 1970 controlled nearly 75 percent of the production. Invariably the top ten stock-holders owned 60 to 100 percent of the company's stock. The banks acted as intermediaries between popular savings and elite investments. Thus in 1970 the Banco del Credito e Inversiones, as previously noted, gave 30 percent of its total credit to five enterprises, all controlled by the Yarur family.[2]

The family aspect of control led to an almost com-pletely irrational structure for the textile industry, accord-ing to a 1969 report by a group of engineers who blamed this irrationality on the "reluctance of the present owners to leave the administration of the plants in charge of technical managers."

With such wealth and power the Yarur family could—and often did—indulge every whim and caprice. Jorge Yarur's mansion on the outskirts of Santiago has sixty rooms. It has a private theater, a stable, and dozens of bedrooms because Jorge enjoyed sleeping in many different beds during a single night. The doors of the bedrooms are inlaid with gold, as are the faucets of the bathtubs. Saba

Yarur, a great sports enthusiast, used the family radio station to relay a special sports round up at 4 A.M. when he was in Miami.

When Allende gained power, Yarur fled.* Even before the victory was assured, Yarur, like many other rich businessmen, stopped paying off creditors, paralyzed sections of the factories, began laying off workers, and did not bother to replace parts of machinery that broke down. By the time the Government stepped in, huge amounts of money had to be loaned from public coffers to pay back wages and to get machinery into full production again. In addition to full production the Government's first order of priority was to change the types of fabrics produced. Although Chilean agencies have for years established quotas for different types of fabrics manufactured in that country, they were rarely enforced and almost universally ignored. Thus, for example, the production of flannel dropped from 300,000 yards in 1967 to only five thousand yards in 1970. Production of cloth for work clothes (such as overalls) plunged from 200,000 yards in 1967 to an incredible fifty yards in 1970. Meanwhile, the quantity of expensive lingerie material and imported synthetics expanded enormously.

With the expropriation of the textile industry as well as the copper, cement, and steel industries, the question of worker control became important, for the Government pretended to be a government of and for the working class. At the plant levels, many of the same things that were occurring nationwide took place. The divisions between

* There is an interesting story circulating in Chile, which may be a product of wishful thinking. It is said that when Yarur fled to Argentina with most of his wealth intact, he bought a huge house and began living in his accustomed style. The Fuerzas Armadas Revolucionarias, an Argentinian guerrilla group, in an act of friendship toward their Chilean comrades over the Andes, broke into the house one night, held the family at gunpoint, and denuded the house of its treasures.

blue collar and white collar gradually became meaningless. In the cement industry, for example, this division was terminated with a public ceremony opening the previously restricted country club. One worker noted: "This club was the most obnoxious expression of the division of the classes inside the business." The club had tennis courts, a dining room, gardens, a swimming pool, lounges, a theater—all for only the white-collar workers.

The question of worker participation in these huge industries became a strong national issue, which began to be expressed as "state capitalism versus socialism." As seen by the Chilean Government, there were roughly four basic alternatives. First, there could be a system like that in the United States, where the workers participate by bargaining for wages and working conditions through a union. Second, there could be shared power within the plant, with the management and the workers represented on the board of directors and both working together to set prices, quality, production goals, and so forth. A third possibility would be full worker control, with management being elected representatives of the workers, subject to removal at the workers' request. Fourth, there could be participation by the workers in running the plant with a superior body, probably the state, making overall policy decisions with respect to types of products maintained, prices set, and so forth.

Allied with these broad alternatives was the question of what the vehicle for worker expression should be. Should there be, for example, a grass roots organization with rotating officers? Should there be representation through political parties? through traditional trade union organizations? through elected Congressmen?

The Government has formulated certain guidelines, although it recognizes their temporary nature. It has decided for the moment that in the large industries and the state-owned enterprises workers should have plant participation but that the state, which supposedly represents a much broader section of the population, should have control over broad economic policy. As Oscar Garreton has written: "The principal problem in the incorporation of the workers to power doesn't lie so much in the enterprise itself—although there must be participation there also—but rather in its incorporation into the state, the government, and its principal instruments, through the organizations and parties." Garreton believes that worker participation is crucial, but that the state should be "dominant . . . as representative not of sections or parts of the social classes, but as representative of all the social forces."

From theory to practice is a long haul, and problems have cropped up almost continuously. In one case, in the textile factory of SUMAR, with eight thousand employees, the interparty rivalries cause problems. One union official explains: "The Christian Democrats speak of full ownership by the workers, others speak of co-ownership, and the most radicalized segments of the Communist, Socialist, and Popular Action parties insist on the Government's model for worker participation." With the parties controlling the trade union organizations, having pre-empted all the main positions on the issue, it is difficult for rank-and-file members to have any important role in decision making; they can only sign up for a previously delineated position.

The tension is constant between *reinvindicalista* demands, or bread-and-butter issues, and political stands. In the copper mines, for example, the miners went on strike in midwinter, demanding a 50 percent increase in wages, far above the cost of living and far above what the Government felt it could pay, given the low price of copper. The complexities of the situation are reflected in the copper industry to perhaps a greater degree than elsewhere because the copper industry has a long tradition of radicalism. As long ago as the early 1960s the copper workers were demanding takeovers by the Government, saying that they had the ability to run the mines themselves, and could do it even better. In mid-1969 the president of the copper miners' federation, Hector Olivares Solis, demanded participation in decision making by the miners. He declared that "those who have the power of decision making are many times ignorant foreign bureaucrats," and added: "The workers, employees and Chilean technicians, without foreign aid, are those that put in march the productive processes of these minerals."

But when the Government nationalized the mines, problems occurred almost immediately. For one thing, the Government decided that Chileans would no longer be paid in dollars. It had been a common practice in Chile, especially in the mines, for foreign industries to pay some of the workers in North American money. Payment in dollars meant almost a 50 to 100 percent overpayment, for dollars could be retained as an investment or sold on the black market for almost twice and sometimes three times the official rate. In the copper mines there was a small group of people called supervisors who were paid in dollars. This group, contrary to the implication of their title, were not only technicians but also chauffeurs, cooks, and others who, it seemed, were whimsically picked by management for the favor. When told they would not be paid in dollars, the supervisors promptly went on strike. They caused a huge rift, with the Government threatening to send in troops and the copper miners threatening to run the mines themselves. The rift was patched up delicately. A few months later the miners went on strike. The Government this time felt it could not confront the strikers directly. Instead it pleaded with them to accept what other workers already had accepted and angrily began calling them aristocrats, for the miners were indeed paid more than the average Chilean worker. "But," the miners retorted angrily, "look at the houses we live in." Poblacion Las Latas in Chuquicamata is aptly named. *Latas* means tin cans, and the houses do look like so many tin cans with dusty roads in between. The miners declared that food prices were higher in the northern deserts and that it was more expensive to live there. They quite rightly pointed to the high incidence of silicosis among their profession, saying that their life span was shortened by their work in the mines. And they pointed to the high profits of the copper companies that they themselves had helped to gain, saying they wanted a greater piece of the action now that they participated in management. After months of negotiations they finally agreed to compromise terms. But the issue was a public indication that there were many splits in the worker-Government alliance—human, reasonable splits, understandable differences.

The bureaucracy in Chile, which has been the butt of so many jokes, is an evil that everyone opposes. Even as early as January, when the Government had just begun to intervene in industries, the workers were hopeful but wary. Harold Roa, a steelworker, explained: "There are some problems, but you have to remember this is a period of transition." One of his fellow laborers, Pedro Briceno, was not so optimistic. "The administration of the enterprise is the same," he noted. "The problems are merely processed. A solution is not sought. Problems go from one level to another without being resolved."

Six months later, these same complaints were being echoed by others. One worker in the steel industry angrily declared: "The management of the iron and steel industry retains the same bourgeoisie mentality as it has always had. All the measures come from above and that cannot be." In another steel factory the workers, most of them under thirty, tried to remove a manager and found that they had to deal with higher authority. "We have struggled a long time," they complained, "to achieve the control of this enterprise, and we are not going to accept either the CAP [the national steel corporation] or the Government giving us less."

Although the Government has brought workers into the directorates of banks, pension funds, social security agencies, and national economic planning bodies, the question of what constitutes a worker state is still an open one in Chile. One Marxist professor recently wondered out loud about the actual meaning of the phrase "worker power," when the newly created regional planning body for the textile sector included representatives of everyone except the textile workers themselves. In the case of Bellavista-Tome, the Government went to the heads of the University of Concepcion to obtain preparatory courses for the workers. Many wondered why the process was from administrator to administration rather than from students to workers. In fact, in that factory the bureaucracy became so bad that the Government had to remove its own intervenor and begin again at the level of plant discussions as to the future structure of the factory.

Still, everyone in Chile is hopeful. The difficulties are enormous and the complexities even greater. With powerful foreign interests still involved, with foreign reserves dwindling, with huge underemployment, and with huge debts to pay off, the problems are bad enough. Add to that the petty dogmatism of the Communist party and the entrenched bureaucrats of the CUT with interests to protect, the fragmentation of the party system into so many varied fiefdoms, and the disparate interests among the peasants, the landed small peasants, the miners, the urban unorganized, and the unemployed, and the overall picture is overwhelming. Yet despite it all, the Government moves along, confident that the problems will resolve themselves through experience. Garreton explains: "The concrete experiences of interventions and expropriations that have been realized or that will be realized in the future . . . will indicate to us our errors and our successes, the forms that should be adopted, the criteria that should be used, etc."

Times are changing in Chile. Company books are now open to all, to verify for the first time the economic reality of the enterprises. But the road is a difficult one. The new Minister of Family sums it up best: "We must construct the socialist road as we walk it."

6

Peasants, Indians, and Agriculture

I want to tell you that the race that defended it-self with heroism, from the initial beginnings of our history, has been losing its lands, has been forgotten. . . . I want to tell you that it is a national obligation, it is an imperative of our conscience, not to forget what Chile owes to the Araucanian nation and race, origin and base for what we now are.

—From a speech by Salvador Allende

Chilean Indians

Señora Campusano speaks in a soft, weary, yet strong and proud voice as she stirs the pot of water and flour that will be the noonday meal for her and her three children. Her weathered face shows clearly the blood of Mapuches, descendants of the Araucanian Indians who ruled in Chile before the Spaniards entered from the north. She's alone, suffering the personal isolation that society imposes on its lowest class. "My husband was accused of a crime he didn't commit," she explains, "and was taken to jail. I can't visit him because the jail is far away and the bus costs thirty escudos ($1.00). I don't have enough money. My two daughters left when they were eighteen to become maids in Santiago. I didn't want them to go but they wouldn't listen to me. One left her baby and doesn't even send me the child support allowance she receives for its care."

The babies will grow up in a one-room hut with a dirt floor, patched together with anything handy—mud, wood, tin, canvas, straw. Their meals will be monotonously consistent, both in substance and in lack of nutrition. Although Señora Campusano has hens, she does not feed their eggs to the children; instead, these precious items are sold for more filling, although much less nutritious, fare. Because of the lack of nutrition these children, like most Mapuches, will probably die before age fifteen. They will undoubtedly be less intelligent, less alert, smaller in stature, and weaker than other Chilean children. So severe is the problem of malnutrition that many psychologists see it as a primary factor in mental aberrations. In upper-class residential districts there is a 3 percent incidence of mental retardation, but in the slums surrounding Santiago and in the rural areas 40 percent of the preschool-age children have IQs of less than 80 (90 to 110 is considered normal).[1]

Even if a child survives, he will be continually vulnerable to the most common diseases, for malnutrition lowers the body's resistance. Illnesses that in developed countries with widespread medical care are considered minor annoyances are often fatal or incapacitating in rural Chile. Typhoid, pneumonia, diarrhea, measles—all are deadly. In parts of rural Latin America the mortality rate from measles may be two hundred to five hundred times greater than in the United States.

Racism, Chilean Style

If the Mapuche child survives the purely physical gauntlet he runs early in life, there lie ahead the psychological injuries that Chilean society inflicts on this minority. It is an especially ironic situation, for Chileans pride themselves on their lack of racism. But as in other countries, the minorities disagree. In one factory I visited, the Indian laborer was quickly pointed out as being "our black man," signifying that in many ways the trials and tribulations of the Mapuches in Chile are similar to those of the black people in the United States.

A Mapuche professor, one of the very few Mapuches who hold advanced education degrees, described his road to success:

I went to grade school in Lumaco. I used to walk nine kilometers back and forth in order to attend school. My mother used to give me a small bag of toasted flour that I divided into two portions. Halfway through the morning and again in the afternoon I popped one in my mouth and wetted it with creek water. At that time there was no school lunch or anything like that. When I entered the high school at Concepcion my whole body broke out with boils. I was not accustomed to meat, nor fish, nor fat. But I grew. Not much, certainly, but some. The food, and the fact that I no longer had to walk so far to school made me happy, although on the other hand I suffered a great deal. My school companions made fun of my name. The teachers never used to help me enough because they were impatient that I didn't know the answers right away. I knew the lessons but I didn't understand Spanish well and it was difficult to answer clearly.[2]

He said that often in his prayers he asked God to make him "a little whiter and more like the other school kids."

While the Mapuche boys struggle through school the girls make their way to the urban centers, as Señora Campusano's two daughters did, swelling the ranks of what are euphemistically called domestic employees. A study done a few years ago by Joseph H. Fichter, a Jesuit sociologist, showed that 93 percent of the female domestics had migrated from rural areas. Their workday stretches from 7 A.M. to 10 P.M., about ninety-two hours weekly, with two days off a month. The average take-home pay in 1971 was around $17 monthly, which included room and board.[3] It is a killing, degrading occupation, even if the employer is kind and sympathetic. More often than not it is but a temporary way station for women who move deeper into the entrails of society by choosing another outlet for lower-class aspirants—prostitution. In 1960 the Santiago police found that 70 percent of the city's prostitutes were formerly employed as housemaids. When arrested they frequently voice the belief that "anything is better than being a house servant."

Perhaps the best indicator of the subtle yet powerful racist tendency in Chile comes when one asks how many Indians there are. The guilt of the conqueror is often assuaged through minimizing the extent of the problem. Chile is no exception. Alejandro Lipschutz, a professor at the University of Chile and winner of the National Science Prize, tells the story of a 1967 conference of high school teachers who, when he raised that question, promptly answered "ten thousand" out of a population of nine million. Recent studies, however, set a more accurate figure of around 600,000. Yet these hundreds of thousands of Indians are almost invisible, subsisting on two or three acres outside metropolitan areas or in back rooms in breadmaking shops in the center city. The only contact the average Chilean might have with Mapuches is when one or two small boys enter the public transportation buses to sing a song for a few cents or peddle some buttons or other paraphernalia.

Mapuches, Peasants, and Agriculture

Only ninety years before Allende took office, troops moved into the area of what is now called Temuco, some four hundred miles south of Santiago. They established a fort for the express purpose of "pacification of the rich lands held by the Araucanians." During the next century came the Indian wars and the gradual but inexorable chipping away at the landholdings of the thousands of small Indian communities, or *reducciones*, where generations of Indians had lived on communally owned property. In 1928 a law was passed that made the liquidation of the community obligatory if it were demanded "either verbally or in writing" by any *one* of the members of the community. In 1960 this law was modified so that one-third of the members of the community were needed to solicit liquidation. But ironically, when in late 1968 the peasants were given the right to organize and the agrarian reform law was passed, legislation concerning Indian communities became even more oppressive, stating that "the judges and the Department of Indian Affairs, in qualified cases . . . will be able to order the liquidation of a community. By the mid-1960s, after decades of harassment, legal persecution, and changing legislation, only about three hundred of these small communities remained.

As the Indians' land was legally stolen from them, the concentration of arable land was aggravated. In the rich central valley where a majority of Mapuches are concentrated, one percent of the landowners controlled 43 percent of the land. In Cautín Province as of January 1, 1971, there were 23,296 proprietors of small farms who owned between one acre and 250 acres. There were 2,177 with land areas of between 250 and 1,000 acres and only 250 with plots of more than 1,250 acres.[4] That area in Chile is often called its granary. It produces the most foodstuffs, but it is also the area with the highest rate of malnutrition in the country. And even though its output is quite high, production per acre is low. Inefficient utilization of land resources often is carried to ludicrous extremes. In one example, a farm of 700 acres had only two workers, each paid a little less than the equivalent of a dollar a day, which they received only every two months.

Agriculture is Chile's albatross, socially and economically. A look at the breakdown of farm holdings may give a good idea of the situation in the late 1960s. At that time the number of farms was 150,000. Of these, 76,000 were a little more than 5 acres each. They were subsistence plots, and their owners usually had to work on other farms to supplement their income. Another 54,000 farms had an average land area of 80 acres; about one third of these were also only subsistence lands, but others produced some extra goods that could be sold in the market. Some 15,000 farms averaged 500 acres, and these were usually dedicated to growing cereals, fruit trees, and the like.[5] Three thousand farms had 1,500 acres apiece, and it was there that the highest productivity per acre was found. Another 2,500 farms had 5,000 acres or more, and these were usually worked poorly and used mainly as the basis for gaining credits or for financial maneuverings. Finally, there were the huge farms, some 700 large landholdings of over 50,000 acres, which were universally unworked except for small portions that were kept for pasture.[6]

If we assume that a family of four is a basic farm unit, about 300,000 people were living below a subsistence level while 2,800 people owned farms totaling 50,000 acres (although even these inequalities are underestimated, since some farms were owned by different members of the same family).

This disparity has been translated into the political arena through the representation of the National Agricultural Society, which until quite recently wielded great power, often with intimate connections with political parties. Also until quite recently, the Communist and Socialist parties have been urban based and have disdained the rural *lumpenproletariat* as being unorganizable and having little revolutionary incentive. The Constitution of 1925 had permitted rural unions to form, but in the late 1930s, as a result of pressure by the SNA (National Agricultural Society), the Liberal Government stopped such organizing through the simple administrative act of not accepting any more applications for union recognition. In the late 1940s this ruling was reinforced by the passage of the Rural Labor Law, which contained numerous conditions for union organizations on farms. No unit could be larger than a farm. No federations were permitted. Organizers were given no legal status. In each organization there had to be at least twenty members, each of whom had worked on the farm for at least a year and was at least eighteen years old. At least ten members had to be able to read and write. The owner of a farm could oppose the formation or functioning of a union there. If a union was begun, the state inspector had to approve its formation, its internal elections, its administration, and the cashing of its checks, and could dissolve the organization by simple decree. Strikes were prohibited during the harvest and sowing seasons, and a union was forbidden to raise strike funds with its budget.

Only a superhuman effort could have built even the shadow of a labor organization under these conditions. In fact, from 1947 to 1964 a mere twenty-two unions, with a total of three thousand members, were established.[7]

Although rural laborers were effectively stopped from organizing, they became increasingly important in Chile for their voting power. Before 1958 each party could print its own ballots, since the ballots were uniform. Often each party printed its ballot in a different color. The farm owner was able to pile all his workers into the farm truck, take them to the polls, and watch carefully to see which colored ballot they voted. In 1958 this printing practice was eliminated, causing owners to think up more ingenious, but far less effective, methods of controlling their workers (one example is the farmer who gave each of his workers one shoe before the election and promised the other if the right candidate won).

Between 1958 and 1964 the voting rolls doubled, and in 1964 the victory of the Christian Democrats, with their strong peasant support, forced the Left to re-examine its previous noninvolvement in rural areas. José Campusano, leader of the Communist Peasant Federation, explained in 1965:

We believe the awakening of the peasants has not been sufficiently capitalized on by ourselves, the communists, because we have followed the same routine methods of leadership, and, principally, because we have failed to understand the revolutionary value of agricultural workers who, in increasingly greater numbers, move to and from the city, and who we had confused with the peasant proprietor, who has a different mentality.[8]

Frei and Agriculture

While the Left belatedly began organizing among the rural population, the Christian Democrats moved strongly toward agrarian reform. Eduardo Frei and his advisers understood quite well that agriculture had become Chile's albatross, draining the society of resources that could be used to better the average person's standard of living. The concentration of land and income in agriculture caused a lack of productivity and thus a severe strain on foreign exchange because food had to be imported. Frei understood that the poverty of the peasants could only be eliminated if there were major reforms in the rural areas. Yet, partly for reasons of ideology and partly for practical considerations of political power, Frei opted for a gradual program of agrarian reform. The two major precepts of the program were that the actual redistribution of the land would be used primarily as a threat—to force large landholders to utilize their resources better and to raise productivity (the agrarian reform law stated that even large farms, if worked effectively and efficiently, would not be expropriated)— and that the large landowners would be compensated handsomely for their land and supplies. This program was also a result of practical and ideological considerations. Christian Democracy respects the meaning of private property and therefore respects the right of a landowner to be compensated, no matter how grossly he misuses the land. This compensation includes not only the land, but the house, the cattle, the tractors, and so on. Frei also realized the difficulties of undertaking radical transformation in agriculture at a time when the Government did not have sole control over the economy. Thus he decided to compensate the owners handsomely for their cattle rather than have them slaughter pregnant cows, as was to happen when Allende decided against high compensation (Also, compensation was a means by which the Government could buy off the upper-middle-class landowners)

Yet by proceeding with this concept of agrarian reform, the Christian Democrats almost immediately found themselves slowed to a crawl by the accompanying restrictions. Chile, not being a rich country, could not afford the high compensations. So by the late 1960s the Government program had to choose between investing in the agrarian reform program and investing in other equally just areas of social concern such as housing or industrial expansion. In view of the fact that the large landowners were not considered the enemy in the Frei ideology, and in view of the internal political pressures that came from those Christian Democrats who held large farms and from the rightists who had supported Frei in 1964, it is clear why the agrarian reform program eventually succumbed to pressures for a slowdown. As early as 1966, Radical Senator and large landholder Roberto Wacholtz could tell his friends that he was continuing investments in land. "Don't be frightened," he counseled. "The moment will come when the government will not be able to continue expropriating; then the agrarian reform will stop."

The politics of the program eventually became clear. Some 60 percent of the expropriated farms were found in the seven provinces of central Chile.[9] Almost half the country's agricultural workers were situated in those seven provinces, in addition to almost two-thirds of the *inquilinos* (those who have small plots of land that they are given on the owner's land). On the other hand, only 18 percent of the proprietors and their families lived in those provinces. Thus relatively few large landholders were affected.

The Government's concern with getting the large land-owners to increase production rather than with providing land to the landless became apparent from other statistics during that era. When landholders did increase productivity, it was usually as a result of heavy mechanization and resulting unemployment. A study done by the University of Maryland showed that between 1965 and 1969 landholders not affected by the agrarian reform program had increased their investments by 120 percent—a clear indication of a great capitalization of agriculture. This increased mechanization was made easier by investment credits handed out by the state. The Government doubled credits that the state bank handed out (from an average of $2,000 per loan in 1964 to $4,000 in 1968) and tripled the amount that CORFO dispensed.[10] Both organizations catered primarily to the large landowners. Organizations such as the Agrarian Reform Institute, which catered to small farmers and cooperatives, had relatively few resources. They had, for example, only 30 percent of the veterinarians and agronomists.

One final comment on the politics of Frei's agrarian reform program. The focus of this reform was the *asentamientos,* the peasant-controlled cooperatives forged from previously large farms. The *asentamiento* was to be composed of peasants who earlier had been part of the work force on the farm. The problem with this vision of the final product is that it condemned those living outside the farms to poverty. What it did was broaden the capitalist class in rural Chile by making owners only of those who worked on large farms. In turn, these peasant landowners would employ, at wages and living conditions little better than their historical counterparts, those who lived on the subsistence plots and the thousands of migrant laborers in Chile. Thus Frei's agrarian reform program would have created a peasant middle class but would not have disposed of the problems of the lowest class.

By late 1968 it was still difficult to judge the results of Frei's program. Many aspects of it, like the planting of millions of forest trees and fruit trees, would take years to show results. There seemed no real evidence that in the preceding three years there had been an increase in production. Yet there seemed to be evidence, although the statistics are somewhat intuitive, that the status of the *inquilinos* and others who had been thrown off the land had worsened as a result of mechanization. In some cases, on a farm that had used perhaps fifty laborers, a wheat harvester had reduced the number to two or three. A terrible drought hit Chile in the summers of 1968 and 1969, decimating a large part of the herds and causing widespread economic disaster. The workers, of course, were the first victims of such a disaster. By late 1969, with the agrarian reform program slowed down, a growing number of union officials had been fired, peasants were being killed, and a growing repression was hitting rural Chile, a repression introduced under the cloak of a drought-imposed austerity.

It would be absurd, nevertheless, to condemn the Christian Democrats for their shortcomings without applauding their innovations. They did start an agrarian reform program that ranks as one of the major reconstructions of agriculture in Latin America. The idea that the rich did not have the right to own land and use it only for summer vacations was a new concept and one that would be strengthened by the victory of the Socialists in 1970. But the most important aspect of Frei's administration was the organization of the peasantry accomplished mostly by the Christian Democrats. The new labor law signed by Frei in 1967 improved immeasurably the chances for formation of peasant unions. The 1948 restrictions were eliminated. Employers had to pay wages to officials who spent time on union business. Federations could negotiate for union members and their local unions. Payment of union dues was obligatory for all members (a check-off could be demanded). Employers were forced to put into a fund 50 percent of what their employees contributed. Employees who did not want to pay dues to the union deposited them in a special fund of the Ministry of Labor, part of which went to a national federation and part of which was used for worker education and training. Rural workers were given the right to strike and the right to organize on more than one farm. A two-thirds membership vote for a strike was necessary. In the event of such a vote, the employer could not continue work on his farm except that which was of "urgent necessity," which would then be supervised by a labor inspector. (A part of the legislation that would be used extensively by Allende gave the President the power to force a farm owner to start up his farm after it had been shut down by an illegal strike or a lockout if either occurred during the harvest season, since either could cause shortages of food for the general population.)

The number of Indians in unions rose dramatically, from 3,000 in 1964 to over 250,000 in 1968. Yet although Frei saw organization as a way of channeling social discontent, that very organization of peasants produced an internal dynamic which generated its own momentum. In 1960 there were only six petitions for better working conditions on Chilean farms. But in 1965 there were 395, and in 1966 there were 527. The number of strikes rose from three in 1960 to five in 1963 to 142 in 1965 to an astonishing 586 in 1966. In 1967, the year the Government doubled the agricultural minimum wage and enacted an agrarian reform law, the number of strikes rose still further, to 655—proof that the passivity of Mapuches and other peasants was increasingly a thing of the past.[11]

The Present

With the election of Allende and the disappearance of the Grupo Movil, coupled with Allende's warnings to the police that in cases of social and political unrest persuasion rather than force was to be used, the burgeoning rural revolt exploded. By early 1971 hundreds of farms were being seized each month by groups of peasants. There was an almost continuous exchange between the Minister of Agriculture, Jacques Chonchol, and the Opposition over the extent and severity of the rural crisis. The peasants organized their own congresses and began discussing those issues that heretofore they had been too frightened or passive to discuss. Overriding much of the conflict was the Mapuches' dislike and distrust of the *huinca,* their special word for the white man. But there were conflicts among the peasants, too. There were fights between white peasants and Mapuches, between *inquilinos* and those who lived in *reducciones,* between the small landholder and the migrant worker. One such dispute occurred in early 1971 and was indicative of the internal turmoil even in this oppressed class. The lands of Jorge Lavandero, a well-known Christian Democrat Deputy, had been seized. The leader of that seizure, Bernarda Moreno, a woman with both white and Indian blood, spoke of the incident:

> We are of the *reduccion* Chucaupo, composed of eighty Mapuche families, a total of 320 persons, the majority of them children. My grandfather, Ignacio Moreno, was owner of these lands that today are occupied by Mr. Lavandero. Seventy years ago Mr. Lavandero's grandfather took over all my lands and the entire community diminished little by little until now it is reduced to one or two hectares [one hectare is equal to two and a half acres] per family. The *reduccion* is composed of the communities of Ignacio Moreno, Juan Lincoleo, Juan Llanquileo, Luis Ranileo, and Juan Canio. Here, different from in other takeovers, political factors are not present. Mr. Lavandero was going to sell these lands to his *inquilinos,* and if that were done, it would have been very difficult for us to recover them.[12]

Lavandero's workers, who were going to be given ten acres apiece as a Christmas present, were tense and angry. They also needed the land. The struggle between these two groups of miserably poor Indians was tragic. It was a tragedy played out again and again. It was a tragedy that looked like chaos to an outsider, but it was really a desperate race by the Government to try to educate the rural workers and small landowners alike that they need not be enemies, that the enemy was the 2 percent of absentee landlords who controlled Chilean agriculture.

To deal with the shortcomings of the *asentamiento* system, which had created a lower middle class of peasants who had previously worked a given farm and yet had hardened the misery of the migrant workers, the Government created the Agricultural Centers. The *asentamientos* had by no means ended the relationship between capital and labor. They had, rather, created a new peasant capitalist class. Thus, when Allende took office, some 30 percent of *asentamiento* labor was coming from outsiders. The Agricultural Centers tried to change this by expropriating entire regions at a time rather than proceeding farm by farm. Plans for entire valleys were laid out, with supply and distribution centers, huge state farms, and buying centers. It was a concept that made a lot of sense economically and that was appropriate, given the class analysis of the Socialists. But it was also a bit premature and difficult to enact. The Christian Democrats, with their powerful peasant federations that had been established earlier, had no trouble convincing their members that state farms where goods and land were held in common and only a small plot and a house were given to each individual family represented communism in its worst form. For those who were about to divide up the land of a large farm, or for those who held land already, any assurances from Allende that small landowners would not be affected were not accepted readily, although it was certain that Allende himself desired this and never intervened in small landholdings. In Chile, as elsewhere, the peasant (or, indeed, the urban slum dweller) who held a little land, no matter how small or unworkable, or who had a shack, no matter how tiny, considered himself a part of the middle class and refused to sacrifice the little he had in a gamble on an uncertain future. With the Socialists talking about higher productivity and a better house and the Christian Democrats talking about total state control and Stalinism, the peasant became confused and tended to fall back on the little plot he held already. As we shall see, this problem became evident in the by-elections in early 1972, but it was apparent even in the early period of the new administration.

Although for the majority of peasants the question of Agricultural Centers versus *asentamientos* would eventually loom large, even during the first few months it was the active segment of the peasantry (usually urged on by the Revolutionary Peasant Movement, offshoot of the MIR) that held the public's attention.

As the takeovers mushroomed, the middle class in Chile became hysterical. There were stories of kidnapped landowners, raped wives, terrorized families, rural chaos, and disrupted production. Undoubtedly some of them were true. But as Frei had said many years before to the wealthy landowners who were obstructing his agrarian reform program at every turn: "In order to save a few cents you are going to lose your heads." The landowners had fought against agrarian reform for a decade, knowing full well that eventually they would lose. The time had come. No longer would the police be sent in to fire on peasants taking over land. Police were to use persuasion. Thus state power was absent and a sort of anarchy ruled. But anarchy, as political theorists understand well, is not chaos. The picture of Indians taking over a farm by standing quietly at the entrance a mile or so from the main house and stopping trucks from coming in, having armed themselves with long poles to which they had attached makeshift arrowheads, was fearsome only inasmuch as it touched the sensitive nerve that many Chileans have when the lower Indian classes are involved. The fear that Indians are the criminal element, drunk, stupid, lazy, and thieving, is pervasive. The headlines in *La Prensa* screamed in block letters, "Drugged Mapuches Rampage in Chile." The story claimed that wild Indians were being given little yellow pep pills by leftist students, which were activating their basest animal instincts. The Left picked up the story and recirculated it gleefully, without comment. This incident demonstrates how polarized Chile was becoming—the story caused terror in some and laughter in others.

Even the delicate Government coalition began to

founder on the rocks of rural unrest. The Radical party (probably the most conservative group, but having changed with the times, backing Alessandri in 1958, Frei in 1964, and Allende in 1970) was more interested in order and legalism than in rapid reconstruction. Especially galling to them was the apparent influence of the Young Socialists, the MAPUistas and the MIRistas, in pushing the Government to the point of disorder while the Radicals' own strength seemed to be ebbing. Old bitternesses were uncovered. One Radical deputy said: "There is unrest in our party. We, the Congressmen, were not agreed with the distribution that we were given in the public administration with respect to Ministries." Further, he said: "It appears to me that if the Government doesn't adopt measures conclusive to bringing tranquillity to the countryside, the problem is going to become difficult and critical in a short time." He blamed the situation on "immature sectors within the Government coalition." Another Radical, Senator Americo Acuna Rosas, explained that the takeover "by outside elements is acquiring very grave proportions because of its effect on the economy of the country, the paralyzation of food production, especially milk, as well as the anarchy, the common crimes that are being committed daily and which the central Government does not recognize." Like his colleague, he observed that "infantile revolutionary zeal or a position of blind impatience contrary to the interests of the country can reside in those persons who, outside the public institutions, like CORA, should attempt to irresponsibly realize a social process—which evidently they are incompetent to do—which hurts the image of our Government and causes a loss of prestige in the national and international environment when stories are told of these occupations and their arbitrariness." But he still had faith in the Government: "I am confident that the Government will impose the necessary stability in these farms in defense of the national economy and that the agrarian reform that we are sparking will be pushed technically and responsibly through normal institutional means and through the special organisms created by the legislature."

The Left felt just the opposite. The Socialist party, of which the youth wing took control with Senator Altamirano as their leader in February, thought that the peasants should be given the reins quicker. After the municipal elections, in which the Socialist party did extremely well and the Radical party did poorly, talk began of purging the Government of Radical party factions.

The peasants, too, were unhappy with the speed of the agrarian reform program. Some of them, concentrated in the Revolutionary Peasant Movement, demanded that all farms of more than eighty acres be expropriated and criticized the present agrarian reform as a "bourgeois law." They wanted no more reserves or indemnifications; they said that the organization of workers and peasants on the communal level should decide the use, distribution, and forms of productive organization of the expropriated lands. The reason for such urgent measures, as one of the deputies of the MCR at their first congress explained it, was quite simple: "From now until the agrarian reform reaches us, the farms are going to be denuded. By then, we will be just about dead from starvation, but the rich will have had time to arrange things. To tell us that takeovers must stop is to give the rich a chance to dismantle everything and leave us the shell. . . ."

His intuitive declaration was supported at the time (early 1971) in a study conducted by a team of professors and students in the School of Veterinarian Medicine of the University of Chile, which found that 60 percent of the cows that were in the slaughterhouses in Santiago were pregnant. (Chile has today some three million head of cattle and needs twice as many. Between 1964 and 1970, however, production of cattle actually fell by 0.1 percent. It is calculated that in Santiago's Municipal Slaughterhouse alone, some twenty thousand pregnant cows are slaughtered yearly.)[13] This was a double tragedy because a lack of refrigeration facilities had led Chile to import cows rather than meat, leading to the need for a period of acclimatization and then a period of pregnancy. Therefore, each cow that was slaughtered represented the loss of a cow, a calf, and a full year of time. The farmers responded that of course they sent their pregnant cows to market. After all, the Government was offering them only a dollar or so per cow, and the market, even with its low prices, was offering more. It was a tragedy resulting from the fact that the Government, while refusing to pay high compensation and falling into the trap that had overcome Frei, refused also to move with full mass power into agriculture to prevent the slaughter of these cows. Perhaps too late the Government on April 22 issued a decree prohibiting the slaughter of pregnant cows in the whole national territory. Various teams from universities agreed to mark the pregnant cows and hand them over to the Agrarian Reform Agency, which in turn would hand them over to various *asentamientos*.

Other peasants were more emphatic in their actions. Guerrilla groups began forming in southern Chile, near the Argentinian border. They were headed by an almost mythical figure, Comandante Pepe, who reportedly helped peasants seize more than a million acres in that area by forming peasant brigades with a semblance of military discipline. In an interview with Alistair Horne, he explained his reasons:

Historically, there is bound to be a counter reaction against the Allende government, a right wing coup. And, if you see a man about to hit you in the face, you don't just stand there waiting for the blow. Of course we will defend ourselves, *hasta la muerte*. But we must organize, and we feel there isn't much time. It is likely there will be a right wing coup within the year.

When questioned about Allende's speech in Temuco demanding that the land takeovers cease, Pepe responded: "Those words do not reach us."

The Government was caught in a delicate situation, having sworn to abide by the law, yet knowing that each day it did so increased mass tensions and undercut future gains from agriculture. The popular Minister of the Interior, José Toha, a friend of Allende, cautioned peasants against takeovers and urged them to work within the legal framework. Allende, in a speech to the entire country, asked the peasants for forbearance but also recognized that their miserable living conditions—with thousands of children living totally abandoned, with hundreds of thousands undernourished, with a lack of education and a lack of culture—might deny them that patience. Characteristically, he demanded a higher sense of responsibility from those with "superior culture and education." In an interview with Saul Landau he said: "Mapuches have such a low level of cultural awareness. They have been degraded, humiliated, and destroyed over generations. And they are hungry. We cannot expect them to wait until the law expropriates land that was stolen from them decades ago. Men who are hungry often do not wait to reason."

His harshest warnings were reserved for proprietors. To a peasant gathering in Temuco, he exclaimed:

For a part of the landowners, the fear of social advances brings them first to conspiracy. These great men who gargle with the word "democracy." When they lost the election they assassinated no less than the Commander in Chief of the Chilean Army. This false class of democrats doesn't merit my respect. And I know that they have armed themselves, and I know that they have machine guns, for yesterday, in the presence of a Minister, one man of this zone said that the government would hear the voice of machine guns. Let him be careful. . . . I am here to say to the Mapuche people that they should have patience, that they should wait; the problems of a hundred years cannot be solved in one day. But I also warn the patrones that they should not pretend to use violence because they are going to be confronted with the violence that the President of the Republic can unleash against them.

The rhetoric was at a high level, but so was the social crisis. Several days later Allende moved swiftly when a landowner and his sons shot peasants who were occupying their land. The landowner and at least a dozen of his colleagues were arrested and charged with conspiracy. That caused the Christian Democrats to note angrily in *La Prensa* that violence seemed to be defined as recovering possession of one's own land rather than as seizing someone else's. It was a fascinating example of private ownership versus social change and of how Allende as opposed to Frei—that is, how Socialists as opposed to Christian Democrats—faced the problem. In liberal Chile the problem had been seen in a strictly legal way; the landowner had title and the Mapuches, armed with sticks, had indeed trespassed. In 1971 the Government viewed the same problem differently. It eschewed strict legality, concentrating on broader questions of social justice. There was strong evidence that the area in question had been legally "stolen" from Indian communities some thirty years before. In addition, the land itself had not been worked very well and was not socially productive. The landowner himself lived far away from it, traveling to the farm only during the pleasant summer months to oversee operations and vacation. Finally, it was feared that the wounding of a Mapuche might be the spark that could set off a civil war in the province, causing a military coup or at least a substantially lower harvest.

Bureaucracy and Paternalism

It was not only the law that caused the new Government problems in the rural sector. There was also the problem of bureaucracy and its accompanying disease, paternalism.

We must remember that shortly before leaving office the Christian Democrats had passed a law stating that bureaucrats could not be relieved of office except for gross mishandling of their jobs. We must also keep in mind that the entire agrarian reform bureaucracy had been created under the Christian Democrats.

Bureaucracy is a social disease in Chile, just as it is in much of the rest of Latin America. Jokes abound about how long it takes to do the simplest task—scurrying from office to office, getting the proper number of forms and the proper stamps applied to each one. Chileans have a special word, *tramitar,* which in rough translation means to delay or postpone by going through red tape. Although the agricultural bureaucracy was the most important, it is necessary to understand, as Chonchol did, that agrarian reform is much more than mere distribution of land. Credit structures must be reorganized, which means control over banking institutions. Buying cooperatives must be established, distribution organizations created, farm machinery disbursed, irrigation projects begun, and so on, and they all have to be tackled at the same time. A peasant living on his own farm starves just as quickly as one living on a master's farm unless he has the proper equipment, a market for his goods, and a guaranteed loan at low interest. Since tractors and seed and fertilizer must be imported, draining precious foreign exchange, or must be produced at home, causing a restructuring of the industrial sector, political decisions must be made. Agrarian reform touches everyone and everything. Other bureaucracies are touched, other vested interests are trespassed.

Bureaucracy means, psychologically, paternalism—the belief that employees in offices far from the source of discontent know far better than those who are discontented what needs to be done and how it needs to be done. Bureaucracy means order; its gods are law and reason, forms and rules. It is a difficult thing to have when one wants revolution. But in Chile the bureaucracy was especially difficult because it was coupled with the peasants' own tradition of paternalism, fashioned out of decades of listening to well-educated and powerful patrones and lacking any education or leadership of their own. For generations the Mapuches had been taught to respect the words of the patrones and not to respect the words of their brothers. It was a habit difficult to break. I remember Fidel Castro explaining in a speech the difficulty that he had after the Cuban revolution when he walked into the sugar mills and jubilantly declared to the workers that now the mills would be theirs, that now they could run their own lives and control their own workplaces. The workers, Fidel said, responded reluctantly, saying: "What do we know about running a factory? Why do we want all the responsibilities and problems of the boss?" It was a human reaction, and one that would occur in Chile again and again in agriculture as well as in the factories.

The problem of bureaucracy was recognized very early in the new regime. As socialists who not only believed in Marx and Lenin but had actually read their works, the new Government officials remembered and respected the words that Lenin had written almost fifty years before:

The complete history of bourgeois parliamentary countries shows that a change in ministers signifies very little, because the true work of administration is in the hands of an enormous army of functionaries. This army, nevertheless, is totally saturated with an anti-democratic spirit, is connected by millions and millions of threads with the large landowners and the bourgeoisie and is dependent on them. This army is surrounded by an atmosphere of bourgeois relations. It breathes only through that atmosphere. It cannot think, feel, or work in another manner than the old way.[14]

The Government now tried to resolve the dilemma by bypassing the old bureaucracy and creating a new one, refusing to consult with old officials. Thus, in early January, as the storm of peasant unrest raged in Cautín Province, Chonchol moved his offices there. He created buying centers for wood from small producers, announced the creation of proposed state farms (the first one to equal thirty-three thousand acres), and within a few weeks had moved to expropriate over two hundred farms.

On another level the Socialists tried to establish a shadow bureaucracy. They established the National Peasant Council, which has a role in such matters as agricultural planning, planned expropriations, politics of prices, credits, taxes, and so on. The council makes suggestions and criticisms to the Minister of Agriculture and acts as an intermediary between peasants and Government. The Minister of Agriculture is supposed to inform them monthly of measures adopted. Probably the most important aspect of this council is its representativeness. Of the twelve members, there are two designated by El Triunfo Campesino de Chile, two by Ranquil, and two by Libertad (all peasant federations); two by Eduardo Frei; two by the National Federation of Peasant Cooperatives; and two by small landowners. The representatives remain in office for two years, receive no remuneration, and act by the mandate of their respective organizations, which can recall them at any time. The President of the National Peasant Council is elected from among the members and holds office for one year, with the office rotating among members.

Before issuing opinions, the National Peasant Council must consult with the provincial councils that are established on the same basis. Two representatives of the provincial peasant federations that are recognized by law are given seats on the provincial council. A representative is also designated by the Minister of Agriculture. The provincial councils act as vehicles of information to the National Peasant Council.

Below these are the *comuna* councils, the *comuna*

being the basic election district in Chile. These groups inform and present arguments before the provincial council. They are made up of all the existing peasant organizations and those who are representatives. The Minister of Agriculture also appoints a representative on the *comuna* council.

Every six months, or at any time it is considered desirable, there is a national peasant assembly. This assembly is composed of all the members of the National Peasant Council and representatives of each provincial organization that forms part of the provincial councils.

It is a sound democratic structure and seems to be working fairly well. In the beginning there were complaints from within the Government about left-wing federations trying to keep out Christian Democrat organizations, but this seems to have been resolved.

The attitudes of the peasants varied. There were those in the hills with Comandante Pepe. Others were functionaries, working for or against Chonchol in the Government. Others worked on their farms, aware of but not yet strong enough to participate in the changes that were taking place all around them. Others, especially those who held small plots of land, were afraid the leftists would come and take their land away, forcing them to work on state-owned farms.

The Government was worried only about passivity. David Baytleman, vice president in charge of agrarian reform, one day traveled to a small town outside Temuco to speak with the Mapuches. They met in an old church in the middle of the poor village. He spoke in Spanish, knowing few Mapuche words, and urged their active participation. "You will have to struggle, to organize, and demand every concession." The words echoed Frei's *Promocion Popular*. Agrarian reform, according to the law, is a slow, cumbersome process. Titles have to be reviewed, deeds researched. Many farms have already been divided and subdivided in an effort to avoid cutoff requirements under the law, making the process even more difficult.

The Mapuches listened and applauded politely when he finished. There were questions, and then it was over. He stood to one side, and as the audience dispersed, one by one they came up to him with a personal problem—a hangover from other times and other patrones. One man shuffled forward with his peculiar problem. "My wife is a *huinca* and I am a Mapuche. The Mapuches in the area, in the *comuna* council, voted to take her father's farm from him. He is *huinca,* her mother is Mapuche. I don't have anything against her father but I cannot do anything to stop the council. But she won't sleep with me now. What can I do?" Baytleman muttered some sympathetic nonsense and passed on to the next person.

However, not all peasants are so well mannered in front of government officials. Arriving in Lautaro to a huge banner that declared: "Bread, Land, and Socialism," Jacques Chonchol read off a list of farms to be expropriated, but several of the currently occupied farms were not among them. The peasants angrily reminded him: "We know the land backwards and forwards and we want to decide ourselves what farms are going to be expropriated."

That this confrontation should occur with Jacques Chonchol is indicative of how a revolution can turn on its own. Honest, respected for his consistent political positions on agrarian reform issues by friend and foe alike, Jacques Chonchol is saddled with an agrarian reform law not to his liking and with a position as Minister that tempers what he can do. On the one hand there is the vibrant complaint of the peasant who asks: "And until when, *compañero,* are they going to talk to us of the law? Law which has served for nothing more than to rob us, so that we have people starving, no school for the children, while the rich get richer and gain more lands." On the other is the editorial of *El*

Diario Austral of Temuco, which welcomes his arrival with these words:

> Mr. Chonchol is to private property what a tiger of the jungle is to the gazelle. Since he was designated Minister of Agriculture the proprietors of land lost all hope of working quietly. Mr. Chonchol was a Christian Democrat, today he is a MAPUcista . . . and with respect to political philosophy he is Marxist-Leninist. He is not a man who changes. More than a politician he is a man obsessed, because he considers the circle of democracy in man's history closed. If there weren't a law of agrarian reform, Mr. Chonchol would be the affliction of the traditional agriculturalists, and he would erase them shortly.

In the fall of 1971 Chonchol was the man in the middle. With all his honesty, he had to learn to lie. One day he would state that he had never seen Pepe and doubted that the man was anything but a rumor and a myth, and the next day Pepe would reveal that previously they had indeed been conversing. Chonchol proclaimed rural tranquillity even as takeovers multiplied. He prophesied increased production figures as landowners burned their harvest and slaughtered their pregnant cattle and as untutored peasants participated in the administration of huge state farms. Many during this period said that he was deep into the twilight zone between law and extralegal means—that, having control of credits and loans, he was actually dispensing money to illegally seized farms while urging such takeovers to stop.

Chonchol is perhaps the one white man the Indians might trust. But the issue of race is becoming subordinate to the issue of control. The Mapuches are becoming more and more sophisticated as they cast off generations of ideological burdens, and they now look to the actions of even their fellows with caution and suspicion. Daniel Colompil, Director of Indian Affairs, was questioned by one of the peasants at a meeting that fall. "Until now," the peasant cried, "Mapuche functionaries have been the ones responsible for the robberies. From now on the Mapuche people are not going to suffer further. Therefore we have to be on top of them. We are the leaders. These things must be settled clearly, from the first moment." He was applauded by others attending the small meeting. But one Mapuche bureaucrat exclaimed: "I don't understand your lack of confidence, when we have left the comforts of Santiago and are losing our vacations here." There was a heavy silence which lasted several seconds. Then, according to one eye-witness, a man rose and said without rancor: "All right, that is your business. If you want to go, go. In any case, the agrarian reform is going to be made by us."

A difficult situation. Add to it the bitterness of decades of indifference and exploitation on the part of local and national power structures and the result is a powder keg. When the veil of oppression lifted, the people who had been either terrified or just too passive to speak out in 1965 were willing to be angry over past deeds. And there were many lurid stories. One was of a farm of some 1,000 acres, situated beside an Indian community where 120 adults and 40 children lived on 150 acres. These Mapuches had neither credits nor technical assistance. As one observer wrote:

They had a major road a mile away but the owner of the farm wouldn't permit them to use it and they had to go four miles farther to leave. A short time ago Luisa Milla Montuy and her daughter, Flor Mari, fifteen years old, spent seven months in jail, accused of stealing a horse, a charge which was never proved. While they were prisoners, and while the husband was in Los Angeles, the proprietors stole the hens and tools of the house of Luisa Milla. Before the agrarian reform law this man gave work to the Indians; afterward he alleged that the Government would take care of them, and left them totally unemployed.

Another group told of their efforts to take their labor dispute before courts, officials, and INDAP, only to be notified five years later that they had to leave the farm. Forsaking justice that they considered based on class, not on morality, they seized the lands which had lain dormant for five years. Their demands were minimal: authorization to construct good housing to replace the shacks that were there, conversion of the patron's house into a school, a teacher for that school, and materials with which to build and maintain a medical clinic.

The stories go on and on, one blending into another in a litany of outrages. One of the peasants succinctly responded to the myth of the effectiveness of new legislation: "When the workers of the farm were not organized, they never gained any type of readjustment of salaries or privileges." On one farm, Agua Fria, the peasants told this story:

Work was done as a form of slavery, beginning very early, near dawn, and ending when the sun went down, an average of fifteen hours. All the animals were raised by the people, by obligation, and had to be sold to the patrones at the price they specified. No one was permitted to read the newspapers or listen to the radio, much less have a watch, because the only time that mattered was theirs. . . . When the patrones believed they saw disobedience on the part of the workers, they shut them in a room and punished them severely. . . . The payment of the social security book was never done on time, sometimes being more than six years in arrears. . . . Salary was paid twice a year.

As the peasants gained in awareness and organization, as stories of takeovers spread throughout Chile, the new radical stance threatened liberals who had been working to spread this very independence in rural Chile. One such case involved a small radio station set up by a religious order in southern Chile. It was called La Voz de la Costa, and had been established by the Catholic Church as part of a program to bring information to and communicate with the peasants in that area. The explicit purpose of the station was to raise consciousness and awareness. Three years after its creation, the peasants moved in, led and encouraged by the students of the local branch of the University of Chile, and demanded participation in broadcasts and programming. Violence resulted, with the peasants themselves divided over the issue. One day a group of peasants would occupy the station to support participatory demands; the next day an opposition group would do the same.

The views of the people involved in the dispute are varied but illuminating. One of these people was a journalist who had been fired because his broadcasts had become more and more Marxist and he had refused to reveal their contents beforehand to his superiors for approval. The journalist, Francisco Curilen, explained the situation this way:

I am not going to deny the constructive labor of the radio station. But here there is a process that cannot be stopped. The proposed goals have been reached, but one must push forward. . . . We have been doing our job at the radio station in accordance with the principles proposed by the ideologue Freire, and we believe, if we are faithful to the thought of that philosophy of development, that we cannot awaken the peasant without accepting him when he is awake. We are criticizing the new era of the radio in that the leadership has been taking an attitude that they say is Christian and that, nevertheless, pretends to castrate the liberation of the peasantry. It appears to me that this attitude is generalized and permanent among Catholic sectors. In the case of the radio one gets the impression that the Council of the Foundation knows everything. . . . It is true that the missionaries have a broad knowledge of the people and the problems of the zone. But this does not excuse that in the direction of the station there should not also be effective representation by the peasantry. As a result the radio should not be only for the peasants, but rather should be made by the peasants. They have preached enough with words, now one must pass on to actions.

According to another man, "the radio has played with fire and now it doesn't know how to dominate the spirits that it has conjured up."

The director of the station disagreed. He acknowledged that the radio had been a force for change and that it had played with fire and said that he hoped the fires would burn brighter. But, he added, "The spirits that we cannot dominate aren't the spirits of the *campesinos,* but rather those of the agitators that use peasants for other ends. It appears that not even the Government can control them. They are people of the extreme Left that are harming seriously the program of the present Government and, as a result, are destroying the work of the radio station." When questioned directly about peasant participation, his answer was classic.

In the first place I should assert that the proposed participation in that document of 32 pages is only a screen that hides the true position of the group. Here there is the manifest desire to take over the radio transmitter and give it a new direction of thought. Besides, we don't believe that the thinking elaborated by the occupants of the radio station would have been elaborated by the real peasants. Now, with respect to real participation, there should be as much in the personnel of the radio station as there are among the auxiliaries of the Radio Schools. Around 120 auxiliaries are peasants. But in all this there is the need for organic development. We would be very pleased if, after two and a half years of work, in a zone of total abandonment and neglect, the peasant were in a condition to tell us: "We want to form part of the direction of the radio." This we would consider a great triumph.

The leadership and founders of the station say that they welcome participation but that they think the thrust for participation at present comes from outside agents, not true peasants. Why? Because the argument of participation is only a cover for the real objective—a change in the policy of the station, its programming, its line of thought.

As the peasants become more pressing in their demands and more radical in their talk, the question of private property becomes more important. I remember a dialogue between the Minister of Lands, Humberto Martones, and Alfonso Podlech, a lawyer for the Agricultural Association during a meeting with farmers. It occurred the week before Christmas 1970. Podlech, who weeks earlier had said that Mapuches were "not competent to be farmers" began by decrying the recent takeovers of farms. Martones responded by saying that hunger is a very strong motivating force and that he had seen hunger on his visits to farms. The farm owners told him that on one of the farms the people killed a cow, so they couldn't be that hungry. It was similar to a story on the front page of *El Mercurio,* which told of a prize-winning bull being killed and eaten by the peasants. The story conveyed a deep contempt for people who could not look ahead to see that they should not eat the goose that was producing more geese. Martones said angrily, repeating himself, that peasants have tremendous difficulties postponing physical needs for future returns. Podlech then gave the eternal response to accusations of social misery: "But Minister, you can't solve social problems by weakening the law concerning the private property of people. You cannot."

Interestingly enough, although there has been much panic in rural Chile, the goals of the agrarian reform program, at least in terms of farms to be expropriated, are quite modest. Of 250,000 agricultural properties in Chile, some 1,200 had been expropriated under Frei by 1970. Under Allende, 4,000 more expropriations are promised by the end of 1973. The other 245,000 properties are to remain safe, at least if the organized peasantry leaves them alone.

By the winter of 1971 much progress had been made in rural Chile. The agrarian reform program was almost completed, in terms of actual expropriation. Bottlenecks in credits and distribution were still being worked out. The official figures for 1971 show that production increased about 5.1 percent, although most people think that the figures are wrong and that it has probably decreased a small amount. But there is far to go, and the complaints about the slowness of the bureaucratic and legalistic process are gaining volume. Roberto Moreno, regional leader of MCR, had said in the summer of 1970: "It is not only a question of organizing the peasantry. The question is to mobilize, to make aware, to win over the peasantry to a revolutionary political attitude. Here there are two possibilities: it can convert itself into a bureaucracy, and therefore lose the real direction of the masses or, better yet, it can have a momentum tied (really tied) to the bases, which will take charge of the productive tasks." Months later, at the National Conference of the Confederation of Peasants and Indians (Ranquil), the rural laborers displayed their frustration, impatience, and anger. President of the Peasant Federation of Talca, De La Fuente, explained:

. . . apart from these *momios* that sabotage production, there is the problem, which is the responsibility of our Government and ourselves, that we are drowning in bureaucratism. We have, for example, the organizations of agriculture, those that affect us directly. . . . We know that they are expropriating farms by listening to the *momios* and listening to the desires of the peasants. We know how the functionaries of agriculture distort and subvert the policy of the Popular Unity coalition with respect to agrarian reform. We know about the delay of credits, the delay of seeds for the *compañeros* in the *asentamientos*. . . . We know that the *compañeros* of the countryside see the attitude of these functionaries and that it confuses them; that they are losing confidence in our Government . . . .

Another rural worker, Armando Baez, from a union in southern Valdivia, explained that the process of delays in bureaucratic channels had possibly increased with regard to social security payments. Another speaker urged the workers to get together and throw out the bureaucrats with the wrong sentiments, to tell them that "if you don't fulfill your responsibilities, it will not be the Government of the Republic that will dismiss you, but rather the organized workers who will tell you that you are not serving the people's cause, and that we—the workers, your *compañeros,* our organization—are going to ask them to resign from their posts and give them to persons who will fight for the cause." At the time, the police were beginning to be called into local labor disputes once again, and both MIR and MCR publicly decried this new attitude.

Everyone made a clear distinction between local officialdom and the national Government. And everyone kept the faith with Allende, the captain. Baez explained:

I have no direct or indirect intention of making the government responsible. I have faith and I have respect for *compañero* Allende; I have faith and I believe that *compañero* Allende has a strong disposition to govern for the people, to govern for the weakest, to govern for the workers and for their children and their wives, but there is a group of functionaries that appear hidden in a secure niche, that have appeared recently inside the Popular Unity coalition and have been placed in key posts in the provinces, especially in the provinces of the south, as is occurring in Valdivia.

But by the end of the first year, there were severe splits among the peasants. Some were afraid of the declarations of the MIRistas who were trying to get the minimum acreage that would exempt farms from expropriation reduced from two hundred acres to one hundred acres. Although this reduction would not affect the majority of those working or living on the land, it scared many small landholders. Others were expecting a revolution overnight and were disappointed that heaven had not yet arrived. Some blamed the bureaucrats, others the Government itself. Some blamed politicians in general, others just those in positions of power.

Yet the progress to date has been substantial. By the end of 1973 the agrarian reform program will be completed with respect to its expropriation stage. The reorientation of credit and the redistribution of wealth and power in the hands of the peasants themselves has effected an enormous revolution in agriculture, a revolution that cannot be turned backwards no matter what may happen at the national level.

7

Justice

One can tell the level of civilization of a society by visiting its jails.

—Mark Twain

Those prisons in which the major part of Chile's prisoners are located are antiquated, when not dilapidated, with a prison population that at times more than triples the original capacity; deprived of the most elemental means of hygiene and sanitation, the prisoners live stacked together in degrading misery, accepting a promiscuity that prevents all re-education plans and makes the prisoners regress morally until they reach incredible levels—incredible, that is, for those who do not see it occur.

—Report of the Chilean Institute of Penal Sciences, 1966

Chilean prisons reflect the society's disdain for all those convicted of transgressing its mores and customs. Julio Pena Nunez, a lawyer and ex-director of the Prison Service,

213

reports: "Around 20 percent of penitentiary construction is of adobe, 35 percent is of wood, 20 percent of brick, and only 25 percent of concrete." In 1968 the Minister of Justice stated that 54.6 percent of the prisons were in advanced states of dilapidation and that only a little less than one-fourth of all construction could be described as in an acceptable state.

Rehabilitation was a laughable proposition, even by 1970. Only 2 percent of the prison population had the possibility of working while in prison, and often that work was only busywork, contributing nothing to the national economy and contributing next to nothing to the training of the prisoner in any skill or craft that would allow him or her to gain employment upon leaving. The Prison Service had only one psychiatrist and four psychologists for a penal population of more than twelve thousand.[1]

Many people in Chilean prisons really don't need incarceration. Prison sentences are too often given for the most trivial crimes. Director of Criminology Marco Aurelio Gonzalez has said: "In Chile the only penalty is deprivation of liberty. Today in the whole world there is a tendency to diversify the penalties. In Holland 90 percent of the sanctions are fines. In the U.S. 60 percent of the convicted comply with their sentences outside of prison thanks to the system called 'probation'. . . ." This flexibility does not exist in Chile. In fact, the reliance on prisons often leads to ridiculous situations. I recall a day when I was eating in the U.S.-owned Savoy Restaurant in downtown Santiago. My host, a Chilean lawyer, rapidly wrote out a check to the waiter and rose to leave. I mentioned casually that there must be a very low crime rate in Chile, for to do that in the United States one would have to have a credit card or some other means of identification to show. He laughed and explained that the trust stems from strong sanctions; in Chile a bad check leads directly to jail and therefore there are relatively few of them. Astonished, I said that that smacked of debtor's prison, something long since abolished even in the most capitalist of countries. I asked how an imprisoned person could pay off his debts. He admitted that once closed, the circle was extremely difficult to break.

But prison is only the last link in the chain of justice that begins with the enactment of new laws, with the codification of a way of life. In a practical sense, justice begins with the policeman on the corner, the sanctions of the community and neighborhood, and the court of law. When, as in Chile, the outlaws come to power—those who had started their lives by organizing among the lower classes and who had often themselves been the objects of repressive legislation and jail sentences—there should be no surprise that the entire concept of justice and its application should be changed. This is especially true when the new-comers to governmental power view justice as stemming from the economic conditions of the society. Take the man who is forced to steal because he is hungry, is caught because he is too malnourished to plan the robbery well, and is tried before a judge who is of another class and speaks another language (Latin) and defended by a lawyer who often looks askance at a defendant who does not have enough money to pay a regular attorney. To a socialist, this man is a victim, not of justice, but of *capitalist* justice. When Allende took office, some of his first measures were meant to alter this procedure.

Allende's first step was to disband the hated Grupo Movil. Next he requested all policemen to use persuasion rather than force. He initiated a six-year plan for prisons, converting existing workshops into regular businesses which produce goods salable to a wide range of consumers. He planned for more prisons. Minors, who had previously been imprisoned with adult offenders, were to be housed separately. Probation was to be permitted for sentences of under three years (at this time, probation was possible only for misdemeanors). Rural penal colonies were to come under the agrarian reform program and hopefully would be eliminated.

Perhaps the most dramatic step taken by the Government in its early days was the decision to lower all prison sentences. Those who had already served twenty years or more were freed and those sentenced to less than twenty years had their sentences reduced proportionately. It was concrete evidence that Salvador Allende, among others, believes that a prisoner is but the product of his society, that in a capitalist society the jails are full of those who commit crimes because of lack of employment, lack of education, hunger, and above all, lack of money to buy high-powered legal talent. As Allende has said: "Many times the delinquent man is pushed to commit the crime through the economic and social reality which condemns him."

The socialists, like the capitalists before them, had a dual system of justice, but it was almost the opposite of the capitalist system. Under a capitalist system the rich and well educated tend to be favored and the illiterate and hungry to be judged more severely, especially because the latter are the ones most likely to commit crimes of physical violence. Under a socialist system the rich and well educated are the ones judged more severely, because it is felt they have a higher duty to know and honor a law written in their language by people of their own class. Examples of this abounded in the first six months of the new Administration. When the peasants were organizing to take over farms in southern Chile, Allende cautioned them to go slowly, to wait until the Government's bureaucracy could sift through the data and divide up the farms. But he well understood the peasants' difficulty with restraint after having waited so long. He understood the grim social and economic forces that drove the Mapuches to bend or break the law. Thus he was lenient with them but tough with the landowners, who did not suffer under the same pressures as the peasants and who knew well in advance that they would have to give up rural dominance. In one major speech Allende declared: "If we demand of the Mapuche, of the native, of the workers of the earth, that they respect the law, we will demand implacably that those who have a greater obligation because of their culture and education should respect it." Law is a flexible instrument and those better equipped to understand both its substance and its tradition should be more responsible for obeying its directives.

When the Government began distributing free milk to children and pregnant and nursing mothers, it used this dual system of justice once more. Allende knew that the lower-class mothers had often bought spoiled milk and not known how to sterilize it, and therefore associated milk with worms and death, since that was what putrid milk had brought to their babies. Thus he anticipated that a mother who got free milk might very well turn around and sell it to the ice cream man to buy more filling food for her children. Allende understood and treated her accordingly. The mother was to be dealt with by her community, who would teach her about milk preparation and sanction her if she did not give milk to her children in a sanitary and proper way. Shame would be the motivating force. However, as for the businessman who would buy the milk from such a mother, the Government would step in and close his business, either temporarily or permanently. The poor, under pressures of the most basic drives of hunger, warmth, and security, were to be treated compassionately and educationally for their crimes; the businessmen with their level of education and culture, driven by what socialists consider the most base of all human desires—the desire for profit—were to be dealt with much more harshly.

Since the lower classes generally steal by means of physical violence, whereas the upper classes can steal through financial manipulations, it is usually the lower classes who get the longer jail sentences. The socialists in Chile, like their counterparts throughout Latin America, have a concept of violence that goes beyond physical manifestations. They speak of institutionalized violence, of the violence of the system against the oppressed, of the violence of the powerful against the powerless, which forces the poor to pick up the gun. Physical violence is placed within its social and economic context. Today government leaders in Chile look to the motivation and goals for the violence. Thus, in his message to the nation in early 1971, Allende gave amnesty to the workers of SABA and the young MIRistas who had been jailed by Frei for robbing supermarkets and banks and explained why:

> I desire tranquillity and social peace; I believe that those youthful militants of the Left, with whom we have had tactical differences, acted erroneously, but out of a higher desire—a desire for social transformation that condemns them because they attacked some banks. They did that, that is certain, and I know it, but they did not hurt anyone, and did not assassinate anyone; they did not spill the blood of any *carabinero* or of even one employee or one worker; they risked their lives for an ideal.

Allende did not agree with their strategy but he understood the basically selfless motivation for the robberies. Robbing banks under a capitalist system in which 2 percent of the creditors get over 50 percent of the bank credit, in which the banks invest money in foreign corporations and are usually controlled by familial groupings that use the money for personal aggrandizement, is not considered a crime worth jailing people for. When the expropriated bank's money is given to the slums or is used to form peoples' militias, the robberies become, in effect, socially beneficial acts.

But there is another sort of bank robbery that is quasilegal, on the very borders of legality, and it was to this sort that Allende turned directly after discussing the release of the MIRistas:

On the other hand, others have assaulted the bank vaults with the tranquillity of delinquents who know that they are going to remain immune from punishment, and the day that the list of those who have taken credits without right from the State Bank is published, the country is going to understand the difference there is between some and others.

For those people there would be indictments and full prosecution. Robbing a bank and distributing the proceeds to the poor was deemed a much less heinous crime than robbing a country of millions of dollars at a critical period after a socialist victory. Although one robbery was committed at the point of a gun and the other through complex financial arrangements, Allende called the one violent and criminal and the other misdirected and idealistic.

The new Administration not only moved to change existing legal semantics, but also explored the possibilities of demystifying the entire court process. It wanted reforms in the Organic Code, proposing age limits of sixty for Ministers of appeals courts and of sixty-five for Ministers of the Supreme Court. (This proposal caused great laughter in the ranks of the Opposition, whose members were quick to point out that under that age criterion the Minister of Justice himself would have to retire from his post.) The almost holy terms *Su Excelencia, Su Excelentisimo,* and *Su Senoria,* all more or less equivalent to "Your Honor," were to be discontinued in order to transform the court process from one in which mortals speak through interpreters to gods to one in which they speak to fellow human beings in words they can understand in order to defend themselves.

The Government proposed not only changing the language of the courts, but also radically altering their structure. Thus the concept of neighborhood courts was debated. Such courts, it was proposed, would judge neighborhood residents on offenses not usually covered by the ordinary body of criminal law. They would be established in every district of the country. They would be composed of three titular judges and three substitutes. One of the three titular judges would be designated by the Governor of the Province and the other two would be chosen by the community through free elections. The prerequisites for a judgeship would be that the person be at least eighteen years old, a resident of that district, and a participant in some neighborhood organization (such as the Neighborhood Center or a Mothers Center), which supposedly would indicate at least a minimal level of community involvement. Public officials such as senators or deputies would not be eligible. Also, those who had been imprisoned or who were physically handicapped (mute or deaf, for example) could not serve.

These courts would have jurisdiction over minor crimes such as intrafamily squabbles, nonsupport of dependents, and public drunkenness. Trials would be public. Judges would be assisted by advisers who could be either lawyers or students of law. The penalties to be meted out would range from public censure to forced labor or fines to jail. Forced labor would include work on community projects such as cleaning the streets, standing guard, and arranging gardens. Small fines could be imposed, but only in relation to the amount of money the person earned. If a jail sentence or fine were imposed, the court would have to consult ordinary tribunals and the defendant would have the right to appeal the sentence to regular courts.

As soon as these courts were proposed, the Opposition stepped in to do battle. Christian Democrats joined hands with the right-wing parties to declare the measures unconstitutional, especially because the judges would not have to be trained in the study of law. They pointed out that such courts could quickly degenerate into political bodies, possibly kangaroo courts, where jealousy, envy, and anger would intervene between reason and sentencing. Government supporters answered that Opposition adherents lacked faith in the common people, that the new courts would certainly ensure a trial by one's peers and would give the rich no advantage over the poor, and that the process of justice would be rapid. According to the Undersecretary of Justice, Viera Gallo: "The Peace Tribunals will have quick and intense proceedings, a jurisdiction of more or less two hundred persons, and they will coexist parallel with agricultural communities, which, it is hoped, will be substituted for the present jails."

Since the Opposition had a majority in Congress, Allende was forced to withdraw the measure from the legislature in the face of certain defeat. It constituted the first major defeat for a Government reform proposal. Not surprisingly, it was also the first major attack on the institutional integrity of Chilean society.

Although widespread popular tribunals were not implemented, in various areas of Chile such courts were arising spontaneously, as a result of either outside intervention by MIRistas or internal needs for some form of justice when outside legal authorities were absent. The shantytowns around Santiago are usually without police, high in crime, and incredibly high in the incidence of drunkenness. This combination of lawlessness and drunkenness was the point of attack usually used by MIRistas entering a community for the first time. They would march in (in at least one case with machine guns strapped over their shoulders) and paternalistically impose prohibition on both the consumption and sale of alcohol. A MIRista told me that the results of these actions were often surprisingly good. The first allies were the housewives, who no longer had husbands coming home drunk, yelling and beating the children, and spending hard-earned money on liquor. Afterwards, the villages often set up their own security systems, consisting of crude wire tightly wound around poles on the boundaries of the community and watchmen and watchwomen guarding the entrances, checking on strangers and loiterers. As community consciousness increased, courts were often established.

A recent study of such courts[2] drew some interesting conclusions. In most *poblaciones,* especially where there had been no struggles involved in gaining the land because the Government had handed over finished houses to the people, there was a passive attitude. In those communities the residents felt that tribunals, lawyers, and policemen had nothing to do with them and therefore did not go to such people for protection. Rather, a resident was seen as inclined to approach some paternalistic figure, someone to whom he "attributes some degree of influence useful in solving a particular problem."

In other, more active, *poblaciones* the external system of justice was often merely supplemented by an internal one. Various methods were employed. Sometimes vigilante groups would be established, but only as wings of the central police bureau. Sometimes the security system was devised and prepared by the Investigative Service, with the slum dwellers acting as deputized citizens. Apprehended persons were handed over to the police.

In other slums residents tried to act as mediators, to resolve differences by talking them through. What happened in these instances was interesting. A dual set of standards usually prevailed, separating the community from the society as a whole. Thus, for example, criminal activity would not be condoned within the community but would be rationalized when it took place outside because of the lower income level of the community itself.

Also, according to this study, a growing number of *poblaciones* often had to cooperate closely with each other in order to gain turf with which in turn to demand housing. They established new and autonomous groupings which attempted not merely to extend or supplement the existing judicial system, but to replace it altogether. Through struggle for their land in the face of Government opposition, these people tried to create an entirely new judicial system within the newly taken over pieces of turf. As the authors of the study put it:

The generation of their own institutions destined to exercise judicial functions, just like other forms of organization, emphasize overall the necessity of generating a new mentality in the community, a mentality that gradually would eliminate individualism, isolation, and negative competition as forms of living together, and would replace them with others which support egalitarian communication, the increase of democracy between leaders and the led, and cooperative and educative ability.

One of the members of such a community gave this description of the process:

We share the pains and also the joys. The percentage of companions who really participate is quite considerable. This situation could only be achieved through our plans, through our political analysis. . . . This situation permits this to be a type of school for the *compañero*.

In this type of community the exemplary resident is not the one who best obeys the law or who earns the most. Rather:

The concept of exemplary worker still isn't well defined, but I believe that he is a person who has demonstrated a greater spirit of sacrifice toward the community, who has a greater consciousness of class . . . who has absorbed a greater consciousness of his condition . . . with respect to this class which is trying to liberate itself from all those traps that it has fallen into until becoming a type of twentieth-century slavery.

Criminal activity is redefined. In communities where there has been little cohesion, where the traditional police agencies are merely extended, the traditional laws and rules of society are carried over into internal community affairs. Acts that the society at large judges criminal are so judged within the community. In the *poblaciones* that sprang up as a result of social conflict and struggle, where more autonomous systems have evolved, new crimes are discovered. As one member explained: "One of the things that is considered a serious crime here is the lack of participation and cooperation among the dwellers, and, over all, with respect to sanitary problems." Those who are lax in controlling flies, in keeping the area clear of garbage, are viewed as indirect killers, carriers of disease, and are treated as criminals. The punishment is usually a public warning and public educative sessions.

Thus, although the Government has been unable to get most of its legislation through Congress, its refusal to interfere any more with social experimentation has resulted in an increase of such experiments, even in the area of justice described above. The lack of Government power in the sector of law and justice is revealing. The neighborhood courts proposal was withdrawn from Congress. The old Law of Checks, under which writers of bad checks could be sent to prison, was also looked into but eventually ignored. As soon as the Socialist Administration came to power, 4,000 prisoners wallowing in penal misery as a result of this law, acting on behalf of 100,000 Chileans who they said were still being processed, wrote an open letter to Allende, saying in part that the Law of Checks was an "aberration . . . written and promulgated under a capitalist regime and in defense of those interests that they [capitalist regimes] represent." They called it an anachronism in socialist Chile and asked for its repeal. However, as Allende discovered, the laws of a capitalist society couldn't be changed without also changing its economics. The Radical party, representing small businessmen, was not pleased with a proposed revision of this law, feeling that it would at best merely lead to something like the present system in the United States, where only professionals with credit cards can cash checks. The Government agreed to study a revision but left that duty to a congressional committee, in effect abdicating responsibility for the issue.

Again and again the Government discovered that it was difficult to reform halfway. It would arrest landowners only to have them freed immediately by judges operating under a system of law written by those very same landowners. The Government ordered the police to use persuasion, but the very fact of having a policeman in a slum area meant giving him discretionary power, which more often than not was misused. The most public incident showing this lack of power over the judiciary occurred early in February 1971. The Government was still sifting through the available evidence about who was involved in the assassination of René Schneider. Congressman Raul Morales Adriasola was asked to answer several questions. He refused, citing his congressional immunity. A military panel overwhelmingly supported the Government, but the Supreme Court, by a 9–2 vote (the two were Cabinet Ministers appointed by the President) overruled that decision. The country exploded. The University Student Federation published a letter declaring: "The Supreme Court, with its decision, has declared itself the greatest obstacle in the way of administering justice in Chile through legal channels." The letter was answered by the Christian Democrat youth organization, which disagreed with the correctness of the decision but felt that the Supreme Court as an institution merited respect. The Communist youth brigade Ramona Parra donned their full-length raincoats, toted buckets of paint downtown, and during the night artistically covered the walls of Santiago with pictures and slogans calling the Supreme Court a cover-up for sedition, traitors, and so forth. The Opposition then demanded of the mayor that the walls be whitewashed. They were, but not very promptly. The Lawyers' College supported the Supreme Court—again, not for its decision but for its right to make the wrong decision. One prominent lawyer with whom I spoke that day was jubilant. "You have come at an historic moment, at a precise moment. I am proud this day, proud of the impartiality of the judicial system." To him it was a reaffirmation of the Court's independence of the Government and another example of the Court's use of reason in the face of public hysteria.

The average Chilean found the whole affair inexplicable. The Commander in Chief had been murdered and Morales was to answer a few questions which now, because of some legal nitpicking, he would not have to answer. The next day *Puro Chile,* a flamboyant and popular daily newspaper that perhaps could best be described as a Marxist New York *Daily News,* called Morales a traitor. Morales went to the courts, and *Puro Chile* was punished under Chilean law by having its publication rights suspended for four days. But the next day the newspaper was still on the newsstands; only its name had been changed. On the first page, in huge block letters, the customary masthead said *"PURO CHILE,"* and underneath, in small letters, *"no salio hoy"*—"was not published today." The impish cartoon character that always graced the front page of the paper was laughing hysterically. The message was clear. There is a spirit of the law and a letter of the law. *Puro Chile,* like the Supreme Court, had abided by the letter of the law.

Although the Chilean sense of humor won that round, forestalling violent attack on the Supreme Court by simply laughing at its conduct, the whole concept of laws, police, courts, and justice in Chile today is a top-priority problem for the Allende Administration. It is difficult enough to use laws written by the rich to take away the power and wealth of that class. But to try to build an entirely new system of justice while still abiding by the old one, transforming it piecemeal, is a task that will take years. The new Government has the ideology and the will. It is a question, in the final analysis, of power—electoral, congressional, and armed.

8

Education

The development of the universities leads to the disappearance of the universities; in other words, the institution's own maximum development will lead to its disappearance.

—Fidel Castro

With the rise to power of the Christian Democrats came the belief that education was to be something more than a finishing school for the elite. The Christian Democrat technicians rose to power under the influence and with the assistance of the Alliance for Progress and during an era of increasingly sophisticated economic concepts. Above all else their party stressed modernization, with all the limitations and advantages such an attitude entails. The nationalization of society under Frei reached into all levels and all corners, from the introduction of uniform working hours to the prohibition of drinking during certain hours of the day, from the land reform program to the opening wide of Chile's borders to foreign capital. Efficiency was king. Obviously such a vision of development would stress education.

Certainly Chilean education at the time Frei took office was nothing to be proud of. To some the entire educational system seemed geared to producing failures. Leonard Gross writes:

Of a hundred Chilean children, eleven never enter school. Of the eighty-nine who do, only twenty-five finish their primary education. Of these twenty-five, six enter vocational schools, but only three of the six stay three years or more; twelve of the twenty-five enter secondary school but only three finish. Of those three, one begins work with a general education, but no real skills. Two enter a university. Of these two, one finishes.[1]

In secondary schools, if a student got a bad conduct rating he was expelled. If he failed a semester he was expelled. There was a compulsory test taken at age fourteen to see if a person had an aptitude for scientific, academic, or technical work. The test results had to be followed.

Perhaps the most glaring deficiencies were in the universities. There it was that the major thrust of the educational reform movement under the Christian Democrats took place. According to Catholic University Professor Raul Urzua, Chilean universities were "characterized by a combination of a formally strong and rigid structure of authority with a decentralization of the teaching functions which at times brings with it virtual autonomy." Universities were traditionally divided into *facultades* (colleges), and these in turn into *escuelas* (departments). The departments developed their own study plans, had their own professors, their own permanent, chaired faculty, their own installations and administration. But this administrative local autonomy was combined with a rigid, authoritarian governing body. Maximum authority rested with the Rector, who was advised by the Higher Council. In most cases university authorities were appointed from outside. The Higher Council was composed of ancient, tenured professors elected by their ancient, tenured colleagues.

The problems in the educational sector were not limited to administration, although obviously any such rigid structure would make even minor changes difficult to achieve. In addition there were the problems of underenrollment, of enrollment in disciplines irrelevant to a developing nation's needs, and of an overconcentration of educational facilities in and around Santiago.

Frei's legions dealt with underenrollment effectively and dramatically. Expenditures zoomed. In 1964 education received 12.6 percent of the budget; in 1968 it received 16.1 percent (and this when the budget in real terms increased some 72 percent). The resulting increase in classroom space and facilities led to a rapid expansion in enrollment. Chile's university population grew from 19,800 in 1957 to 56,591 in 1967—in other words, from one student for every 341 inhabitants to one for every 157 inhabitants.[2]

The second problem, that of shifting the student population from the traditional fields of law, medicine, and philosophy to the more locally vital fields of natural sciences, engineering, and teaching, was also tackled effectively. During Frei's term 80 percent of the new slots were in the latter fields. From 1957 to 1967, for example, only sixteen new places were established in the field of law, but 10,200 went to teaching. In the same period the number of those who aspired to be doctors of medicine rose by one-third, and the number of those who wanted to be doctors' aides increased more than fivefold.[3]

During the 1960s higher education, which had always been a state enterprise, changed from a capital to a national phenomenon. In 1957 90 percent of the university student population had come from universities with headquarters in Santiago or Valparaiso, the large coastal city forty miles from Santiago. Yet in 1967 one-third of the students were in the provinces; the two state universities that in 1957 had had only 20 percent of the students in the provinces now had 56 percent.[4]

As universities prospered, investigative institutes were established. It was an embarrassment to the Freistas that they had little hard data upon which to base future programs. The majority of investigative institutes in Chile even by the end of the 1960s were less than ten years old.[5] This situation made for an amazing ignorance of domestic conditions. On another level, the effects of the lack of competent research led to a distortion of national priorities, since Chilean theories, Chilean programs, and Chilean Government policy were most often based on studies and information gleaned from developed countries, the validity of which when applied to different environments had not been properly evaluated.

To accompany all the successes of the Christian Democrats in the field of education, the winds of change brought disputes that had neither been sought nor desired. The first major controversy arose over who was to vote in university elections. The Christian Democrats were against the monopolization of the Higher Council by a small clique of tenured professors. They wanted the entire faculty to have voices and votes in university governance. But this desire inevitably led to a discussion of the entire question of expanded university participation. The Christian Democrats in late 1966 led a series of meetings which concluded that students should have five of the twenty-five memberships in the Higher Council. The Communist student organization countered with a proposal that in addition to being members of the council students should participate in electing university officials. The Communists wrote at the time: "Student participation in the generation of authority is the only solid guarantee that the university politics will line up toward the goals that the Chilean people desire." The question was put to a vote in a special referendum, and the students voted against the Communist position.

But events in the last decade in Chile have shown that progressive ideas cannot long be buried, even by popular vote. In this case the very decentralization of authority within the university facilitated the crisis. The catalyst was the College of Education and Philosophy. It was by far the largest college in the University of Chile. The students on the average were from lower social levels than college students elsewhere. The faculty was paid less than colleagues in other colleges. On the whole, as one observer noted, "It is the part of the university where the institution appears less as a springboard to social ascent or vertical mobility." In late 1967 this college supported student participation in university elections. In early 1968 the idea began to be put into practice within the college. What followed was an intra-university struggle, with other colleges criticizing the move, buildings being taken over, and finally a fifty-day student strike. After that, student and staff participation in university elections became the conventional wisdom.

Although I have chosen the University of Chile as a specific example, similar reform movements were spreading throughout Chile. In most cases such movements linked off-campus issues with student activities. Although traditionally Chilean and other Latin American universities have been considered inviolable by Government authorities,* national and student politics mirror each other. All the political parties have university constituencies, and the student presidency is considered a choice plum. Politics permeates Chilean universities. I remember walking into a bathroom in the College of Economics at the University of Chile. The stench of urine and the broken stalls and overflowing toilets were familiar, but scrawled on the walls were, instead of the sexual slogans and drawings ubiquitous in North American

---

* Traditionally police were not permitted on university property. This tradition began in the early 1900s but seemed to be breaking down in the late 1960s. In Argentina, Venezuela, and Brazil universities have been invaded again and again. In Chile the tradition was broken in 1969 when Frei sent the police in to search room by room for MIRistas. But still the myth prevails.

college bathrooms, political slogans supporting and opposing the Government.

Student elections are watched very closely as predictors of national voting patterns. In the early 1950s, for example, although the Christian Democrats had only one Senate seat, they won a majority of student university presidencies. In the late 1960s the trend was leftward. Luciano Cruz Aguayo, elected head of the student body at the University of Concepcion, was later to go underground to lead an effective MIR network of cells. A Communist was elected President of the University of Chile. Leftists also gained control of the State Technical University.

Although the Christian Democrats viewed university reform movements as separate from other national reforms, some students did not share such a view. University students were especially conscious of the increasing turmoil outside the university. The arrest of the SABA workers, the rising wave of agrarian unrest, the rapid encroachment of foreign investment, the split in the Christian Democratic party—all were issues that brought home to already highly politicized student bodies the critical nature of Chilean life. It was a turbulent, confusing era. The rhetoric was heady, and political infighting was intense. Institutionally, however, little was accomplished. Universities moved toward reforming themselves at a glacial pace. In June 1969 the Movement for University Reform expressed deep misgivings about the process of reform. The group found the university community still too often looking outward, beyond Chile's borders, or inward, to petty departmental disputes, and not utilizing its skills and knowledge for the great mass of Chilean people. In a very few instances there seemed to be serious efforts at reform. At the Catholic University the Center for the Study of the National Reality, CEREN, was established, under the aegis of Jacques Chonchol. It was an attempt to establish an interdisciplinary approach to researching current Chilean conditions.

By mid-1970 Catholic University was also thinking of implementing a complicated plan for equalizing salaries. After long sessions with faculty, students, and staff the idea of economic units was proposed. Economic units were a compromise between those who wanted complete equalization and those who wanted to retain some inequality. Thus the criteria for salary included nontraditional ones such as size of family and age, but also familiar ones including degree of responsibility, amount of education, and number of degrees. Whether the plan will succeed in redistributing income within the university is an open question.

After the election the new Government immediately set out to top all previous efforts in the field of education. In some cases it was a question of quantity—more schools, more classroom furniture, and so on. In other cases it was a question of reordering priorities so that education would no longer be a class-based phenomenon. Only 5 percent of the university enrollment by 1970 came from the working classes, and the new Administration found it difficult to live with that figure. Buses were converted into temporary classrooms which traveled to the dusty *campamentos* surrounding Santiago. The Government decided to give two notebooks to each incoming student (the notebooks were to be made by prisoners as a way of integrating them into the national economy). Sixty thousand scholarships were handed out, double the number of 1970.[6] But as even the most vehement socialists discovered, changing the class nature of education was a comprehensive problem that was not easily resolved in a short time and that raised the most personal questions about policy. For example, a woman was discussing scholarships with me. She said that among her colleagues there was a division of opinion about whom to give such scholarships to. Should they be given to the most needy? Some of her colleagues thought that the most needy, who often had suffered malnutrition throughout their childhood, might have brain damage, be less intelligent and more listless than their counterparts, and therefore be a less advisable investment in the sense that what they could return to the society would be less. Given scarce resources, a choice of priorities had to be made. But others held that these children had been discriminated against once and that to pass them up a second time because of the effects of the first discrimination would mean that their plight would be forever ignored and that their upward mobility would be postponed. It was not an easy question to resolve.

Allende's Government went further than Frei's in resolving certain educational dilemmas because it saw the total transformation of the economy as its goal. For instance, under previous administrations scholarships had been available for buying books, but there had never been enough (scholarships or books). Under Frei the Minister of Education, Juan Gomez Millas, attempted to use the Editorial Juridica, a publishing house, to produce inexpensive texts for schools. His idea met active resistance by those who feared a uniformity in teaching material if such material were determined by the Government. Under Allende's Minister of Education, Mario Astorga Gutierrez, a much broader scheme was proposed, according to which a state publishing house would publish educational material as well as other things. With the nationalization of Zig-Zag this became a reality.

When Allende took office there was the fear that many private schools, especially religious ones, would have to close down. Such a fear proved unfounded, although as Astorga explained, "It is natural for there to be strict control of those establishments which receive state subsidies, because it is an investment that belongs to all Chileans. . . . Equally all the establishments in the country should be subject to the plans and programs dictated by the Ministry. If this were not done freedom of teaching, which is fully supported, would become license." This statement was not made any clearer by the fact that the costs of admission to schools had been frozen when the Government took office, a possible threat to private schools.

With respect to content there was little doubt that school libraries would stock, and required reading lists would include, more books on the Vietnam War, the Cuban revolution, and imperialism, but in general there was no clear party line on education. Mario Astorga asked for "a great national debate in which we would redefine the objectives of Chilean education." Such a debate was quickly begun, although usually actions replaced words. Some facets of universities altered their programs to fit the changing national rhetoric. CEREN, for example, decided after the election that its purpose should be one of seeking ways to effect socialism rather than merely researching what it is. Workers' education courses were established, as were short-term courses leading to paraprofessional careers. A workers' university was established in Santiago, with a strictly Marxist orientation. Eventually two extreme positions became clearly defined in the national debate. On one side were the Opposition parties in Congress. The Christian Democrats had forced Allende to sign an agreement before the election to respect the autonomy of the university, and Congress later reinforced this with a law that prohibited the Government from intervening in universities in any political way. On the other side was the Committee of Students Without a University (CESU), newly formed by MIR. This group explained its position in a long, detailed statement, noting that in 1970 49,244 students applied to Chilean universities and some 28,753 were turned away. Plans in 1971 called for an expansion of space to permit 9,000 additional students to enter, but that would leave 35,000 outside. CESU argued that the lack of space was not a technical question but a political one. Lack of space, the members believed, was "only true if we accept the current conception of a University." The organization added: "It is because the University separates theory and social practice that it has limited space. . . . It is because the University constructs 'hospital schools' instead of taking the students to learn in the public health services, that admissions into a career in medicine are limited." CESU demanded an end to the concept of the professor as an oracle of truth in favor of the concept of work teams utilizing advanced students and teaching aides as well as professors. It demanded night courses, televised classes, the creation of teaching corps, and the development of teaching activities outside the classroom.

The issue of the university's integration as an institution into the national political arena has still not been resolved. In an important election for Rector and Higher Council in June 1971 at the University of Chile, the left-wing candidates, who were asking for a politicization of the university, were defeated narrowly by the Christian Democrat candidate. But the leftists won a slight majority on the Higher Council.

On noninstitutional levels there has been more experimentation. One student from the School of Sociology at the University of Chile supported the left-wing candidate lukewarmly and only because he thought such an election would give students and workers more time to organize. Yet already in his college, where the Federation of Revolutionary Students (FER) is in the majority, an agreement to establish a workers' university was worked out with an organization representing the majority of industries in a suburb of Santiago. The proposed university would have a literacy program, an analysis of Chilean history and an analysis of the capitalist system and its productive processes. As FER explains, "This will include the role that industry plays, what the work laws are, unions and their limitations as instruments of power. Besides, we will analyze the problems of the workers, and, especially, of unemployment. All this will be done with the ultimate purpose of shedding some light for the masses on the way to reach power." FER hopes that the left-wing candidates, or the UP, will embrace such programs. But as one student explained, "In any case, we are already doing it. Besides, this type of work is almost impossible to do at the University of Chile, because of the bureaucracy. We believe that these sorts of activities are the province of student centers, in cooperation with sectors that are not administrative with some professors."

Perhaps the most broadly participatory program of student involvement was the voluntary work program. Begun under Frei, the program's summer projects in rural and slum areas of Chile greatly expanded under Allende's Administration. More than fifty thousand students participated in the works the first summer, under the guidance of Government Ministries. It was quite an experience for many. The attitude of the villagers to the influx of youthful workers was often, in the beginning, one of hostility and coolness. But as the students proved to be hard and serious workers the villagers opened up and welcomed them. Such works were a method of forming contacts between students and the most oppressed sectors of the population and also of spreading the gospel of socialism to all parts of the country. Students from Peru, Bolivia, Argentina, and Cuba came to demonstrate their solidarity with the new Chilean revolution. They were welcomed by the Government, although the Opposition loudly criticized such open politicking. International support groups for oppressed students and guerrilla groups throughout Latin America were formed. Ideas were exchanged. What the Christian Democrats had ushered in with their wide-ranging programs of expanded enrollment in the mid-1960s had expanded until the role of students and the educational system had become one of the areas in Chile with the most experimentation and the most debate.

9

Health and Medicine

The only privileged ones will be the children.
                    —Slogan of the new government

In Chile one-third of those who die each year are children. This is a slightly better than average percentage for all of Latin America, but it is far worse than in the United States, where only one out of every sixteen people die before the age of fifteen.[1] In the United States the average consumption of animal protein is 66 grams; in Chile the average is 28. In the developed countries the average daily caloric intake is around 3,600, whereas a peasant in Curico takes in only 1,895 calories per day.[2] Malnutrition affects 40 percent of all Chileans and brings with it not only high mortality rates but significant social problems. Diseases that ordinarily would be mild become deadly when the body is undernourished and has few strong defenses against disease-carrying germs. Dropout rates from school, as well as poor scholarship, can often be traced to listlessness and lack of attention stemming from an inadequate diet. Juvenile delinquency is often the result of a combination of low education and mental retardation, both caused by malnutrition.[3]

In fact, malnutrition is the first sign of social class in Chile. An adequate diet is difficult to obtain for most working-class people. In a recent study it was found that the minimum diet requirements for a family of five (according to the United Nations model in 1970) would take about 75 percent of the average Chilean worker's monthly income to purchase. Of course, the Chilean must pay not only for food, but also for transportation, clothing, rent, health care, and so on. And the situation has been getting worse. In 1965 a worker earning an average wage could buy five portions of the minimum diet daily; by 1969 he could buy only three.

In the working-class *poblacion* of José Maria Caro, 142 of every thousand children die before their first birthday. More than 40 percent of the children from three months to six years of age are undernourished and 60 percent of the school-age children have an intellectual coefficient inferior to normal. These same children at five years of age weigh twelve pounds less and are four to five inches shorter than their counterparts from upper-class districts in the same geographical area.[4] As Dr. Fernando Monckleberg, a physician who has done much research into malnutrition and its effect on the body, has observed: "Twenty-five percent of our poor children have an inferior brain size. . . . Malnutrition in the first months of life leaves irreparable brain damage, even though there is apparent recuperation, especially with respect to weight. Height and brain size don't recuperate and the intellectual coefficient remains definitely harmed. . . . Malnutrition then, produces underdevelopment, and underdevelopment produces malnutrition."

This situation was not just recently discovered in Chile. The entire health crisis has been known for many years. In 1952 the National Health Service (SNS) was established to disburse medical care and attention to those who could not afford to see private doctors. Yet by the mid-

1960s almost everybody accepted the fact of its failure. Chile had not produced enough medical personnel. In 1958, for example, there were eleven thousand nurses and matrons in Chile while in Sweden, with a comparable population, there were fifty thousand. During his 1964 campaign for the Presidency Frei pointed out that 28 percent of the babies and 41 percent of those who had died in Chile that year had lacked any kind of medical assistance. By the late 1960s, the inadequacy of the health system was recognized de facto by the creation of rival service institutions. There were separate health services for the armed forces, for those employed in the railroad industry, and for white-collar workers. Many in Chile preferred not to go to a doctor except in emergencies or to pay for medical services rather than get inadequate attention after miserably long waits in the public health service.

The inefficiency of the health system is a result of many factors. One important factor is an overconcentration of health personnel in and around Santiago. Sixty percent of all health professionals are located in metropolitan Santiago, whereas only 6 percent are located in towns with populations of less than twenty thousand—towns that constitute 50 percent of Chile's total population. No doctor wants to work where there are no facilities, few comforts, and little public entertainment. In fact, there are those who use the same argument to escape working even in Santiago. Thousands of doctors emigrate to other countries, especially to the United States, and each such emigrant costs the country of Chile the huge amount of money that was allocated for his training and education.

Another complicating factor is the swollen and bloated bureaucracy that has sprung up in the health system. In 1967 6,487 medical professionals (doctors, dentists, pharmacists, and so forth) worked for SNS, whereas administrative employees (health inspectors, chauffeurs, administrators, cooks, and so forth) numbered 40,656.[5]

This bureaucracy has been the cause not only of a shortage of trained personnel, but in many instances of inefficiencies that have cost lives. Stories of such inefficiency abound. Perhaps the finest example is the Supply Center for Medical Equipment and Medicines, located in Santiago. If a doctor needs anything from this center he must fill out the proper forms in triplicate and await his order. Dr. Francisco Villegas, ex-Minister of Public Health, notes: "It is a popular saying that the best way of getting equipment or instruments in our National Health Service is to visit the Supply Center and take them personally, a situation which gives those living in Santiago a decided advantage." Another physician with whom I spoke told of a medical colleague who "asked for a radium machine which was needed for a series of upcoming cases. The letter was sent, and there was no response. Then the letters were sent once more, with the proper stamps, proper signatures, in triplicate, and word finally came back explaining that there were three machines available, but that they were lined up against the back wall in the basement, and thousands of containers of powdered milk were piled in front of them. It would be at least three months before they could be reached." In still another case (the examples are myriad), a doctor asked for penicillin and the Center replied that they had none but would be getting a supply soon. Needing it right away, the desperate physician went downtown, made friends with the ambulance driver, and got all the penicillin he could carry.

Doctors often respond to allegations that they are not working as hard as they might be with a reminder that they get paid very little and only every other month. It is by no means rare for their paychecks to fall behind by three months or more. The doctors are required by law to work a certain number of hours each week in a state hospital, but the law is openly violated. One physician explained: "Doctors like to work in the hospitals because there are no time cards." Hospital services are offered on an irrational basis, only part-time. In one instance a room for surgical operations was open only from 8 A.M. to 3 P.M. three days a week and from 8 A.M. to 12 noon three days a week. Thousands were turned away as a result.

The almost incredible misallocation of resources in Chile's health system has contributed to a mortality rate higher than in most other Latin American countries, even though, ironically, the system is relatively advanced—on paper, at least. According to a 1968 study by the Pan American Health Organization, Santiago had proportionately more deaths associated with pregnancy, appendicitis, and pneumonia than did Mexico City, Lima, Caracas, Bogotá, and Guatemala City.

But aside from the obvious problems of money, organization, and misallocation of resources, the greatest problem in the health system in Chile, as seen by the new Government, is the problem of attitude. The Government sees the health system—as it sees justice, or almost any other aspect of a society—as part of an economic and political system. Sickness and death are often the result of economic oppression or political weakness. Too often medicine, partially because of its profit potential, is based on curative rather than preventive practices. Treating health as a technical problem gives only temporary and limited success, and only then at a huge social and economic cost. Thus, Government officials point out, during the years between 1925, when the first primitive health system was created, and the early 1950s, when the next one was established, the infant mortality rate dropped somewhat and pediatric clinics and the use of antibiotics stemmed some diseases. But since the early 1950s, despite almost a hundredfold increase in clinic visits, infant mortality has remained high. Socialists in Chile believe they have the answer—preventive medicine, medicine that starts in the home with the preparation of food and improvement of living conditions and only as a last resort involves going to the clinics. Monckleberg has written: "Behind the diarrhea and the pneumonia, frequently, lies the shack or the slum . . . that is to say, the earth floor, the humidity, the parasites, the black water holes, the promiscuity, etc."

As the summer of 1970 approaches, the *poblacion* of La Pincoya, with its sixty thousand inhabitants, prepares for the months of disease. It hasn't had water for ten months. Its children are literally dying of thirst, although the community is located but a mile from downtown Santiago. Ten children are already hospitalized with dehydration and hundreds are suffering from typhus, dysentery, and diarrhea, which they got from drinking from the dirty pools of rainwater that fill the pockmarked unpaved road. The *poblacion* has few paved roads and no electricity. People line up at the intermittent water pipes between three and six in the morning, because at that time water sometimes trickles out in a cruel, tantalizing gesture. For most, it is merely an exercise in human hope and futility. The new Government finally put a water tank in the community, but it doesn't work any longer, "a crude joke that we cannot afford any more," says one of the residents. The only relief comes when a water tank from the police force comes by, but that only occurs every three days or so and for parched mouths and dying children the relief is negligible.

On an individual basis, some doctors have begun experiments in slum areas to try to abolish situations that occur regularly in *poblaciones* like the one in La Pincoya. In these experiments the doctor is an adviser who helps and assists paramedical community residents. One experiment that is succeeding is in Nogales, a fifteen-year-old *poblacion* located on the inner ring of the shantytowns circling Santiago. On the wall of its polyclinic, which is also its auditorium, is a sign drawn by one of the residents showing a seesaw with a child on one side and a sack of money on the other. It asks: "How much is the health of your child worth? Don't sell the milk!" The reference is to the free milk given daily to all children under fifteen and to all pregnant and nursing mothers. In this way, Nogales residents are experimenting with the theory that health begins at home.

Under the leadership of middle-aged, tireless Dr. Fortunado, whose gray crew-cut hair accentuates his smooth boyish face, the community organizes itself. Fortunado discusses his own background candidly. He used to be, he admits, like any other middle-class doctor, helping those who came to his office. Yet he gradually came to understand better than most that one can only help those who help themselves, and that one can only help people to help themselves when one knows their problems. He joined a local drinking society and found from the conversations of the workingmen that the problem of health translated at the local level into the problem of garbage, flies, and dirty rivers.

Fortunado believes that middle-class people, especially medical personnel, have the skills to help the poor, but that these skills become meaningless in the face of their ignorance of the slum dweller's reality, their prejudice against the lower class, and mutual suspicion and distrust. As he bluntly puts it: "The National Health Service is terrible; it doesn't come to the people. The bureaucracy is overwhelming. If a child goes to a doctor and the doctor treats the child cruelly or without warmth or understanding, the child will not return." And that, for Fortunado, is a tragedy.

One Chilean journalist told me: "Too many doctors here treat the children of the poor with disdain—they pronounce them sick, that's all." Then they prescribe medicine that the poor can't afford and send them back to the slums, where the disease germs await the exhaustion of the antibiotics.

In Nogales the solution was outlined as follows: first, control the garbage and the flies and educate the mothers in how to prepare the milk; second, divide up the community into sectors, with each having a coordinator, an out-clinic, and a medical team; third, educate the people in each sector to bring their children to the clinic on a regular basis, whether they are sick or not. For the first time in Nogales there is now an accurate census; for the first time it is known with some certainty how many children there are in each sector (call it a neighborhood, although the divisions are a bit more arbitrary than that) and how many are dying each year. Organization, education, and controls have already produced results. Four months earlier, thirty children had been dying each month. Now, even with summer approaching, there had been only one death in the past month.

As I sat in the Nogales community center and listened to various community and Government participants discuss their attitudes toward medicine, I gained a good idea of how politics and ideology in Chile are translated into practice. After residents and nonresidents made speeches, I was quizzed by my Chilean friends as to which speaker belonged to which political party. For a North American who couldn't tell the difference between a Democrat and a Republican, even during a campaign year, I did pretty well. Fortunado was a MAPU because of his clear use of principles without rhetoric and humanist speech wrapped in Christian rather than Marxist vocabulary. The bureaucrat from the National Health Service was probably a Communist (I guessed wrong there) because he spoke eloquently for five minutes, extolling the potential of the Government and the ideals of socialism, without actually saying anything. The middle-aged man from the community who spoke so well and long about practical problems, such as the need for a campaign to clean up a nearby canal and an adjoining part, who spoke of the Government as an opportunity to be used by the masses and not as an end in itself, was a member of the Socialist party.

Nogales is not the only example of progress in decentralizing and changing the concepts of medicine. A *poblacion* of seventy thousand people was also divided into sectors, each under the control of a doctor, who was bringing to these Chileans for the first time the concept of a family or neighborhood doctor who would know intimately their case histories and problems in the community. In 1969 only ten of the 4,357 infants supervised died, or 2.3 per 1,000—one of the lowest figures in the entire world. These children were checked, whether sick or not, on a regular schedule. As a result of the neighborhood-oriented approach, solutions to medical/criminal problems were often creative and unique. For example, there was a family in which a drunken father had raped his nine-year-old daughter two months after the mother had abandoned him and their four children aged one to twelve. In this case the daughter was placed with another family after a medical and psychiatric examination; the father, after being imprisoned for his act, was released and given treatment for alcoholism and a psychiatric examination; and the children were matriculated in the local school and protected and cared for by families in the neighborhood.

The new Government relies on these local experiments very heavily. Sergio Infante, a socialist who is the head of SNS, is trying at present to do two things at once, with somewhat contradictory reactions. He is trying to unify the disparate health services, so that all Chileans will have the same quality and quantity of health supervision. At the same time, he is trying to decentralize operations. It is still too early to evaluate his success, but as he says: "For the first time, we have incorporated the community into our labors, not just as objects of health actions, but as subjects, as actors. . . . Around fifteen hundred to eighteen hundred health volunteers have been placed throughout the country." The Government has also taken over the distribution of drugs and has taken control of a large pharmaceutical firm. The feeling was that this firm was making phenomenal profits and that a Government-run operation could dispense medicines at a very low cost. Some feel that this operation will get as bogged down in bureaucracy as others the Government has undertaken, leading to the worst of both possible worlds—high-cost medicine and inefficient distribution. Others say it will provide more equitable distribution of drugs and medicines, most of which have never been dispensed in adequate quantities to poor people.

Socialists, however, do not limit the concept of health to such obvious factors as drugs and medical personnel and hospital programs. The environment, the family, entertainment, and vacations all contribute to psychological and physical well-being. Socialists despise the capitalist system in which the rich get one kind of food and the poor get another, in which the rich buy fresh oranges and the poor buy watered-down orange juice, in which the rich buy good bread and the poor buy white bread, in which the rich buy milk with the cream kept in and the poor buy milk with the cream taken out. Before the socialists took office in Chile there were two types of bread: *pan especial,* sold to middle-class people, and *pan popular,* a cheap kind. There were two kinds of milk, in red containers and white, the former with the cream kept in, the latter with it taken out. The Government lowered the price of milk and put quality controls on it. It also lowered the price of bread and eliminated the two types.

The Government has established many tourist spas for working people, with low-cost travel and lodging arrangements that are within the budget of the average Chilean. The thought that more Argentinians and North Americans were seeing beautiful southern Chile than working-class Chileans was galling to the new Government. Moreover, it was felt that vacations aid in giving workers a sense of well-being, a break from the grueling workday and congested neighborhoods. Although this program was just getting started when I was in Chile, I managed to get aboard one of the guided tours around Puerto Montt, in the volcano and lake region of Chile. It cost less than half what the commercial tours cost, but it was also certainly more primitive. The tour bus was an old school bus that probably was still being used as a school bus on alternate days. The windows fogged up as we started out, and for the first fifteen minutes the sun wasn't warm enough to evaporate the moisture. The road was poor and the ride was bumpy. Heat was either nonexistent or reserved for the comfort of the driver; we were very cold. The boat that took us to the main island was small in comparison to the commercial one. On the island, the commercial tourists dined at the hotel; we sneaked around the side to a little schoolhouse and wedged our legs under short tables for a tidy repast. I doubt that it will capture the North American tourist trade, but it was well worth it for anyone who would settle for camaraderie (our small group was very close) rather than commercial comforts.

The Government believes that the basis for a new system of health, as well as for reconstruction of Chile's social system, lies in the family. To socialists in Chile, this extremely important institution has been distorted and broken up as a result of the pressures a capitalist society imposes on man and wife. Chilean men are generally thought to be worth less than Chilean women. This is an accepted fact among middle-class families, but is especially believed among lower-class women. Some Latin American friends of mine had just had a baby, and their Chilean maid looked at him one day as he was lying on his back staring stupidly at the ceiling. "This one is Chilean," she laughed. Other working-class women agree—the Chilean man is lazy and drunken, he dresses in baggy pants, and he is often tragic. The drunkenness charge is unfortunately true. Wine is both Chile's blessing and her curse. Chile has almost 300,000 acres of grapevines and produces almost 450 million liters of wine. The wines produced invariably take international awards. Yet only 4 percent of the wine is exported. The rest is consumed within the country. The results: almost 20 percent of the population is considered seriously affected by alcoholism; 8 percent are considered alcoholics. Eighty percent of those affected are heads of households, thus affecting the entire family. Eighty-two percent of the country's fatal accidents are caused by alcohol. Eighty percent of the people who do not show up for work on a Monday cite hangovers as their reason. Forty percent of police arrests are for alcoholism. Sixty-three percent of the prisoners are alcoholics. Thirty percent of the beds occupied by men in hospitals are occupied for sickness of the liver, with 90 percent of these stemming from alcohol consumption. In working-class areas the problem is even worse. In Poblacion La Victoria, for example, 19 percent of the fathers are alcoholics and another 35 percent drink excessively. Among the women the figure is between 5 and 8 percent.[6]

Although men bear the social stigma of alcoholism, it is the women who often bear the burdens imposed by a country in which men have virtually all the political and economic power and the Catholic Church has strong influence. As noted in the chapter on peasants, most peasant women who come to the city work as maids, and most prostitutes have once been house servants. In 1961 alone, there were 129,000 abortions—one for every two live births—even though abortions are illegal in Chile. Induced abortions terminate 35 to 40 percent of all pregnancies, and a high percentage of hospital beds are taken up by women with internal bleeding as a result of brutally self-induced abortions.

The Government recognizes the extent of the deterioration of the average working-class family in Chile. As Salvador Allende has said, the social fragmentation that characterizes underdeveloped Chile "has its reflection in the familial environment." The Government has proposed a new Ministry of Family, to be headed by Gloria Aguayo, formerly a member of the Christian Democrats and now a member of MAPU. In my limited time in Chile I gained the impression that this Ministry, if created (there are vested interests that do not want another Ministry to usurp certain powers, and the Opposition in Congress has slowed down the legislation), would probably be the most progressive in the Government, outside of the shadow agricultural bureaucracy established and composed of peasants. This new Ministry would be staffed mostly by women, and most of them would be socialists. They would probably blame the disintegration of the family on the capitalist system and on the limitations that the Catholic Church imposes on women. Felicitas Klimpel, lawyer and Secretary General of the National Council of Family Education, faces the problem of the "mercantile myth of marriage": "In a survey that we did a while ago, we proposed to a group of mothers the possibility of choosing as a son-in-law either one who was unknown but had a car, or another who was known and had a bicycle. The majority chose the unknown." The workingman is drunk and lazy; the poor man is even less desirable.

The yet-to-be-formed Ministry of Family (now supported by money given from Salvador Allende's private budget) will likely promote such things as bills to legalize abortions and divorce. It will not be easy to do this in the face of violent Catholic opposition. In fact, when the Government proposed a new divorce law, the Church came out against it with the almost unbelievable argument that "it is a fact that every divorce law brings more and more divorces, multiplying them in a progression both continuous

and alarming in all countries where such legislation exists."
In other words, divorce laws would increase the number of
divorces, so there should be no such laws. Interestingly
enough, the Church resorted happily to Karl Marx to support its argument. Marx had once said: "If marriage were
not the basis for the family, it would not be an object of
legislation, as for example, friendship is not." He added:
"No one is obligated to become married, but everyone who
does get married should be obligated to observe the laws of
matrimony." The Catholic superiors add to this their own
unique view of history: "Of the multiple forms that men
have given sexual life, love and conjugal society, history
confirms that stable monogamous marriage is a principal
motive for the ascension of humanity toward superior forms
of life. The moral perfectioning of a society carries with it
an evolution toward monogamy and stability." In fact, the
Church opposes all parts of the Government's policies with
respect to the family. "A family policy that raises the
banner of birth control, of legalization of abortion and
divorce merits better the name of an antifamily policy."

Of course, in matters of health and the status of
women and the role of the family, the real changes will
come from mass organization of people, not by Government fiat. There is a Confederation of Chilean Women,
whose express purpose is to educate women about their
rights and to lobby for increased participation of women in
the political life of Chile. It is apolitical but heavily composed of left-wing women. Chilean women are in an
ambiguous situation. They are more liberated than their
Latin American sisters and better educated; the proportion
of them currently entering universities is close to 50 percent. But there is also the Latin American concept of
machismo, which means that the man rules both in his
home and in public life and that women are to be taken
care of and protected. Even among the somewhat liberated
hippies of Providencia, who smoke dope and listen to acid

rock and try to emulate their North American youth compatriots, a vast majority said in a recent survey that they would not marry a woman who was not a virgin. The political parties are all led by men. These parties in turn select representatives for various national organizations, and usually they are men. Rosa Valdez de Cothin, President of the Chilean Federation of Women, told me that when the National Committee of Education was first created it had no women members. After a long and bitter fight, the federation managed to get one representative on that committee. At the worker level the same sort of discrimination occurs. In the largest industries where there is now worker participation, women have almost no representation. Even in the textile industries, where women make up a majority of the labor force, there is little participation. In one corporation none of the eight people in the leadership were women. In another firm only one out of twenty in positions of leadership was a woman.

There are labor laws on the books that aid women, although few women are educated enough to know about them or organized enough to fight for their recognition. Laws passed many years ago state that an employer who has more than a dozen women working in the plant must provide day-care services. A woman who is pregnant may take off six weeks before the birth and six weeks after, with full pay. If she chooses not to return to her job for the first year after the birth, the employer must hold the job open for her. With respect to the man, the Chilean woman has certain rights also. For example, a married man must have his wife's signature in order to sell the family goods. Thus, according to Chilean law, the house is not the property of the husband to do with as he sees fit. The money the wife earns outside the house is solely hers. She can put it in a savings account or buy personal property with it, all of which belongs to her alone. In Chile there has also been, for decades, a family allowance for children. A certain amount goes to the family each month from the employer. The law says that if a wife finds that her husband is not giving her the correct amount she can go to the husband's employer and be paid directly. If the woman is separated from her husband, she still gets 50 percent of his salary.

These laws are fine—on the books. Enforcing them is another story. Therefore various groups of women are going into working-class neighborhoods and out to the rural neighborhoods to explain the rights women have and to offer services if these are needed.

Health workers, too, are organizing throughout Chile. In Santa Maria nine health workers—none of them doctors, seven of them women—took over the local clinic to press a complaint. One of their fellow workers had been convicted of injuring another worker (although these people thought it was a frame-up) and had been fired even though he was free on bail. The nine people took over the clinic, opposing their own union leaders and the director of the clinic. They managed to hold out for a few hours, enough time for the Government (representatives from CUT, the Ministry of Interior, and the Ministry of Work) to come scurrying. The issue, like so many others occurring throughout Chile, was put to the vote. The union members voted on a proposal to reintegrate the man into the work force. It was accepted, 63 to 45. To the Christian Democrats writing in *La Prensa* it was one more instance of anarchy, with the masses imposing their hurried judgment on the clear thinking of the director who was trying to keep the hospital free of hoodlum elements. To the Government it was another demonstration of people being permitted to judge for themselves, as much as possible, whom they would work with and under what conditions.

In Santiago the Federation of Health Workers sent a petition to the hospital authorities asking that certain doctors and technicians be removed from their positions. At the same time, the Federation of Professionals and Health

Technicians retaliated, threatening extreme measures if these people were actually removed. The lines were drawn —medical versus paramedical personnel. It was also a political dispute, because most of the doctors were opponents of the Government and most of the nurses and health workers were supporters. The conflict has not been resolved to date; it still simmers. Ricardo, a young doctor, who is quite leftist in his politics, had second thoughts about democracy in the hospital. "This country is not prepared for socialism overnight," he explained. "It lacks a socialist conscience." He told of doctors belonging to the Communist party who, when the Government placed a ceiling on salaries, began seriously considering migrating. He himself is determined to stay "until my freedom is curbed." But his reservations are clear. He spoke critically of the hospital workers. "In one hospital the nurses, instead of putting the thermometer under the armpit, were making up the temperatures, and when they were discovered and criticized, instead of apologizing they went out on strike." He spoke critically of the change in the curricula in medical schools. "They're teaching now more social science and less medicine. Now the graduates are leaving with little knowledge of how to diagnose a disease, but are much more socially aware," he complained. He was sympathetic to the new health program but once again was reserved. "My speciality is the heart, but what does the socialist Government say? No, the three worst killers in our country are diarrhea, tuberculosis, and alcoholism. But you don't need a doctor to cure those ailments. They say my studies cost too much, and the valves and other equipment must be imported from the United States, draining precious Chilean resources."

Then Ricardo added, somewhat defensively: "Eighteen hundred Chilean children die of heart trouble each year." That he feels the need to justify the acquisition of expensive medical equipment on the basis of how much suffering it would alleviate is an indication of the subtle changes in the field of medicine occurring even in the first year of the new Government's tenure. And that the most brilliant doctors study heart transplants while alcoholism damages livers and malnutrition affects 40 percent of the young is proof to the Government of the distorted priorities in Chilean medicine. With a doctor as Chief Executive, the health of the people takes on top priority.

10

The Media and Culture

The bank is being taken over by the state—a fine achievement for our Government. We will nationalize the natural resources. Excellent! It deserves the support of all Chileans. But if they do not nationalize, at the same time, our customs, our spirit, our culture, all the rest will be useless. . . .

—Statement by the workers of Espectaculo,
A Chilean theater organization

Imagine for a moment that Japanese is the most popular language in the United States and is taught in the schools; that the most popular cars are Toyota and Honda; that the news services are Japanese-run; and that most movies come from Japan and have subtitles in our language. Imagine further that the most popular singers are Japanese and that the songs themselves are in their language. Imagine a whole generation of young Americans walking down the street dressed in kimonos, singing popular tunes in Japanese.

Hard to imagine, no doubt, but it is exactly the case in Chile, where United States commodities and culture have taken over.

Bonanza, Lassie, and *Along Came Bronson* were among the most popular television programs in Chile when I was there. Almost 70 percent of the fare shown by Chilean theaters consists of North American movies, ranging from old, dubbed Walt Disney films to subtitled first-run features. The top recording artists while I was there were Tom Jones and Frank Sinatra, although there was a growing market for acid rock. The news came from UPI and AP.

What is the effect of this cultural dominance by a country with a different set of values, a different history, and a different political framework? The Workers of Espectaculo, a local theater organization affiliated with CUT, put it this way:

> Our folklore, our history, our customs, our way of living and thinking, are being strangled before the uncontrolled invasion of the unfortunately famous "packaged" program. We are handed the fleeting and violent history of a "gangster" and are denied the brilliant and solid life of our own heroes. They impose on us banal lyrics, lacking in any content, to replace our own lyricists, our own writers. Hundreds of thousands of dollars are wasted in foreign histories, and not even one escudo is given us to learn our history.[1]

I often went to the movies while in Chile. All Chileans attend movies fairly regularly. The price of admission is relatively low and the range of films from which to choose is phenomenal. Theaters are three-quarters full at 2 P.M., at 5 P.M., and at 11 P.M. First-run features, ten-year-old movies—it doesn't matter. I remember going to see *Getting Straight* one night, a movie that had been packing the crowds in for three weeks. It had been impossible to translate into Spanish; the title worked out roughly to "On the

Edge of the World." I was struck by the obvious irrelevance of the movie to all but perhaps one percent of Chileans. The language was hip and slang-filled. The scenes took place in a modern, upper-middle-class university in the United States. The protests were sexual, not political. The dialogue between whites and blacks was slangy and irrelevant to the Chileans, whose minority, the Mapuches, certainly doesn't parallel the blacks in the field of education. Finally, the theme of the picture was, on one level, man's struggle against the oppression and emotional stifling caused by the mega-university. The climax was a wild free-for-all in the president's office, with the hero planting a kiss smack on the mouth of one of his thesis advisers. He had finally cracked as a result of idiotic cross-examination having to do with D. H. Lawrence's penchant for homosexuality. The whole thing couldn't possibly have made sense to Chileans except as a fantasy view of another world. Only a few weeks after the film's appearance the MIR, which was known for its guerrilla attacks on banks and its organization of people's militias in southern Chile, created an organization called Students Without a University, which demanded more space in the universities, the use of television, larger class-rooms, and evening classes. In other words, they were fighting for everything the Berkeley uprising and dozens like it later eschewed and protested against. Without stretching the point too much, I would say that *Getting Straight* was representative of about 65 percent of all movies seen in Chile and of the type that had the highest attendance. They were the newest, the slickest, those with the best photography, the sexiest scenes, and the crispest dialogue. As I was sitting in the theater I thought of the foreign movies that had come into the United States. The Apu trilogy came to mind as a picture that supposedly represented the Indian way of life; it was shown to a very small audience in art theaters. But North American movies such as *Getting Straight,* which supposedly represent the

American way of life, are shown to mass audiences. I can't help but think that foreign movie audiences come away from such entertainment with values and fantasies inappropriate to their own situation.

In the past few years a small group of Chileans with a great deal of influence on styles, fashions, and values has sprung up in imitation of the hippies of the United States. These are the middle-class and upper-middle-class young people who stroll the fashionable streets of Providencia, shop in boutiques that would do justice to Telegraph Avenue, and eat hamburgers and ice cream cones in nearby cafés. Just a few weeks after Allende's electoral victory, before his inauguration, Chile had its first rock festival, a mini-Woodstock held in the upper-class suburbs of Los Dominicos. When the music died down and the audience slowly returned home, eight girls were missing and the sickly sweet smell of marijuana was wafting over the Chilean countryside. With alacrity the Chamber of Deputies ordered an investigation. The Office of Student Relations of the Ministry of Education reluctantly released a study indicating that 60 percent of Chile's high school students smoked marijuana. Hippies had come to Chile.

The Left in Chile hates and fears the hippie phenomenon because it is an import from the United States and mainly because it may sap the political energy of the middle- and upper-class youth. Six months after the Socialist Government took office, a movement called "Youth Power" was fostered in Chile. It was backed by the Right and was a movement similar to the 1967 Haight-Ashbury scene in Berkeley. The demands included freedom for individual creativity, relaxation of sexual mores, and creation of values commensurate with a leisure class. Yet this was not happening in the United States, where the problem of growing leisure time was in fact becoming important, where productivity was so high that millions of workers were doing busywork just to maintain a semblance of a labor force, but in Chile, where there were still the serious social ills of poverty, malnutrition, and inequality. Among left-wing youth in Chile the worst type of epithet one can use on a fellow is *marijuanero,* which means roughly that he is a pseudorevolutionary, a bourgeois middle-class revolutionary. I remember talking to leftists until I was sure they were exaggerating the description of the pseudorevolutionaries in Chile. Then, during one of my brief stays with a lawyer working in Chile for the Ford Foundation, a Chilean couple came visiting and there was an impromptu party. These guests were students of the Technical University, and the man proclaimed himself a socialist. He was studying architecture. When I asked him what he would do after graduation he said he would go to study in New York. The couple had brought with them a portable record player. All their records were in English—from Aretha Franklin to Joe Cocker. And of course we all smoked dope. It could have been downtown Manhattan or the hills of Berkeley. I can almost hear the MIRista telling me: "See, I told you so. The North American orientation comes out in many ways—the choice of music, the choice of careers, what people take into their bodies."

Newspapers

Chile is often cited for having one of the freest presses in the world. If we define freedom as diversity, then this is true. In terms of the range of opinions printed and available to the average citizen, Chile is perhaps ahead of all other nations. There are few forms of censorship, and these mostly relate to either political libel or pornography. In Santiago there is on every block a kiosk brimming with a wide range of literature. It is a fantastic display, especially as compared with the United States, where most newsstands in the nation's capital carry only three or four middle-of-the-road dailies.

Thus, when the Inter-American Association of Journalists criticized Allende for strangling Chile's free press, the reaction was a kind of laughing anger. It should be noted that the past president of the association was none other than Agustin Edwards, one of Chile's richest businessmen and owner of *El Mercurio,* its most widely circulated daily paper. Edwards had been a favorite target of Allende during the campaign, and when Allende answered the association's charges (which, by the way, were not echoed by any Chilean newspaper, either right-wing or moderate) he ended by noting: "It would be interesting if you would communicate to one of the most conspicuous leaders of your association, Mr. Agustin Edwards, that he should come to Chile to accept responsibility for the financial manipulations of his bank, manipulations which have put the general manager in prison."

The press in Chile is so diverse possibly because it is so political. No self-respecting newsman would say he was objective if objectivity were defined as expressing all sides of an issue. All newspapers have a political axe to grind, and most are subsidized by political parties. No Chilean newspaper would have the audacity to proclaim as its motto: "All the News That's Fit to Print." For example, when in early 1971 the Committee on the Alliance for Progress made public a report on Chile, the report contained two parts. The first part quite critically described the last years of Frei's Administration. The second part analyzed the new Socialist game plan and found several inconsistencies. *La Prensa,* the Christian Democrat newspaper, printed the second part and ignored the first. *La Nacion,* the Government's paper, printed the first and ignored the second. *El Mercurio,* supporter of Alessandri, printed both parts. In order to find out what is really happening in Chile it is essential to read all three newspapers, plus from time to time either a Far Left newspaper like the MIR's *El Rebelde,* or a Far Right journal such as *Portada.*

But diversity of the press has not been the problem for the new Government. Rather, the problem has been the question of who controls the press and what it is used for. Just before the new Government took office, a published study showed that three businesses—*El Mercurio,* SOPESUR, and COPESA—controlled 65 percent of the newspaper publication in the country and that two groups— Edwards and Zig-Zag—controlled almost 98 percent of the magazine publications.[2]

Many leftists believed that the newspapers were nothing more than business corporations, controlled by those who held large quantities of capital and sold like merchandise, using slick writing and sensationalized stories to capture a part of the market. Of course, commentators noted that the low level of journalism was not limited to right-wing newspapers—left-wing tabloids also suffered from this. Armand Mattlehart blamed it on the capitalist system. "The sensationalism, the low level of leftist newspapers, are in many cases the abortive children of the law of the jungle imposed by the capitalist competition in the field of information distribution." Conservatives and liberals in Chile differ with him. They believe that all capitalism means is that the consumer is sovereign. Indeed, the director of a liberal daily views subscription rates of newspapers as a sort of vote of confidence:

All of you are against freedom of the press, arguing that it is freedom of property, but the facts prove you wrong. In effect, to sell each day 300,000 issues constitutes a true plebiscite. Now, then, this plebiscite is the ultimate expression of freedom of personal choice.

The Left, of course, does not agree with that. From their analysis of journalism as nothing more than another big business dominated by a few large economic groupings, the leftists have decided that freedom of the press is quite similar to freedom of the marketplace. As Eduardo Rivas, President of the Santiago Regional Council of the School of Journalism, said in 1969: "Freedom of the press is a myth in Chile; it is a freedom that ends in the management of the enterprise."

Once having decided that newspapers are large corporations, the next step is obvious—create class consciousness among the workers. The workers in this case are the journalists, those who write the stories, who get paid very little, and who are often fired if they don't toe the line. In late 1969 Eduardo Rivas urged his fellow journalists:

> Now is the hour that the School of Journalists should stop being a celestial organism, enclosed in a marble tower, and should assume its true role as defender of the dignity and office of a journalist, which is, after all, a job like any other, and which puts us in the working class and not the exploiter class. Ours is the class of the workers, of the peasants, of the students. . . .

He assumes class solidarity with other workers:

> Now is the time that we should stop being spectators and fight for our class, the same class as the peasants, the workers, the students. . . . The large landholders came to express their solidarity with the School of Journalists; we refuse it because there can be no solidarity between the exploiters and the exploited. They can never unite with us nor us with them.[3]

The language was strong, but Rivas was not alone in using it. In *El Sur* and *La Mañana* journalists won the right to express their own opinions in columns signed by them. Within various newspapers, including *El Mercurio*, supporters of the Government established committees demanding greater autonomy for the workers and greater control over editorial policy. Among the staff of the evening paper *El Clarin,* which has the greatest national circulation, a recent union election in which the Front of Revolutionary Workers was opposed by the Communist party resulted in the former defeating the latter by winning four out of five positions of leadership. Alejandro Ortega Canelo, the union president, explained their victory. He said the owner of the paper had vacationed for four months throughout Europe while loans of five hundred escudos were being denied to workers. "Workers are hassled if they belong or want to belong to the union. Journalists' stories are censored." Ortega believes the content of the paper should come under the journalists' control. He sees the Sunday supplement, with its combination of pornography and sensationalism, as proof of the paper's existence as merchandise rather than information. He tells of a recent tour taken by ten workers, including photographers, typesetters, and collators, to Antofagasta, and of what the workers in the mines there told them:

They brought back the general criticism that newspapers don't represent them at all. They cited as an example the salt-peter miners, who had helped overcome a fire at a plant; the story was not reported by the press. The efforts to win the battle of production, the voluntary work effort, in fact, everything they are doing, is not reported to the extent it should be. They said that workers are mentioned on the pages of the dailies only when they are involved in police matters.

Some newspapers have not reacted kindly to this new effort to explore labor issues beyond working conditions and salaries. At *El Mercurio* several workers were dismissed for "agitation." Sonia Edwards, sister of Agustin and vice president of the newspaper, took the side of the workers, explaining her position this way:

The only future that *El Mercurio* deserves is nationalization under the control of the workers, with a regime similar to the textile enterprises transferred to the social area.

She added that, although she was vice president, she had been isolated from the workers. Workers who approached her had been fired. Things had become so bad, she said, that she was not even permitted to see a union member unless accompanied by a representative of management.

The struggle of the workers to gain control over the newspapers they were designing, writing, and publishing inevitably led to a general discussion of the content of newspapers and news service bulletins.

Information, for capitalists and socialists alike, means power. But socialists hold that information is useful only if it is placed in an understandable context. The best known and most brilliant theorist on communications in Chile, Armand Mattlehart, has made these comments about Chilean communications content:

> The reader passes without transition from a takeover of land, to the invasion of Laos, to the assassination of a football player, to the latest assault of the Tupumaros.

The news is given no meaning because it has no context:

> In order to overcome the overflowing and chaotic river of news flow, in order to select and classify, in order to be able to gather useful conclusions to orient individual and social conduct, the mind of the listener would have to function like a computer. In fact, if we might be permitted to play with the two root derivations of the word, information "uninforms" and, finally, does "not form." It supplies the audience with a group of facts taken from a reality that is defined as ephemeral, transitory, and disjointed, and doesn't supply the context of the news or, that is to say, the elements that would permit the listener to internalize it in an accumulative line of active knowledge. In effect, news, in order to fulfill this mission of formation would have to drag the reader from his passivity as a consumer and convert him into an element of action. It would contribute thus to fortify the process of mobilization.

Mattlehart sees no accident in this disorganization. To him it is part and parcel of a conspiracy by the capitalist press everywhere:

In the final instance, the disorganization of the news benefits the cohesion of the apparatus of domination; divide and conquer is one of the fundamental principles of the power of manipulation of the masses. The law of the jungle of a capitalist society converts the organs of bourgeois information into a jungle. Now, then, from the foregoing, we can deduce that such anarchy is the rule of functioning of an order. Therefore news is anarchic only in appearance; it receives its coherence from the social order, from the values that underlie that order.

Thus the conspiracy is not one of individuals, but is endemic in a capitalist system where the goal is growth, where the marketplace is the final arbiter of justice, and where the present is but a step into an increasingly hopeful future. The only enemy is instability; a chaotic news flow produces a stable, apathetic citizenry.

Television

Information is no longer limited to the written word. In modern societies, perhaps more is learned from movies, television, and music than from books. Certainly this is the case in Chile, where comic books, television, and films rate much greater attention than books and magazines. With these forms, however, the same problems exist; there is a mixture of dependent economics and cultural disintegration.

Many television programs, especially movies shown on television, come from the United States. Television movies cost Chile dearly. One TV technician explained: "An imported film costs between $600 and $900; that is money which leaves the country." A national program is cheaper since it reactivates the local economy. In early 1971 65 percent of the programs seen on Chilean television were imported (not all from the United States).

Although popular in Chile, television has not reached the heights of fanaticism there that it has in the United States, partly because of its newness, partly because of cultural differences, and partly because it is too expensive to have widespread distribution. There are no networks. There are three stations, one controlled directly by the Government and reaching the entire country, and two run by the two major universities in Chile, the University of Chile and Catholic University. Programming begins in early afternoon and goes until about midnight, except when there is a soccer game in progress or a late movie. With all my ethnocentrism, I once asked a Chilean woman why there was no TV in the mornings. Shocked, she asked: "Who would want to watch TV in the morning?" It was, to her, like drinking in the morning.

Questions concerning freedom and censorship also cropped up in relation to television when the new Government took office. It will be remembered that the Christian Democrats forced through Congress a flood of legislation pertaining to the media just before they abandoned office. After six months of Allende, Juan Hamilton, a Christian Democrat Senator, denounced what he called the "politicization" of the Government television station:

We made this announcement because the subject is a serious one, and not with a desire to harass journalist Olivares [head of the station] but rather fundamentally to call to the attention of both the Government and the citizenry the fact that, at some future time, the right that the people of Chile have to be informed with objectivity and with respect for the truth might be threatened by denying the access of different currents of opinion to a medium like television.

The question of censorship was indeed serious, particularly when Manuel Cabieses, who was director of Channel 13, declared quite explicitly:

> When socialism arrives the means of communications, just like the means of production, are going to be in the hands of the state, or, that is, of the workers through the state. That is a goal for which the men of the Left in this country are struggling, and struggling unwaveringly, frankly, and openly.

The fear was that this laudatory objective would be only half accomplished, with the result that power would be centered in a vengeful, bureaucratic elite of Government administrators with Marxist notions of purity. Such fear was not wholly irrational—the Communist party was well known for its authoritarianism where cultural purity was involved. It held back a showing of *The Confession,* a film that dealt with torture during the Stalinist era in Czechoslovakia. There was nothing subtle about this quasi-censorship; it occurred at the same time as the April municipal elections. *El Siglo* explained that such a film distorted history, concentrating on the bad aspects of communism and forgetting the good parts. When the Government television station showed *1984,* the Communist party was furious. It couldn't understand why a station controlled by leftists would show what it considered an anti-leftist film. Leftists, however, saw no similarity between Stalinism and socialism.

But the question of political content in programming as raised by Hamilton can be discussed on a much higher level. It was on such a level that Manuel Calvelo, a technician for the Government television station, answered Hamilton's charges. When asked whether national television was becoming political, he gave this characteristic reply:

> Yes, I have received letters to that effect. I answer them by saying that national television has always been political. . . .

there is an explicit and an implicit politics. Not to make politics explicit is to make it implicit. This channel is going to make programs that reflect the popular mobilization and the process of structural changes that exist in the country. If it didn't do this, it would still be political; it would have the politics of evasion and complicity that is the politics of certain musical shows and of all the serials.

Some people see television as primarily a medium for entertainment, not education. The tired laborer comes home, shucks his shoes, reclines on the sofa, and chuckles delightedly to the programming, exercising his limited choice by twiddling the knob. To others, entertainment often is synonymous with vacuity—or worse, reactionary politics. Just as Mattlehart thought disorganized news was reactionary politics, so Calvelo believes that vacuous programming leads to reactionary life styles:

Currently, television is the perfect "idiot box." It is the "Roman circus," an instrument of ideological penetration, of perversion of the cultural values of the Chilean population. It is creating artificial needs. It doesn't reflect the national reality, but rather, foreign ways of living, and is perverting the mentality of the children.

Reactions and Solutions

The criticism of all types of media is pervasive. Increasingly, leftists are asking the Government to step in and nationalize cultural resources. The Workers of Espectaculo put it this way:

The bank is being taken over by the state—a fine achievement for our Government. We will nationalize the natural resources. Excellent. It deserves the support of all Chileans. But if they do not nationalize at the same time our customs, our spirit, our culture, all the rest will be useless; we will never be able to liberate ourselves from the subtle and hidden wires with which imperialism is accustomed to choke and exploit our people. We should begin with the head, with the motor of human beings, in order to achieve a real, a genuine Chileanization.

The Government has responded to the criticism in certain areas. Perhaps its most dramatic measure during the first year was the imposition by decree of an order whereby radio stations had to devote 40 percent of air time, spread out equally over the entire day, either to music interpreted by Chileans (25 percent) or Chilean folklore (15 percent). It was a desperate measure to stem the overwhelming flood of North American and British music. Evaristo Lopez Almuna, a Chilean poet, gave a typical response: "The Chileanization of radio programs comes at a moment of absolute cultural exhaustion. I sincerely believe that Chileans will turn their eyes once again to Chile and stop thinking, singing, and dancing in English." Chilean artists were understandably jubilant over the measure, but radio stations were more subdued in their response, pointing out that there was not enough Chilean music at the time to fill up the required percentage. One station asked if Bach and Beethoven could be considered imperialists. *El Siglo* asked that the measure be altered slightly to count as air time the introductions to the records. The average Chilean, however, did not rise to this level of sophistication. One maid with whom I spoke told me candidly: "I don't like Chilean music. I don't like those *cuecas*." Her favorite was Tom Jones. Many middle-class Chileans, although ashamed of their desires, honestly enjoyed listening to the Beatles or to Frank Sinatra. Undoubtedly that's why the Government relied on decree rather than persuasion. By the time I left Chile two months later, tastes were already changing as surely as they had changed in the ubiquitous presence of the Beatles in 1968.

Later in the year the Government took majority control of the RCA facilities in Chile and began cutting many discs of Chilean folksongs and of national groups interpreting international songs. I remember accidentally meeting a former MIRista one day after the original announcement of the takeover. He was about to go to Argentina to push his latest record. I asked him what the songs were about. "Romantic, inconsequential songs." Why? "Because first I need to become known to the *pololas,* the young girls, and their boyfriends. After I gain fame, maybe," he added wistfully, "I can record songs that have meaning." Then he added: "Maybe with the new Government controlling the recording company I won't have to compromise myself first." Indeed, even in the first months after the Government's election, music had responded to political changes. A few years before, a five-man group of folksingers called Inti-Illimani had formed. They were former music teachers at the Technical University who decided that since they taught music, they knew it well enough to recapture the spirit of Latin America in their songs. They succeeded admirably; with their beautiful harmony and the Chilean sense of humor, they traveled throughout Latin America after the election as troubadours of socialism, getting thrown out of at least one country for discussing the Chilean experiment with students. Just before I left they released a new record with such titles as "Song of the Agrarian Reform," "Song of Social and Private Property," and so on. The latter, interestingly enough, was written in collaboration with the Minister of Agriculture and has as its first refrain: "Now the countryside will not be for the few; the public will receive all the harvests."

The Government understands well that to reach the youth it must use the popular media, especially music. The Federation of University Students has met with popular singers in order to request their collaboration and support in such efforts. Just before the summer of 1971 the popular singers issued a call to their fan clubs to support the revolution and begin doing voluntary work in the summer. One popular singer, Ricardo Garcia, commented: "The principal thing . . . is to link the artists, who have lived untied to reality, to the happenings that are occurring in Chile now, in order to permit them to give their support to the construction of a new society." A single came out shortly thereafter, cut by Jorge Rebel. Called "The Work of the Summer," it began: "This song, is a song of youth, with the testimony of our uneasiness."

Other experiments were picked up and supported by the new Government. One concerned the publication of a left-wing comic book. A few years before, a group of people had gotten together and had begun publishing *La Chiva,* a comic book that dealt with the mythical yet oh so very Chilean village of Chamullo, with its local shopkeeper, its drunken inhabitants, their complaints about the Government, their dreams of success, and so on. It is without doubt one of the Western Hemisphere's finest efforts to combine humor with real social discussion, and as far as I could tell, it is extremely effective. During the political campaign the cartoonist of *La Chiva,* together with students in the School of Economics at the University of Chile, began circulating to the people mimeographed comic strips that debated the concepts of freedom, the charges of the Opposition against the Government coalition, and so forth. The characters, like those in *La Chiva,* are obviously Chilean; they speak the idiom of the streets, yet ask such questions as, "What will happen to my refrigerator, or my children, if the Communists win?" Later the mimeographed sheets became more organized, and when the Government took power, enough money was given to the project to put out a cheap comic-book-type format. In late October Allende himself gave his seal of approval: "For their graphic expression, and the clarity of their concepts that translate faithfully the psychology of our country, I consider them a valiant aid to the

work of the committees of the Popular Unity Government."
The comic book is now named *Firme,* but it retains the old
characters. The books, which are handed out free to discussion groups in the neighborhoods, discuss major points
in the Government's program. Some of the first issues discussed included the nationalization of copper, the budget
of the new Government, and the stereotype of women. The
people who put out the comic book say it is extremely
difficult to produce. Getting a balance between contempla-
tion and laughter is not simple. Marxist professors in the
universities simplify national issues and come up with basic
facts and concepts which they feel people ought to know.
Then the writers and cartoonists take over and try to create
the slang and the humor and the situations that will best get
the point across.

The Government, which last year took control of the
largest publishing house in Chile, has recently been discussing publication of a sort of left-wing teenage rock magazine
that would give teenagers information about the international rock scene and local popular singers while educating
them to the concepts of socialism. Government supporters
are finding the task as challenging and as difficult as the
comic book format.

Chilean leftists are beginning to realize that socialism
is a fine theoretical concept, but that, come the revolution,
it is not so easy to put the concept into practice. They have
discovered that not every Marxist thinks alike and that
artists especially are likely to feel quite differently about
culture when they have no access to public coffers than
when they do. Hernan Valdes, a well-known writer, describes the chaotic scene after the election, when the intellectuals met in conference after conference to decide what
to do now that a dream had come true. "It appeared," said
Valdes, "that the new Government was only waiting for the
utterances and concrete plans of the intellectual sectors in

order to unleash a process of revision and total transformation of the cultural ideological values of the bourgeoisie, unleashed with the same sense of importance that the process of socioeconomic changes had." But the conferences quickly broke down, bickering arose, and separate meetings began. Too often these artists operated from the same mental set as their predecessors in positions of literary influence. In discussing the individual artist, Valdes notes: "Because of the sole fact of having been rejected by the bourgeois system, the artist and writer of the Left demanded recognition (by a left-wing Government) and began thinking that the state was responsible for dissemination to the popular sectors of cultural materials that private enterprise had rejected because of lack of demand." Later he explained:

Privately, the majority of the participants in these types of meetings thought that the time had arrived when the state, animated by socialist principles, would give them a considerable number of clients, because of their progressive political positions.

For many writers, rejection by a capitalist system meant automatic acceptance and sponsorship by a left-wing Government. This egoistic feeling was so pervasive that at times, according to Valdes, there was the belief that "cultural underdevelopment came about because of the great quantity of poets and writers who had not been published." If only the masses had been exposed to an inexpensive copy of this writer's or that poet's missives, the period of underdevelopment might have been greatly foreshortened.

Others rejected this view but accepted one that was only superficially different—that the present group of artists in Chile were highly trained and could adequately translate into popular rhetoric the highly sophisticated Marxist concepts. That is, "writers should change themselves in order to express the popular interests." The skilled would be the interpreters of the popular will.

Members of the Far Left, however, thought both these interpretations of the role of the writer and artist in the coming transition to socialism were off base. They called such attitudes "paternalistic" or "elitist." They disliked the notion that culture must "arrive to" the masses, that it never arose from them. During the summer of 1971 there was a "train of culture," stocked with folksingers, dancers, and so on, touring rural Chile. As the engine wended its way down the single-track backbone of Chile, it became an embarrassment to the country. It was bringing much-needed entertainment and publicity to rural Chile, but not culture. One writer observed: "A culture doesn't exist that is ready to be bottled, formalized, and distributed, one which needs only to be put within reach of the masses." To many left-wing students culture was a thing to be rediscovered by the masses while they were struggling to develop their own consciousness, from their own communal roots. The Writers' Workshop at Catholic University added that artists and writers should be utilized only as coaches for giving the masses the skills necessary to seek—and publicize—their own feelings. In some MIRista circles, even this was going too far. In downtown Santiago the children of the poor were invited to paint on the walls, and the paintings were so beautiful that many leftists considered them proof of the old theory that the *lumpenproletariat* would, because it was less inhibited than the middle class under capitalism, be more artistic.

Things are changing very quickly now in Chile with respect to what the people hear, what they see, and what they read. The Communist Youth Brigade paints marvelously colorful political murals all over Santiago to raise the consciousness of the people, and moreover, it changes these murals every few days. The new Government publishing house prints hundreds of books and pamphlets about left-wing theory that had previously been published only in Argentina or Mexico. The movie theaters show Cuban and Russian films. The government television station is trying to use North American newsreel footage of demonstrations. Street theater pops up here and there as a way of spontaneously educating people. There is, of course, the natural political infighting among different sectors. Valdes explained the great preoccupation among left-wing intellectuals that "persons who weren't members of the Popular Unity parties would have an input into the direction of cultural politics, which would be natural since a great number of intellectuals on the Left are not affiliated with parties." But there are others who learned from the Cuban and Chinese experiences, where culture was found to be extremely important in teaching people new values. The head of the Actors Union in Chile noted that "Cuba, when it was busy with the revolution, abandoned the artistic part; after four years it returned to it, but it was too late; the actors had emigrated to other countries. Cuba had to begin forming new actors. We don't want that to happen here." Socialism is, above all, a change in attitudes, and in Chile the Government, especially through those on its lower levels, has been experimenting with new forms of media expression and new methods of communication.

11

The Revolution Continues

Every social system thinks itself eternal until history sets it straight. Throughout history, every social system that has been attacked has defended itself, and has defended itself with violence. No social system has dissolved itself of its own free will. No social system has resigned in favor of the revolutionaries.

—Fidel Castro's final speech in Santiago, December 1971

The slogan of the Young Socialists before the 1970 election had been: "We shall win the election in order to win the Government in order to take the power in order to make socialism in Chile." A long and complicated slogan, true, but it was written in shorthand over walls and windows throughout Chile during the first year. The Left has gained two of those objectives. It has won the election and it has won the Government. Such successes have given it considerable power and considerable influence on Chile's future. The Government has used that power extensively in all areas of the society—in the media, in the factories, in the courts, in the neighborhood shops, in the copper mines. The Government has already accomplished more than half of the forty goals of its popular program. It has taken control of most monopolistic sectors of the economy; it now controls banking; it has abolished the tactical police force; it has established distribution centers and created buying centers; it controls advertising; and it has nationalized the copper mines. In doing all this the Allende Administration has brought into the Government for the first time either workers or representatives of the working class. In all nationally controlled industries, workers have participation and, in some cases, indirect control over the industry (the leadership of large corporations usually consists of six Government representatives and five labor representatives selected from the industry; given the constituency and composition of some left-wing parties in the coalition, at least some of the six Government representatives could well be workers also). Most institutions now have at least begun to move in the direction of more control by the community or the work force. The social security funds are now controlled by the workers and the recipients. The newspapers are beginning to have participation by the unionized staff members. Although such concepts as neighborhood courts have been defeated in Congress, others, such as the establishment of a democratically constituted agricultural bureaucracy, have been successful.

The figures from the first year are impressive. Unemployment has been reduced from over 8 percent when Allende took office to a little more than 4 percent in February 1972. The cost of living, which rose by 36 percent in 1970, rose in 1971 by only 23 percent. The GNP increased by nearly 8 percent in 1971. And, above all, there has been a significant redistribution of wealth. Food prices have remained low because the Government has not devalued the escudo, and imported food is very cheap. At the same time, real wages have increased by 30 percent. With respect to agrarian reform, the Government expropriated 1,300 farms in its first seven months in office as compared with 1,200 farms expropriated during Frei's entire term. The agrarian reform program, at least with respect to the expropriative phase, will be completed by the end of 1973.

And all this has been done, as Allende proudly points out, without a single political prisoner languishing in Chilean jails. Freedom of expression, individuality, and diversity have been maintained. Most observers agree with Allende's statement. *Panorama Economico,* a well-respected economic journal, has maintained: "Seldom in our history, or any history, has such substantial change in a power structure taken place with such a low social cost." Fidel Castro congratulated Chileans during his visit for "doing more in your first year than we did in ours."

Nevertheless, there are still serious problems, some resulting directly from the progressive changes that have been made. Chile's industry has always been geared to the consumption patterns of the upper class, and machinery cannot automatically be converted to the production of socially useful goods. Automobile factories, for instance, cannot suddenly be changed to produce shoes. (In at least one case, however, this was possible—when the workers of the textile industry voted to produce school and army uniforms instead of fancy lingerie.) The fantastic redistribution of land in the rural sector will bring higher productivity only in three or four years. (The Government, by opting for a rapid, inexpensive agrarian reform program, has come up against the very problems that Frei tried to avoid. Farmers who must choose to sell their cows to agrarian reform agencies for two or three dollars a head would rather ship them to market, even at the low market prices, and even if the cows are pregnant. Some have even burned their wheat fields and slaughtered their cattle in response to low compensation and as a political protest to the Government.) The price of copper has fallen precipitously, from a high of over 80 cents a pound in the last months of Frei's Administration to around 50 cents a pound now. At the same time, production costs of copper have increased—because of the exodus of engineers and technicians when the Government stopped paying in dollars; because of the dilapidated condition of the mines when the Government took them over; and because of the huge wage increase that the copper miners gained after a long strike last year.

Last, but not by any means least, Chile must face the problems of any weak country in an international monetary and trading climate dominated by big capitalist powers. I remember the president of the First National City Bank in New York blithely noting that Allende's nationalization of their small office in Santiago wouldn't hurt the bank a bit, but "Where does he think he's going to get money from now?" United States loans and aid have mostly been curtailed, except to the military (with whom the United States still wants to retain some influence), and except for some grants and loans to university programs. The Export-Import Bank has dropped Chile's credit rating to a "D" category, lower than Yugoslavia's. Because of Frei's renegotiation and postponement of loans in 1967, Allende will have $3 billion worth of loans falling due in 1973. When Allende took office he had a huge surplus of foreign exchange reserves—around $335 million—but now those reserves are close to being exhausted; they hover at around the $75 million level. He has begun talks with international bankers concerning possible renegotiations of the loans, but any such agreement by international financial agencies will be dependent on Chile agreeing to certain stipulations, any one of which could undoubtedly be antithetical to the socialist nature of the Chilean revolution.

The economic pinch has certainly hurt. Already the free milk program has had to be cut back. The prices of basic commodities are beginning to rise steadily, and there are those who think that the low inflation rate is only artificial, that within a year or two it will rebound to the highest levels of the early 1960s or the mid-1950s.

In addition to the economic difficulties, there is an increasingly difficult domestic political situation. The Opposition is now welded together in a formal coalition. What in late 1971 was a tenuous alliance in support of electoral candidates has turned into a more serious congressional offensive against the Government. The first move came when the Opposition voted to impeach Minister of the Interior José Toha, a competent and well-liked member of the Socialist party who is a personal friend of Allende. Although Allende postponed the inevitable by switching Toha to the Defense Ministry, Congress eventually had its way. More serious, however, has been the series of congressional amendments presented to Allende. These have drastically reduced funds for public agencies whose operations are essential for agrarian reform programs, industrial development, housing projects, and even some public services. Congress is currently trying to enact a constitutional amendment that would prohibit Government intervention in the affairs of private companies without congressional approval and is trying to make this retroactive to October 1971.

But Allende still has the advantages of being President; he can veto such a bill. It is doubtful that the Opposition could get the two-thirds vote necessary to override his veto. But it is clear that if Allende does not get a majority in Congress, his programs will gradually be undermined and strangled. He has gone as far as possible without the help of Congress. During his first year in office, although Congress did not pass one bill of importance, Allende managed to alter radically the nature of Chilean society. It is obvious that this struggle cannot continue.

Allende's political problems, however, come not only

from external parties; there have been divisions within also. The coalition, which was surprisingly durable during its first year, is slowly breaking down now. The parties now number eight, with both the MAPU party and the Radical party having split. Each of the eight parties has a portfolio, at least one Ministry in the Government. Thus, if any Minister dies or resigns or is impeached, the whole Cabinet might have to be rearranged. For example, when Congress voted to impeach Toha, it caused delicate negotiations within the Government. Toha was a Socialist party member, but when he was switched to the Defense Ministry he was replacing a Radical. Thus the Minister of Defense was switched to the Education post from which a member of the Radical party had resigned. The Minister of Interior post was filled by another Socialist, designated by Carlos Altamirano, the secretary-general of the party.

One Chilean high official once told me succinctly: "The Chilean revolution is so very, very complicated." These internal negotiations are just part of the complications. There are others. The honeymoon between the Communist and Socialist parties has come to an end. The Young Socialists and MAPU adherents are now challenging the Communist party to move toward revolution. The fear is that the Government is trying to consolidate past gains and is losing its momentum.

The economic and political strains in Chile are by no means easily separated. Sometimes what the Government is wary of doing for political reasons it must nevertheless do for economic reasons. For example, there is a shortage of meat and other goods in Chile. The Opposition blames the Government's poor handling of national distribution and its economic policy; the Government blames a conspiracy of the upper classes to buy up all the goods and cry scarcity. Whichever is correct, there is clearly only one solution—a system of rationing. The upper classes in Chile have refrigerators and therefore can buy meat at the beginning of the month and store it. They also have cars to travel to distribution centers, which the Government established in neighborhoods in order to stop the rich from getting a disproportionate share of the food products merely because they could buy more. But rationing smacks of dictatorship. It is also an eventuality that the Right had been predicting as far back as January 1971, only two months after the Government took office. Therefore an attempt at rationing would be political suicide. Even within the Government there are sectors that don't like it. I was talking to a Social Democrat who had just traveled to Cuba and had discussed the situation there. She had asked a Cuban woman how much bacon she could buy in the store. A quarter of a pound was the answer. "But I can buy as much as I want," said the Chilean woman. "But can the poor?" asked the Cuban. And the Chilean woman realized that although in Chile one had the freedom to buy as much as one wanted, it was a freedom based on the assumption that everyone had enough money. In Cuba, everyone ate bacon. In Chile, only some gorged on it.

The Government was dealt a severe political blow when it lost, by substantial margins, two by-elections in January 1972 that it had expected to win. The Left lost by 6 percent in the senatorial election and by a huge 16 percent in the election of Deputies. Although these elections involved only 5 percent of the electorate and the Government did better in them than it had in the 1970 national election, they still represented a stunning psychological defeat. Close analysis indicates that although the Government gained a majority in the towns in and around the copper mine of El Teniente, it lost heavily in the rural areas. Some blamed the MIRistas, who had leafleted the area, urging the Government to reduce from two hundred to one hundred the minimum acreage one could hold and still be exempt from provisions of the Agrarian Reform Act. This had scared many small landholders, who were afraid it would be the first step toward eliminating all private property. Others thought the vote was a protest against the Government's new agricultural program, which stressed agricultural centers rather than *asentamientos*. In the former, migrant laborers and all classes of rural Chile were integrated. In the latter, only those who had worked on the farm that was expropriated got land. Many *asentados* didn't want to have to share their farm with migrant laborers.

Above all these political and economic considerations looms the specter of the army. No one doubts that the final question of any revolution is the question of power, or that the army still holds the military power in Chile. And no one doubts that the Government, if it stepped outside the constitutional framework, would invite military intervention. The MIR believes that the need for armed confrontation, in order to bring the revolution to a higher level of combativity, is as strong as ever. So far, according to the MIR, Chile has been living in a prerevolutionary stage, a stage of preparation for the armed conflict. Allende disagrees, believing that the army can support a genuine revolution if such a revolution comes about through constitutional means. He has placed military personnel throughout the Government. In return, the army has warmly supported him during times of crisis. For example, when in December 1971 the Opposition organized protest marches against the presence of Fidel Castro in Chile and broke into Communist party offices to decry the presence of a dictatorship in Cuba, the army was called on to intervene and save democracy. Instead, Allende was presented with a replica of the sword of Bernardo O'Higgins, the hero of the War of Independence. It was an unprecedented honor for a President so early in his term of office. Maybe Allende is correct. Maybe a revolution can occur with military support—but only if it is effected within the constitutional framework.

And that brings us to the current dilemma of the

Government. It is caught in an economic situation that is worsening at every turn, and yet to deal with this situation effectively it would need to step outside the Constitution, thus courting a military coup. The alternatives are fairly clear. First, the Government can move outside the Constitution. The MIRistas argue for this alternative. They discuss the natural long-term assets of Chile. These include the largest copper reserves in the world, a strong asset when a rise in copper prices is being predicted. Also, Chile has many powerful trading partners, including Russia, Eastern Europe, China, and Cuba, that probably are willing to barter, obviating the necessity of having dollars with which to do business with other countries. Chile also has a wonderful climate, its seasons being the opposite of those in the Northern Hemisphere. With a climate much like that of southern California, Chile could produce and sell fruit and wines during the winter months. But all these assets are long-term. It will take years before fruit trees bear fruit; it will be a long time before trade advantages show up on the economic ledgers. Yet the Far Left believes that the short-term economic burdens of Chile can be lifted. They want Allende to refuse to pay any compensation to expropriated North American companies, feeling that these companies have gained their original investment back many times at the expense of the Chilean people. Furthermore, the Far Left is asking for cancellation of the international debt. The Government paid only a small compensation to the copper companies when it took them over, but it agreed to honor the $700 million in debts that the companies had contracted. The Far Left demands that all such debts, including those made with international agencies, be canceled, arguing that these loans never really aided Chileans, at least not the great majority of them who are working people. Such loans often went, either directly through subsidy or indirectly through infrastructure works, to aid North American companies or rich Chileans whose industries were geared to the upper-class luxury markets. The Far Left argues that with the drain on revenue temporarily reduced by canceling debts, the country could get back on its feet again. For example, Chilean farmers agree that the country could be exporting food and producing enough milk to take care of internal requirements, but that it would take five years.

Yet by overstepping the Constitution the Government would clearly be pushing the country beyond its political framework. There is the possibility of intervention by the army—which, although strongly apolitical, has strong ties with the United States and with the Opposition parties in Chile. The MIRistas would welcome such an intervention. It is what they have been preparing for for three years. Some MIRistas claim that they could put from twenty to thirty thousand people into battle immediately, armed with weapons stolen from armories during the past three years and trained during people's militia training sessions during the past year. (The MIR has already demonstrated impressive strength—in 1971 its leader accidentally died and thirty thousand people marched through the streets of Santiago in a funeral procession.) They figure that with the support of the organized labor class this group could in fact win over the army; the only way the army could win would be to kill hundreds of thousands of Chileans, a prospect that the Far Left believes would split the army itself.

Another alternative is to operate within the constitutional framework, trying to alter it from within. This might be called "revolutionary pragmatism," and it is characteristic of Allende's way of doing things. I remember his speech at the University of Concepcion, where the student president, Nelson Gutierrez, had just challenged Allende, fraternally and warmly, to push the revolution still further by giving power to the masses directly. Allende's response was characteristic and classic. He doesn't believe, he said, that the revolution begins after the army is defeated, nor does he think that it can be over in one day. Rather, it is a process. He explained how the students fit into the process at a different stage of development than he had in the 1930s:

> I want to point out the substantial difference between the generations that preceded you in these university halls and yourselves. We criticized the capitalist regime; you are fighting to change the cultural dependence, to conquer the scientific and technological backwardness, and that implies, although it is not completely understood, not only to criticize the regime, but also to contribute to the substantial changes that Chile demands and needs, among other things, in order to raise the scientific and technological level.

When the students started whistling their disgust at such an attitude, implying that the revolution had not yet come and that students must therefore look to armed confrontation rather than long days in the libraries, an angry Allende cited Lenin's dictum that "Revolutionary extremism is a traitor to socialism." He declared: "You are whistling at Lenin, not me." And then, for perhaps the thousandth time since his inauguration, he talked of the long, painful process of revolution:

> What stage is Chile living in now, young comrades and guests? It is living through a stage to which we have arrived not by accident. The victory accomplished in September and reaffirmed in April signals a process of political maturation that began long ago. The majority of you were not born—I refer to the students—when already great worker and student struggles occurred in Chile in order to make possible political victories that we must preserve. If there is a fact that we should not forget, it is that Marxist theory of history teaches us that it is indispensable to overcome progressively and effectively each stage, and that one must permit to survive those positive aspects of society in order to make use of them in the process of creating another society. In the specific case of Chile, we want to transform the political victories into social victories. . . . The

historical reality shows us that here . . . in our country we have utilized a road that our reality has permitted to be employed. This road has been the fight within the voting booths.

He repeated his belief that the history of Chile indicates that a rapidly maturing political electorate can effect radical and even socialist change in the country through their voting patterns. He argued for pragmatism, asking the students not to leap to the next stage of socialist development without having educated the masses to the higher level of sophistication:

> Why, youthful comrades, do you not ask yourselves why the reality is stronger than theory. A country with 900 million has to accept Hong Kong. Why are Formosa and Chiang Kai-shek permitted to survive? Because the correlation of political forces obliges him to accept this reality. Who of you are going to discuss with me the revolutionary content of Cuba? And who of you would dare to ask Fidel Castro tomorrow to take over the Bay of Guantanamo which is in the hands of the North Americans? If he did this, the revolution would suffer its greatest defeat.

For Allende, armed struggle is useful only as a desperate last resort. It is useful only when it becomes apparent that one cannot win through educating the people, because when battle occurs, education stops.

Allende has two possibilities for revising the political system through electoral politics. First, he can try the plebiscite. Only *once* during his term in office can he go directly to the people to ask for their vote on a bill. No one doubts that if this is done, the vote will decide for or against dismantling the bicameral legislature and replacing it with a one-chamber People's Assembly. Allende would be on strong ground in asking for this dismantling. The current congressional representation is based on the 1930 census. Thus rural areas, which are more conservative, have a much higher representation in the Congress than they should. But there are considerations to give Allende pause. The returns of the February by-elections strongly indicate that a majority of people might not support such a plebiscite. It would, after all, be a plebiscite to alter radically a political system that has remained the same for a century. The people, no matter how poor or how miserable, might prefer to stay with what they have than scrap it for the unknown.

Second, he can wait until the spring of 1973, when congressional elections occur, and try to gain a majority in the Congress. This would be a very difficult task, but Allende is already working toward it. In February 1972 he demanded that all the parties in the coalition drop their party labels during the next congressional elections and run on a unified Popular Unity ticket. Although this strategy would seem the most appropriate, there is strong opposition to it. The small parties in the coalition fear they would be swallowed up and lose their identity in a single party. The Opposition in Congress has already passed a bill prohibiting a candidate from running on a party label without having been a member of that party for more than one year. This bill, if passed over Allende's certain veto, would undermine this possibility.

Another alternative for the Government is to continue operating within the constitutional framework and consolidate newly won gains. It is the most attractive and yet the most insidious course. In this case, the Government would continue speaking the rhetoric of socialism, yet would become increasingly conservative, leading the masses astray and providing no leadership at the critical moments of Chilean history. Of course, no party wants to pursue the third alternative without trying the second. But if a plebiscite loses and the congressional election does not bring with it a majority in Congress, substantial portions of the coalition will opt for this alternative. The problem with it, besides the obvious, is that it would lead to the termination of the revolution without yet integrating into it all sections of the population. This is important. Before the 1970 election the working people had the alternative of voting for the Left in order to gain power. Now, in a certain sense, these working people, or at least the organized trade union representatives, do have power within the Government. But the migrant workers in rural Chile, the part-time workers who still ride the buses peddling their wares, and the unemployed do not yet have a voice in the new Government. It would be cruelly ironic if the revolution were to stop at this point, for it would be stopping when at a point where the majority of Chileans actually do have a voice and an influence in Government and the minority of those who most need it would be excluded.

Yet all these alternatives overlook the ingredient most important to a revolution—its people. The people in Chile are on the move. They have always been politicized; now they are organized. Previously taboo subjects such as socialism, abortion, and worker control are now debated in small community groups almost weekly. The people now push constantly against the centers of power, just as Frei wanted them to in the 1960s. And it is this mass movement that will probably give Chile its unique character. The Government has gone far, but still there is much to be done. The slum areas still exist. The system of justice still discriminates against those without an education and without money. The educational system is still geared to producing middle-class technicians. Still no more than 10 percent of the student bodies in colleges come from working-class backgrounds. But the people are on the move. Not all of them, by any means, but a greater percentage than in most other countries. And they seem to have a clear sense of where they are going. Allende once was asked by Regis Debray what would happen if he were assassinated. Allende responded:

It is the . . . belief of the bourgeoisie that personality makes history. This belief is encouraged by the reactionaries and they have converted it into a tactic. . . . I believe that the path which appears most easy for the reactionaries would be this [assassination] but in reality the consequences would be worse for them . . . undoubtedly if this were to happen it would become clear that the reactionaries do not accept the rules of the game that they themselves established. . . . Social progress is not going to disappear because a leader disappears. It may be slowed down, it may be postponed, but in the end it cannot be stopped. In the case of Chile, if they assassinated me, the people would continue on their way; with the difference perhaps that things would be harder, much more violent, because it would be a very clear object lesson for the masses that these people would stop at nothing.

It is quite unlikely that Allende will be assassinated. But his point is well taken, and it is what makes Chile such a hopeful country. The past decade has seen the people take an increasingly strong and influential voice in decision making. At every level of Chilean society the people themselves, backed by national political parties, are making their wants and needs clear, through the polls, through takeovers of farms, buildings, and schools, or through the establishment of new forms of social organization such as have occurred in some farms and *poblaciones* where tribunals and new social constraints have been developed. As long as the Government provides the leadership and gives the people the space to develop, they will. There is a long road ahead, and Chile is just beginning to walk it. Some people are calling the experiment "gradualism"; others are calling it "reformism." I do not attempt to give it a name or a grade, but it must be obvious to anyone reading this book that I wish it well and hope they make it.

Postscript

Writing a postscript on a historical process is a little like taking notes on a tidal wave as it continues to build. It has been almost nine months since I wrote the last chapter of the book, and the revolutionary process in Chile continues its rapid pace. A number of the trends that I touched on in the latter part of the book are becoming much clearer.

The conservative parties and the Christian Democrats have firmly welded their marriage of convenience. They have consistently vetoed Governmental legislation, have refused to finance such measures as the creation of the Ministry of the Family, and have placed strong restrictions on further use of Executive power for nationalization. They have stripped two Ministers of their office (a simple majority in both chambers of Congress is required to do this). They were about to force the dismissal of four more when the October "strike" occurred. The National Party has even been preparing an attempt to force Allende's resignation (a two-thirds majority in both chambers would be needed). The Opposition has agreed to field one slate of candidates in the upcoming March elections, hoping to win a popular mandate and increase its Congressional majority.

The economic situation has also worsened. Prices have risen by 132 percent since the beginning of the year. Scarcities in machinery, parts and equipment are severely hurting the economy. The Opposition blames these problems on poor management and on the speed at which property is being nationalized. The Government points out that in the area where it has moved at the *greatest* speed, the agrarian reform program, Chile's agricultural output has grown by 6 percent in one year, according to the 1972 report of the UN Food and Agricultural Organization; this was the highest rate in Latin America. The parties in power blame internal sabotage and external pressures for the economic troubles. But neither side with its accusations can alter the grim fact that Canadian, Dutch, and United States banks have suspended Chile's credit. Moreover, the Kennecott Copper Corporation has obtained a French court order preventing payment to Chile of $1.4 million owed by French manufacturers for copper produced at nationalized mines that Kennecott had previously owned. And a court in the Netherlands has ruled to allow Kennecott to seize a ship from Chile loaded with 1,250 tons of copper.

Politically, the country is polarized. In 1971 its voting populace was fairly evenly divided along pro-Goverment and anti-Government lines, as evidenced in the university elections and local by-elections. The 1972 alignment has remained about the same, but the activities of the anti-Government segment have become more intense. Meanwhile, the lower classes (traditionally supporters of the Government) have become much more conscious of their revolutionary role. It has been three years since the peasants began taking over land. It has been two years since the workers gained their first opportunity to participate in the running of their own factories and organizations and the slum dwellers seized land and began constructing their tin and wood shacks on the dusty plains outside Santiago. During all this time these groups have gained in self-confidence. They have worked through their initial mistakes and have learned to cooperate in defending their newly won gains.

For the Socialist Party and Salvador Allende, the success of a revolution is not measured in terms of the number of houses built or the number of children graduated from public schools. Those are important indices, of course, but a far greater measure of such success has to do with consciousness, a vague, almost abstract word that is on the lips of Chilean Marxists these days. Perhaps the best example of the level of consciousness the Chilean working class has achieved, as well as of the power and new-found unity of the middle class, has been the October "strike." The strike began as a lockout by the owners of the affected business, an independent trucking firm that was being nationalized; it quickly spread, becoming a rallying point for those who opposed the Government and its policies. Professional associations, the Chamber of Commerce, and the Society of Industries called on the Chilean people to strike. Many small businesses have closed. Although many professionals responded to the call, most workers did not. The willingness of workers to keep working partly reflected the Government's organizational influence within the trade union structure, but it also seemed to indicate that workers were growing aware of the class nature of their struggle. The support shown by the vast majority of workers surprised even the Government in light of the worsening economic conditions. Many doctors honored the strike, but paraprofessionals for the most part did not, so hospitals were open on a limited basis. When the bus and taxi drivers in Santiago struck for one day in solidarity with the truck owners, students stole buses and drove them, along with government officials and workers.

The strike lasted nineteen days, and in that time the country got a taste of what it would be like without the professionals and the middle class. Hundreds of millions of dollars were lost in man-hours, production and sales. The

Government ran supplies of food and medicine from outside Santiago to the slum areas where they were needed (middle-class families are said to have sent their maids to these areas to bring back food). Women's groups became the backbone of the survival effort by collecting medicine bottles and distributing food. A woman in Santiago was reported as saying, "The store owners refuse to work. I can only feel sorry for them." She had just bought her potatoes from the state distribution outlet at a price lower than the store owners had been charging.

The strike also brought to light a growing willingness of the Opposition to go beyond political rhetoric. Young people who opposed the Government roamed through Santiago burning trash and blocking streets. Railroad tracks from Santiago to Valparaiso were blown up, as were transmitting towers. A textile factory in the south was partially burned. Thousands of *miguelitos* (star-shaped objects with spikes) were thrown onto the highways to puncture car tires and block access routes.

The Government, which had declared a state of siege when the strike began, responded to these acts by imposing a strict curfew. People who were found on the streets after hours were arrested. All radio stations were taken over. At one point Radio Mineria, a station in Santiago, broke away from the national radio network to broadcast attacks on the dictatorial nature of the Government and incite the people to rebel. Just as the military intervened, according to one popular account, the radio announcer claimed that people in the area were showing overwhelming support for the station's views. "People are even arriving on foot!" he commented, to the amusement of his listeners, 90 percent of whom didn't have cars.

The strike ended only after Allende accepted the resignation of the entire Cabinet and appointed military men to head three key ministries—the Interior, Mining, and Public Works. The intrusion of the military into the Cabinet prompted a great outcry from the Far Left. There were rumors that Altamirano, Secretary General of the Socialist Party, would resign over such a move. MIR has also been critical. But the Communist Party, pragmatic as always, supports the move. The Far Left fears that military men inside the Government will inevitably exert their influence to support the status quo. Allende and the Communist Party deny that this will happen. Allende further claims that the military appointees to his Cabinet are not figurehead generals. The Air Force General placed in charge of Mining, for example, was once administrator of a state-intervened mining enterprise.

Although Allende promised that the new participation of the military was in everyone's best interests, he quickly replaced the Minister of Work with Luis Figueroa, President of the Trade Union Confederation, and the Minister of Agriculture with Rolando Calderon, Secretary General of CUT and the son of a peasant. It appeared that workers' representatives were being placed directly in positions of power in order to offset the influence of the military—or in order to help allay the fears of such influence.

Whatever the reasons, Pedro Vuskovic and Jacques Chonchol, the intellectual architects of the domestic economic programs and the agrarian reform effort, are now outside the Government. The effect these two departures will have on revolutionary programs is debatable. Some feel that the direction of the programs has been set, and that it is a good idea to have them headed by people who are close to the peasants or the workers. Others, denying that Chile is so far along, wonder who will provide the vision needed to draft the broad alterations that might be necessary.

The next few months are but a prelude to the March Congressional elections. If the Government wins, the victory may quicken the momentum of the revolution. If the Opposition picks up the seats needed for a two-thirds majority in both chambers, Allende may be ousted. Politics in Chile is a life game and is taken as seriously as socialism itself. Most observers expect little overall change in the composition of Congress after the elections. No doubt the Christian Democrats will lose some support from both the Right and the Left. Indeed, as the polarization of pro- and anti-Government forces sharpens, it is difficult to see what role a middle-of-the-road party like the Christian Democrats can play.

When Allende was elected, he told reporters that his was not the goal of effecting socialism in Chile, but that of bringing about the preconditions that would make such a goal possible. The elimination of foreign monopolies and the introduction of workers into positions of power are evidences that he has succeeded in his task. But history marches on. The Frei days seem distant, and even the first few months of Allende's regime are fading into history, but the Chilean revolution continues, entering new stages of confrontation and dialectic on the road to socialism.

November 20, 1972

Source Notes

CHAPTER I—A BRIEF HISTORY OF GOVERNMENT IN CHILE

1. H. R. S. Pocock, *The Conquest of Chile,* New York: Stein and Day, 1967, p. 48.
2. William Weber Johnson and the editors of *Life, The Andean Republics,* New York: Time Incorporated, 1965, p. 121.
3. Donald Dozer, *Latin America: An Interpretive History,* New York: McGraw-Hill, 1962, p. 269.
4. Luis Galdamos, *A History of Chile,* London: Russell and Russell, 1964, p. 368.
5. Frederick B. Pike, *Chile and the United States, 1880–1962,* Notre Dame, Indiana: University of Notre Dame Press, 1963, p. 100.
6. Andrew Zimbalist, *Dependence and Underdevelopment in Chile,* Harvard University, unpublished manuscript, 1971, p. 14.
7. Donald Dozer, *op. cit.,* p. 499.
8. Oscar Weiss, *Nacionalismo y Socialismo en America Latina,* Buenos Aires: Ediciones Iquaya, 1971, p. 154.
9. Enrique Sierra, *Tres Ensayos De Estabilizacion en Chile,* Santiago, Chile: Editorial Universitaria, 1969, pp. 52–53.
10. Luis Vitales, *¿Y Después del 4, Qué?,* Santiago, Chile: Ediciones Prensa Latinoamericana, 1970, p. 21.
11. Enrique Sierra, *op. cit.,* p. 144.
12. *Ibid.,* p. 140.
13. *Ibid.,* p. 145.
14. *Ibid.,* pp. 180 and 202.
15. *Ibid.,* p. 140.
16. *Ibid.,* p. 145.

CHAPTER 2—THE FREI YEARS—THE END OF LIBERALISM

1. Leonard Gross, *The Last Best Hope: Eduardo Frei and Chilean Democracy,* New York: Random House, 1967, p. 10.
2. *Ibid.,* p. 229.
3. Enrique Sierra, *op. cit.,* p. 140.
4. Robinson Rojas, "El Tremendo Avance De Las Luchas Campesinas," *Causa ML,* June 1970.
5. Luis Vitale, *op. cit.,* pp. 16 and 18.
6. *Comportamiento de las Principales Empresas Industriales Extranjeras acogidas al DFL 258,* Division de Planificacion Industrial, publicacion 9, A/70, p. 17.
7. Americo Zorrilla, *Exposicion Sobre la Politica Economica del Gobierno y del Estado de la Hacienda Publica,* Folleto No. 118, Direccion de Presupestos, p. 11.
8. *Punto Final,* December 8, 1970, pp. 4–5.
9. *Causa ML,* June 1969, p. 7.
10. Orlando Caputo y Roberto Pizarro, *Desarrollismo y Capital Extranjero,* Santiago, Chile: Ediciones de la Universidad Tecnica del Estado, 1970, pp. 73 and 79.
11. Luis Enriquez y Winston Cabello, *La Absorcion Tecnologia y el Problema de las Regalias,* Monograph presented to the Department of the Theory of Dependence, School of Economics, University of Chile, 1969.
12. Orlando Caputo y Roberto Pizarro, *op. cit.,* p. 34.
13. Frederic G. Donner, *The World Wide Industrial Enterprise,* New York: McGraw-Hill, 1966, p. 109.
14. Miguel Wionczek, *La Banca Extranjera en America Latina,* Lima: Instituto de Estudios Peruanos, 1969, p. 4.
15. Harry Magdoff, *Age of Imperialism,* New York: Monthly Review Press, 1969, p. 153.
16. Orlando Caputo y Roberto Pizarro, *op. cit.,* pp. 79–80.
17. *Ibid.,* p. 51.
18. Americo Zorrilla, *op. cit.,* p. 9.
19. Robinson Rojas, "Yanquis Invaden la Industria," *Causa ML,* June 1969, p. 28.
20. Americo Zorrilla, *op. cit.,* p. 10.
21. Jose Cademartori, *La Economia Chilena,* Santiago, Chile: Editorial Universitaria, 1968, p. 196.
22. Robinson Rojas, *op. cit.,* p. 28.
23. Jose Cademartori, *op. cit.,* p. 226.
24. From a study by Mario Vera Valenzuela, cited in *Cultural Popular,* No. 1, November 1961, pp. 4–10.
25. *Ibid.*
26. *Ibid.*

27. *Ibid.*
28. *Ibid.*
29. Andrew Zimbalist, *op. cit.,* p. 21.
30. *Ibid.,* pp. 26–27.
31. *Ibid.,* p. 27.
32. Norman Girvan, *Multinational Corporations and Dependent Underdevelopment in Mineral Export Economies,* Yale Economic Center, paper no. 87, June 1970, p. 33.
33. Keith Griffin, *Underdevelopment in Spanish America,* Cambridge: M.I.T. Press, 1970, p. 172.
34. From a speech by President Salvador Allende, December 23, 1970.
35. *Ibid.*
36. Comision Politica Tecnica, Partido Democrata Cristiano, *Proposiciones para una Accion Politica para el Periodo 1967–70 de Una Via No-Capitalista,* PEC Edition, No. 239, July 28, 1967, p. 18.
37. *Causa Marxista-Leninista,* June 1969, p. 29.
38. Study by ODEPLAN, Division de Industrias, 1966.
39. Pedro Vuskovic, "Distribucion del Igreso y Opciones de Desarrollo," *Cuadernos de la Realidad Nacional,* Septiembre 1970, p. 60.
40. Gregorio Samsa, "Los Salarios Actuales Son Menos de la Mitad De Los del Ano 1956," *Causa ML,* October 1969, pp. 17–18.
41. *Ibid.,* p. 12.
42. *Politicas Especificas Comunes A Todo el Sector Industrial, Estrategia Industrial,* Tomo II, CORFO.
43. F. S. Weaver, Jr., *Regional Patterns of Economic Change in Chile, 1950–1964,* unpublished Ph.D. dissertation, 1968.
44. Pablo Huneeus, "Efectos de La Ley de Inamovilidad," *Panorama Economico,* No. 249, October 1969, p. 27.
45. *Estadisticas 1969,* Servicio de Seguro Social and *Ocupacion y Desocupacion en Gran Santiago,* Instituto de Economia, Universidad de Chile, 1969.
46. *Causa ML,* October 1969, p. 19.
47. *Ibid.,* pp. 18–19.
48. Colin Bradford, *The United States and Latin American Modernization: The Frei Administration in Chile,* unpublished manuscript, 1969, p. 22.
49. Jose Antonio Viera-Gallo y Hugo Villela, "Consideraciones Preliminares para el Estudio del Estado en Chile," *Cuadernos de la Realidad Nacional,* Septiembre 1970, pp. 23–24.
50. *Punto Final,* April 6, 1968, II, 52.
51. *Punto Final,* May 20, 1969, II, 79.
52. *Punto Final,* May 6, 1969, II, 78.

CHAPTER 3—TRANSITION

Note:
During the period directly before and after Allende's election every Chilean leftist assumed that the large North American corporations, in conjunction with the CIA, would be trying to produce economic instability in Chile, while at the same time trying to use their contacts with the Chilean middle class and the military to remove Allende from office. Yet support for such assumptions did not come until a year and a half afterwards, when columnist Jack Anderson made twenty-six confidential memoranda from private files of IT&T available to the press. The revelations were by no means surprising to the new Chilean Administration. The memoranda showed how IT&T operatives in South America, as well as corporation executives in Washington and New York, were considering tactics for promoting and financing a right-wing military coup aimed at ousting Allende. The papers revealed that such a plan was recommended by a high-ranking member of the Central Intelligence Agency in charge of clandestine operations in Latin America. The papers further revealed that the corporation attempted to get support from high government officials such as President Nixon's National Security Advisor, Henry A. Kissinger; Assistant Secretary of State for Interamerican Affairs, Charles A. Meyer; and Edward M. Korry, then U.S. Ambassador to Chile. General Viaux seemed to be the pivot around which the maneuverings occurred. Although wanting to move immediately, Viaux was told by Washington to delay because the time did not seem propitious. In return for such a delay he was told he would be given materiel assistance and support from the United States and others for a later maneuver.

Perhaps such memoranda help explain the apparent ineptness of the kidnapping attempt by Viaux and several accomplices. Even in jail Viaux has maintained that he has a "clean conscience" about the attempt, emphasizing his superior morality for acting in the face of danger, even though others were counseling him to wait.

1. Luis Vitales, *op. cit.* Most newspaper quotations used in this section come from this excellent essay.

CHAPTER 4—THE FIRST FEW MONTHS

1. Pedro Vuskovic, *op. cit.*, p. 58.

CHAPTER 5—WORKER CONTROL

1. Enrique Sierra, *op. cit.*, p. 140 and Luis Vitale, *op. cit.*, p. 18.
2. *El Siglo*, La Revista del Domingo, February 1971.

CHAPTER 6—PEASANTS, INDIANS, AND AGRICULTURE

1. Elsa Richard, "El Hambre Devora a Miles de Chilenos," *Mundo*, January 1971, p. 4.
2. "Arauco Discriminado," *Revista del Domingo*, Diciembre 27, 1970.
3. Cited in Leonard Gross, *op. cit.*, p. 41. A similar study, done in 1969, came up with the same results (Tapia A., Fernando, "La Empleada de Casa Particular," *Pastoral Popular*, No. 112, July/August 1969, pp. 6–8).
4. Statement by Jacques Chonchol cited in *El Mercurio*, January 24, 1971.
5. Robinson Rojas, *op. cit.*, p. 22.
6. *Ibid.*
7. *Desal Report*, No. 3, 1970, p. 2.
8. James Petras, *Politics and Social Forces in Chilean Development*, Berkeley, California: University of California Press, 1969, p. 269.
9. Robinson Rojas, *op. cit.*, p. 21.
10. *Punto Final*, May 1969, p. 9.
11. Robinson Rojas, *op. cit.*, pp. 17–18.
12. *Punto Final*, January 19, 1971, II, 122.
13. *Punto Final*, April 1971, p. 21.
14. From an essay entitled, "One of the Fundamental Problems of Revolution," cited in *Punto Final*, May 1971, p. 25.

CHAPTER 7—JUSTICE

1. Taken from a long article on prisons in *El Mercurio*, January 10, 1971.
2. Equipo del CIDU: Oscar Cuellar, Rosemond Cheethan, Santiago Quevedo, Jaime Rojas, Franz Vanderschueren, "Experiences de Justicia Popular en Poblaciones," *Cuadernos dela Realidad Nacional*, No. 8, June 1971, pp. 153–173. Much of the following description of various systems of internal justice in *poblaciones* and *campamentos* is taken from this study.

CHAPTER 8—EDUCATION

1. Leonard Gross, *op. cit.,* p. 54.
2. Jean Labbens, "Universidades Chilenas: su evolucion en la ultima decada," *Panorama Economico,* August 1969.
3. *Ibid.*
4. *Ibid.*
5. Ramirez R. Ronaldo, "La Crisis Universitaria: Contenido y Estructura Para Una Universidad Comprometida," *Revista de Planificacion,* No. 6. Facultad de Arquitectro y Urbanismo, Universidad de Chile, Instituto de Vivienda Urbanismo y Planificacion.
6. *El Siglo,* January 9, 1971.

CHAPTER 9—HEALTH AND MEDICINE

1. Dr. Fernando Monckleberg, "Desnutricion y Desarrolo Socio-Economico," Apartado de la revista *Mensaje,* No. 182, September 1969.
2. *La Nacion,* March 1, 1971.
3. Fernando Monckleberg, *op. cit.*
4. *La Prensa,* January 17, 1971.
5. *Boletin Informaciones Politicas,* Comunidades Juveniles de Concientizacion, January 6, 1971.
6. Sergio Nasser, "Los alcoholicos se ayudan," *Pastoral Popular,* No. 112, July/August 1969, p. 17.

CHAPTER 10—THE MEDIA AND CULTURE

1. *La Nacíon,* March 4, 1971.
2. Armand Mattelart, "Estructura del Poder Informativo y Dependencia," *Cuadernos de la Realidad Nacional,* No. 3, March 1970.
3. From a speech by Eduardo Rivas, August 23, 1969, at a meeting of The Society of Journalism.

A Brief Bibliography

Affonso, Almino, *et al. Movimiento Campesino Chileno*. Santiago: ICIRA, 1970. Vols. I and II.

Cademartori, José. *La Economia Chilena*. Santiago: Editorial Universitaria, 1968.

Caputo, Orlando and Roberto Pizarro. *Desarrollismo y Capital Extranjero*. Santiago: Ediciones de La Universidad Tecnica del Estado, 1970.

Chile Hoy. Mexico: Siglo Veintiuno editores s.a. 1970.

Debray, Regis. *The Chilean Revolution*. New York: Pantheon, 1971.

Lechner, Norbert. *La Democracia en Chile*. Argentina: Ediciones Signos, 1970.

Petras, James. *Politics and Social Forces in Chilean Development*. Berkeley, California: University of California Press, 1969.

Pocock, H. R. S. *The Conquest of Chile*. New York: Stein and Day, 1967.

Sierra, Enrique. *Tres Ensayos de Estabilizacion en Chile*. Santiago: Editorial Universitaria, 1969.

Swift, Jeannine. *Agrarian Reform in Chile*. Lexington: Heath Lexington Books, 1971.

Vitales, Luis. *¿Y Después del 4, Qué?* Santiago: Ediciones Prensa Latinoamericana, 1970.

About the Author

DAVID MORRIS graduated Cornell University in 1966 and went to the University of Florida, where after eight months he realized that learning cannot be done in classrooms. He fled to the Institute for Policy Studies in Washington, D.C., where, as an Associate Fellow, he began integrating some disparate threads which departmentalized schooling had taught him were unrelated. He has worked in northwest Washington, developing a youth community, and has taught at Federal City College. He is currently co-director and co-founder of Communitas, an upper-level, two-year college for community action. Mr. Morris has published many articles on Latin American affairs in various magazines, including *Commonweal, The New Republic, The Nation,* and *American Report.*